Minimal Brain Dysfunction in Children

WILEY SERIES ON PSYCHOLOGICAL DISORDERS

IRVING B. WEINER, Editor
School of Medicine and Dentistry
The University of Rochester

Minimal Brain Dysfunction in Children

PAUL H. WENDER, M.D.
Research Psychiatrist, Laboratory of Psychology,
National Institute of Mental Health
Assistant Professor of Pediatrics and Psychiatry,
Johns Hopkins Hospital

WILEY-INTERSCIENCE
a Division of John Wiley & Sons, Inc.
New York • London • Sydney • Toronto

In memory of my father, an empiricist and eclectic, whose constant admonition was, "Always observe for yourself!"

And to my patients who allowed me—to the best of my ability—to see.

Series Preface

This series of books is addressed to behavioral scientists concerned with understanding and ameliorating psychological disorders. Its scope should prove pertinent to clinicians and their students in psychology, psychiatry, social work, and other disciplines that deal with problems of human behavior as well as to theoreticians and researchers studying these problems. Although many facets of behavioral science have relevance to psychological disorder, the series concentrates on the three core clinical areas of psychopathology, personality assessment and psychotherapy.

Each of these clinical areas can be discussed in terms of theoretical foundations that identify directions for further development, empirical data that summarize current knowledge, and practical applications that guide the clinician in his work with patients. The books in this series present scholarly integrations of such theoretical, empirical, and practical approaches to clinical concerns. Some pursue the implications of research findings for the validity of alternative theoretical frameworks or for the utility of various modes of clinical practice; others consider the implication of certain conceptual models for lines of research or for the elaboration of clinical methods; and others encompass a wide range of theoretical, research, and practical issues as they pertain to a specific psychological disturbance, assessment technique, or treatment modality.

University of Rochester   *Irving B. Weiner*
Rochester, New York

Foreword

Minimal brain dysfunction (MBD) in children constitutes at once a vexing clinical problem for physicians, psychologists, and educators and a source of unending theoretical dispute between adherents to one or another school of thought. More often than not, the quarrel begins with misunderstanding the conditions under which one specialist considers the diagnosis legitimate and another does not; the acrimony is perpetuated by a confusion in levels of discourse (a syndrome defined behaviorly versus an anatomical description). Further fuel is added to the flames by misconceptions of the fixity of "organic" versus "functional" diagnoses. A condition that is perceived as psychological in origin is regarded by some as more readily reversible than one that is biologically based; consequently, the MBD diagnosis is resisted as being "pessimistic." The origins of this erroneous belief are ancient but its untruth is evident if one contrasts the ease with which bromism, epilepsy, or benign meningioma can be treated with the difficulty of curing obsessional traits or personality disorders.

The confusion of tongues between clinicians is best illustrated by the vicissitudes of a prototypical case. John, aged, 7 had been under competent pediatric care since a normal birth. His second-grade teacher, finding him to be restless, distractable, and a poor learner, suggested to his mother that John might be "brain damaged." Frightened by the term and distressed that her pediatrician had failed to detect this condition, the mother sought an emergency appointment in great alarm. The pediatrician angrily responded that the teacher had transgressed on medical prerogatives. He tried to calm the parents by repeating the reassurance he had offered earlier about John outgrowing his "immaturity." At their insistence he scheduled psychological tests and arranged a referral to a neurologist who normally treats adults, there being none with pediatric subspecialization in his town. The psychologist suggested "organicity" from the test findings, but the neurologist dismissed central nervous system disease on the basis of the motor and sensory examination. The EEG was reported as showing "more slow waves than expected for age."

Reinforced by the neurologist's judgment, the pediatrician insisted on the correctness of his original opinion and referred the parents to a child guidance clinic; the parents' complaints about home management problems as well as the school difficulties made it undeniably clear that *something* was wrong with John. At the clinic, a history of parental discord and John's anger toward his older sister led to the interpretation of his symptoms as family-centered. When six months of psychotherapy brought no obvious relief and once the school insisted on retention in grade, the pediatrician sought help from consultation at a prominent medical center where, at long last, the existence of MBD was stated "authoritatively" on the basis of the total clinical picture. A trial of amphetamine therapy brought about striking behavioral changes, a decisive improvement in school performance, and a consequent uneasy peace among the warring factions. It was difficult to argue with success.

Were this an isolated example, it might be ascribed to the incompetence of the principals involved; unfortunately, it is very common. The explanation must be sought at a level more fundamental than the talents or the personalities of the professionals repeatedly involved in such cycles. The teacher had accurately observed a behavioral syndrone which, from the literature available to her, she had ascribed to MBD; however, her limited ability to discriminate phenotype from genotype had, in other instances, resulted in the use of the same label for behavior that had quite different causes. The pediatrician and the neurologist had, in their own terms, been "correct" in denying the presence of gross and localizable structural damage in the central nervous system; their viewpoint, however, was based on a, by now, anachronistic view of brain-behavior relationships; it is precisely the higher level motor and symbolic acts that are sensitive to central nervous system integrity, not the spinal reflexes or the cranial nerves. The EEG was, as so often in this clinical situation, simply irrelevant; gross pathology can be diagnostic, but normal or borderline records permit no firm interpretation.

Though the psychologist had suggested what proved to be the "correct" diagnosis, he had done so from an unreliable data base; performance-verbal discrepancies, subtest scatter, and Bender Gestalt performance are suggestive—not conclusive. The child guidance clinic team had indeed noted real phenomena in this family; their error lay in ascribing causal priority to these issues because of a psychogenic bias whose origin is to be found in the one-sided nature of the clinical training of the orthopsychiatric team. The task of the medical center consultants had been made easier by the interval history, but it was the response to stimulants that "settled" the dispute; in fact, therapeutic response cannot serve as conclusive evidence in this case, since the drug may be effective in psychogenic behavior disorders. Clinically, what mattered to the child, his parents, his pediatrician, and his teacher was the unequivocal improvement in his behavior. And, as Dr. Wender points out, this so frequently follows the appropriate use of stimulant drugs in treating these children that failure to entertain the diagnosis of MBD is a serious breach of clinical responsibility.

Some twenty years of experience as a clinician with just such problems as John's have convinced me of the need for solid clinical account of the MBD syndrome for the more effective education of child care specialists. Wender's monograph is an outstanding contribution to this clinical literature. For that alone, we owe him our thanks. But this book is more than that. It makes a valiant effort to build a theory that can account for the syndrome, a theory based on the available clinical and experimental evidence, but one that goes beyond a descriptive restatement of the evidence to some adventurous guesses about the fundamental psychological and biochemical abnormalities.

Such a theory can serve several useful purposes: as a clinician's vademecum, as a spur to observation, and as a stimulus to observation. How well do Wender's formulations meet these objectives?

When no single symptom or sign or laboratory test is pathognomonic and when the weighting to be given combinations thereof remains uncertain, the clinician must have some central concept to guide his exploration of the presenting complaint. Wender's conception of the basic psychological defects in MBD provides this. It offers an effective device for alerting the clinician to the diagnosis in cases with quite variable initial presentations.

As to the second criterion (a spur to observation), the very effort to make "sense" out of the congeries of symptoms forces critical examination of those aspects of a particular case that do not seem to "fit." This may result in a decision to abandon the diagnosis (and search for another) or may lead to a revision in the theory. In either event, a more searching evaluation of the problem has resulted. At least, this will be so if the theory is regarded as heuristic rather than final, a point stressed throughout.

These two accomplishments in themselves are a considerable contribution. But it is in respect to the third criterion (a stimulus to experiment) that the formulations developed in this monograph are of the greatest value. A number of assertions are put forward, however tentatively, that cry out for test. The theory is operational in that it suggests *specific* tests, both at the psychological and the biochemical levels. The author is himself engaged in undertaking a number of these. By committing his views to print and offering them to what I hope will be a wide audience, he has provided all of us with a challenge for systematic clinical and experimental study.

If one advances a theory, one obviously hopes it is correct. But what distinguishes "good" from "bad" theory is less its "truth" than its susceptibility to disproof. All too many psychological theories suffer either from being so all-encompassing that they "explain" everything (i.e., make us content that we "understand," hence can abandon search) or from being so abstract as to defy operational tests. The key to utility is the ability to *predict* in advance of experiment, not to "explain" after the fact. The prediction, if proved correct, leads the search for mechanism to progressively more fundamental processes; if proved false, it forces a reformulation of basic premises.

Thus it becomes a matter of minor note that I disagree here or there. What does matter is the possibility of refutation, not by talmudic argument, but by resort to data.

For all of this, we are indebted to Paul Wender. I can only hope, in behalf of the many children who suffer from these disorders, that this book will be read carefully, examined critically, and put to the test in the clinic and laboratory. The outcome can only be better care based on improved understanding.

June 1970

LEON EISENBERG, M.D.
Chief of Psychiatry, Massachusetts General Hospital, and Professor of Psychiatry, Harvard Medical School

Acknowledgements

I express my grateful appreciation to Drs. Leon Eisenberg and David Rosenthal who read the manuscript and made many helpful suggestions. I am indebted to Gloria Parloff, for her suggestions as well as for her invaluable assistance in the editing and reediting of the manuscript. Unsolicited thanks are due the residents and students who forced me, by pointing out the obscurities in my logic, to clarify my thinking. Needless to say, all of these persons are exempt from any responsibility for the book's imperfections which they helped to ameloriate. Finally, I thank my secretaries, Margaret Claeys and Ruby Edmonds, who have patiently and stoically tolerated the retyping of multiple revisions of the manuscript.

Various copyrighted materials are quoted in the text by the permission of the *American Journal of Orthopsychiatry,* the *American Journal of Psychiatry,* the *Archives of Neurology and Psychiatry,* the *British Journal of Psychiatry,* Grune and Stratton, Publishers, the *Journal of Comparative Physiology and Psychology,* E. & S. Livingstone, Publisher, McGraw-Hill Book Company, the Menninger Foundation, Oliver and Boyd, Publishers, the *Psychoanalytic Quarterly,* the *Psychological Review,* and Charles C Thomas, Publisher.

Paul H. Wender

November 1970
Bethesda, Maryland

Contents

Minimal Brain Dysfunction in Children

Introduction: Minimal Brain Dysfunction— The Problem and the Approach

Minimal brain dysfunction is probably the single most common disorder seen by child psychiatrists. Despite this fact, its existence is often unrecognized and its prevalence is almost always underestimated. An understanding of the syndrome is obviously of great practical importance; but it is of considerable theoretical importance as well.

The syndrome is of practical importance to child psychiatry for the following reasons:

1. It constitutes a large fraction of the more seriously disturbed population of children.
2. It is frequently misdiagnosed.
3. When it is diagnosed correctly, it is often maltreated.
4. The maltreatment is expensive and by definition ineffectual.
5. The correct treatment is often dramatically effective and is always cheap and readily accessible.

This syndrome is of some practical importance also to adolescent and adult psychiatry because:

1. Though the manifestations of the syndrome change, they sometimes persist until later life.
2. It is quite likely that the child psychiatric syndrome is either the precursor or the first manifestation of a considerable number of seemingly different adult psychiatric syndromes.
3. The recognition of the relationship between the earlier and later manifestations of the syndrome may have therapeutic implications for the later manifestations.

This syndrome is of theoretical interest because it is possible to construct a model which will account for the complex psychological manifestations in terms of simpler underlying physiological variables. I shall propose such a model. It hypothesizes a specific physiological abnormality as an explanation of the etiology of the syndrome in a large fraction of the children

1

diagnosed as having minimal brain dysfunction. Present neuroanatomical and neurophysiological knowledge permits assignment of a possible neuro-anatomical and/or biochemical locus for this physiological defect. From the putative defect would follow certain quantitative deviations and variations in certain psychological functions. From these quantitative variations one can derive—with nonelaborate psychological theory—the varying qualitative psychological variations which are observed in some of these children and adults.

All "etiologists" attribute causal significance to "constitutional factors" in the origin of psychiatric dysfunction. Such general statements, being nonspecific, are not particularly clarifying or useful. The proposed model postulates a direct relationship between specific constitutional variations and observed psychological abnormalities. It provides a scheme by which one can trace the long term psychological effects of early physiological variations. I believe this model is meaningful as well as simple. To me, and I hope to the reader, the model is useful in that it clarifies some very murky areas in psychological development.

Trying to identify such an unrecognized entity among the familiar limited group of psychiatric disorders might produce misleading conclusions. Instead, what I have done is to reclassify the familiar: the biological analogy would be the linking of shrews, duckbilled platypuses, and whales in the category of "mammals." I will assert that there are intrinsic, important, and generally unrecognized similarities among a fairly heterogeneous group of individuals with disturbances that have been variously diagnosed, and that because of their similarities these individuals should be grouped together.

The most similar strategy of discovery by reclassification that I can think of in psychiatry has happened with the category of "schizophrenia." Bleuler —and others since—pointed to an ostensible similarity among a group of seemingly very divergent patients. The group in question includes individuals with diagnoses ranging from "pseudoneurosis" to "dementia praecox": it contains individuals ranging from many of Freud's early patients to chronic hebephrenics. Bleuler's categorization has "stuck," it has been accepted; whether his categorization will be of continuing heuristic value remains to be determined.

In similar wise I propose that a large number of psychiatric conditions of children can and should be included under one conceptual roof. The core disorder is a syndrome that goes by a variety of names: minimal brain damage; hyperactive or hyperkinetic child syndrome; minimal brain dysfunction; minimal cerebral palsy; minimal cerebral dysfunction; maturational lag; and postencephalitic behavior disorder, to mention only a few.

Before proceeding, it is necessary to choose a designation for the syndrome. Since the disorder is a syndrome and has varying manifestations, and since each of the designations tends to name a salient attribute which is variably present, most of the names tend to be partially incorrect and hence misnomers. If the syndrome can be present without the attribute designated by a particular name, one runs into amusing linguistic problems. Since the syndrome was initially recognized in hyperactive children, and since some children with the syndrome are hypoactive, one must either recognize the existence of "hypoactive-hyperactive children" or provide another designation. Of the names provided, each has its own particular problem: "minimal brain damage" and "minimal cerebral palsy" make etiological assertions for which in many cases there is no evidence; many children having the behavioral attributes of the syndrome have no history of and manifest no signs of neurological damage. "Hyperactive" and hyperkinetic child syndrome" both designate a salient attribute in most of these children, but, as noted, the attribute in some instances is absent. "Maturational lag" is a phrase which, again, has etiological connotations which may be unjustified—namely, that the syndrome is a result of a self-limited developmental delay. "Postencephalitic behavior disorder" was an early phrase diagnosing a particular etiological subgroup of the syndrome. "Minimal brain dysfunction" and "minimal cerebral dysfunction" imply an alteration in the functioning of the brain without specifying its localization or nature. Of the available terms, I find these two the least offensive and shall employ the former. "Brain dysfunction" has the trivial advantage of avoiding some localization within the brain. In the present state of ignorance this would seem to be the most conservative position. In the remainder of this book, therefore, the phrase "minimal brain dysfunction" is used, abbreviated as MBD. (The abbreviation is also used to designate the adjectival form, "minimally brain dysfunctioned.")

To anyone who has experience in child psychiatry, the behavior pattern associated with MBD is rather distinct, is easily identified, does not decimate the child population, and certainly does not affect a large number of adults. However, if one wishes to assert the great commonness of the syndrome—as I do—one must maintain that the typical "classical" picture is only one of many variants. One must assume, as I will, that other abnormalities of child behavior that share some features in common with the more classical ones are variants of the disorder—that the "typical" case is an extreme instance. Again, an analogy appears in the categorization of schizophrenia. Severe hebephrenia is an uncommon disorder while "borderline" or "pseudoneurotic" schizophrenic states are relatively common. To a Kraepelinian psychiatrist taking a narrow view of the disorder, hebephrenia is a typical instance of dementia praecox; to a Bleulerian it might be considered an extremely severe and comparatively unusual manifestation of schizophrenic illness. The strategic tack I have taken is foreshadowed by this analogy. Bleuler started with an extreme instance of the dementia praecox syndrome and hypothesized an underlying "primary" defect.[1] The defect was definable and recognizable psychologically and was postulated to be a reflection of an underlying neurophysiological defect. Bleuler then proceeded to illustrate how these primary abnormalities (presumed to be physiologically caused) might interact with life experience to generate the varied symptom patterns seen in the "group of schizophrenias."

Bleuler's strategy, that of postulating a group of primary related dysfunctions (disassociation, autism, ambivalence, affective abnormalities), implies that individuals who manifest only one or a few of these basic dysfunctions may share etiological factors with individuals who manifest the more "classical" syndrome of schizophrenia. I shall propose that the "typical" MBD child is a more extreme variant, and that some of his underlying physiological and psychological defects may be found in a much larger segment of the population of children. As in the case of the schizophrenias, the extreme instance may help us to learn more about the less severe ones.

The book is divided into two parts. Part One deals in traditional fashion with the characteristics, etiology, diagnosis, prognosis, and management of the syndrome. The descriptions of the syndrome and its management are primarily based on my experience in treating several hundred MBD children, but a review of the literature is included. The first part, containing this material and a review of the relevant literature, should stand of its own weight regardless of the validity of the second.

Part Two examines the proposed theory. The spatial separation is designed to facilitate in the reader's mind the separation between probable fact and possible fancy. Here, the proposed model deals with both psychological and physiological levels of explanation, and these two levels are partially dissociable. This is important to note because the psychological theorizing, being more directly tied to fact, is the less speculative of the two. It is capable of standing without its neurophysiological underpinning. Given our present knowledge, the neurophysiological explanations must be far more speculative and less trustworthy. I cannot but feel that such neurophysiological theorizing might well be printed on serrated pages which are detachable from the body of the text. Too often such theorizing is apt to be out of date when published, rendered quaint, and of value only as a potential source of amusement for psychiatric historians of the future.

[1] Although Bleuler (1911) initially described four "primary" symptoms of schizophrenia, he later attributed all four to *one,* more "primary," dysfunction: weakness of association.

For this reason it is important to emphasize the theoretical separability of the neurophysiological and psychological theories that will be proposed.

One final point relates to the audience to whom this essay is directed: it is a difficult one to specify. I have tried to answer the questions of many—for example, the practicing school counselor, the psychologist, the pediatrician, the child and adult psychiatrist, and, finally, the biochemist. In attempting to appeal to all, I hope I have not discouraged those whose primary concern may be with only part of the material covered. I will remain sanguine.

PART ONE

The Minimal Brain Dysfunction Syndrome

CHAPTER 1

Characteristics of the Minimal Brain Dysfunction Syndrome

What are MBD children like? With what problems do they appear? How are they recognized?

Oscar's eight. As we look back, we've been having problems all along but we'd gotten used to them. I'm not sure that we would have come if the school hadn't complained about the same sorts of things we've been used to for a long time. He's always been a strong-willed, negative child who wanted to do things his own way. He was impossible to toilet train or even keep around the house. When he was 2 he wandered away and we had the whole neighborhood and the police looking for him . . . . We didn't find him for five or six hours and when we did he didn't seem to be the least bit upset by his little adventure. He's always been a bundle of nervous energy. He's always fidgety—he can't even watch TV for long. When he was younger you could never afford to take your eyes off him . . . the second you did he would be into things and you'd find they were broken. He wore everything out . . . toys, clothes, everything . . . . He wasn't malicious. He just has two left hands and two left feet. He tripped all over himself and when he was growing up he was constantly bumped or scraped. Fortunately he was a pretty thick-skinned little boy, pretty tough, and never cried very much. As I said, it's always been hard to discipline him. It started with toilet training. That was a nightmare —he still wets the bed occasionally. Sometimes he's purely negative and other times he just appears to be forgetful. It's hard to tell if it's really forgetfulness. He changes so much from one day to the next— he's consistently variable. He doesn't seem to be a daydreamer but sometimes it looks like he just forgets what you told him. That shows up in the way he plays. He's never had much stick-to-itiveness and always runs from one thing to another. He never had trouble at school getting along with the other kids. He's always been really outgoing—if anything, inclined to be a bit bossy, but very friendly. He likes his teacher, too. All the teachers have thought Oscar was a nice boy but he just wouldn't listen. This year his teacher says he's always in and out of his seat, humming in class, fiddling around, bothering the other children, and just seems uninterested in learning. She feels—the way we do—that he could really learn if he tried. When he is interested in something he can really get quite good at it. The trouble with school just seems to be that he doesn't care.

The school suggested that we bring Gary for a psychiatric examination. They thought that maybe his learning problems might have an emotional basis. The accompanying letter from the school psychologist regarding this child with a "special learning disorder" indicated that Gary had normal intelligence with "no indication of brain damage" (because "there was inappreciable scatter" on testing). The problem "seemed to be primarily motivational . . . . A difficulty in complying with authority figures, particularly females, seems to be the major dynamic factor. Psychotherapy for the child and his parents is recommended." The child's school history revealed few details that differentiated him from most children with "special learning disorders" who are not referred to child guidance clinics. Inquiry concerning the referring psychologist revealed that he was a proponent of the psychogenic theory of learning disability; he was apt to refer for psychiatric evaluation all children with learning problems who were not grossly retarded.

Johnny's probation officer told us to come here. He's been a bad kid for years and managed not to get booked for a long time. In the first grade he took stuff from my purse and sold stuff from around the house. The past couple years he's fallen in with a bad bunch of kids who've been leading him—other kids have always been able to boss him around. First it was a bit of stealing from the drugstores, then hubcaps, and finally this business with the car. He's always done badly in school. He was left back twice and been suspended a few times. He couldn't do anything very good in sports either. He's always been trying to get other kids to like him any way he could. He never did what we told him at home. Everything you did would roll off his back. My husband says I spare the rod and that I don't follow through. He ought to live with Johnny. I tell him something 10 times, 20 times, 100 times and he just ignores me. It isn't like he's being ornery. It just never reaches him. I just can't get through. The father added:

"He's not really a bad kid . . . . I wasn't good in school and I had some trouble with the cops when I was a boy . . . . I drank a bit too much but I've finally settled down."

Our doctor thought that Mark ought to get a neurological evaluation. He said that he might have minimal cerebral palsy and recommended us to you for a neurological evaluation and EEG. Mark was a premature baby, had jaundice after he was born, was a bit slow developing, a bit clumsy and awkward, and our doctor always felt that he might have a little bit of cerebral palsy. He's been a very nice boy. He's very affectionate—if anything, he hangs on you too much for attention and love. He's very immature and it's hard for him to do his chores. He's eight now and he really can't tie his shoelaces. He doesn't take care of his room, he just forgets to do what you tell him to. He had to repeat first grade and is having trouble now in the second. They said his I.Q. was low-normal and that he should be able to learn but he still seems to be having a great deal of difficulty. He has a lot of trouble writing and has very messy handwriting. I've tried to help him with that and with reading. He reverses a lot of letters and words and just can't stick with it. You try to get him to sit down and five minutes after you start he's up again. He's a good boy, he just has some problems. Our doctor thought that by finding out exactly what the difficulty was we might be able to get him into some kind of treatment program.

These vignettes are condensations of several cases and portray common variants or subtypes of the MBD syndrome. What do these children have in common? One is "all boy," one has a "special learning disorder," one appears to be a budding delinquent, and the last seems to have organic brain damage. Despite these seemingly disparate clinical pictures, it is very probable that all four of these boys have "minimal brain dysfunction."

If these children may be meaningfully grouped together, the examples illustrate that the MBD syndrome is indeed a syndrome: the behavioral and psychological abnormalities portrayed above occur in a number of areas which are not necessarily affected in any individual child. These areas will be described in more detail later. A further complication, not demonstrated in these histories, is that the affected areas often change over time, with certain abnormalities disappearing and others becoming more salient at different ages. This, too, will be elaborated. I shall also include descriptions of various clinical signs of MBD, of MBD subtypes, of social context, and of a diagrammatic means of representing the overlap of MBD with other diagnostic states in children.

CHARACTERISTIC DYSFUNCTIONS

MBD children manifest dysfunction in the following areas: motor activity and coordination; attention and cognitive function; impulse control; interpersonal relations, particularly dependence-independence and responsiveness to social influence; and emotionality. The characteristic dysfunctions in these areas are detailed below.

Motor Behavior

The principal abnormalities of motor function are a high activity level and impaired coordination (dyspraxia). As "hyperactivity" (the term often applied to the syndrome) implies, many of these children are described as motorically overactive. A history frequently reported by parents involves a child who was active and restless in infancy, stood and walked at an early age, and then, like an infant King Kong, burst the bars of his crib asunder and sallied forth to destroy his parents' house. The description of the child as a toddler is likely to mention that he "was into everything," was constantly touching—and hence, inadvertently breaking—toys and objects, and had to be watched at all times for his own protection as well as the preservation of the household. As an older child, he may be described as being incessantly in motion, driven like a motor, constantly fidgeting, unable to sit still at the dinner table or even in front of the television set. At school his teacher is apt to report that the child fidgets, is unable to sit still in his seat, gets up and walks around in the classroom, talks, jostles, and annoys his fellows. Older children and adolescents will usually be aware of their excessive activity level, which they often characterize as "nervousness" or "restlessness." When successfully treated with medication, they will report a decline in these symptoms which parallels others' report of a decline in activity.

Parents sometimes report two additional early manifestations of excessive activity: "colic" during infancy and sleep problems. Stewart et al. (1966) report an increased prevalence of infant feeding problems and colic among the hyperactive children in their series.[2] The sleeping difficulties are variable: Some children go to bed late, fall asleep with difficulty, awaken frequently, and arise early. Others may have difficulty falling asleep, but sleep profoundly and are difficult to arouse.

The motoric hyperactivity is often accompanied by a verbal hyperactivity. Some children manifest a press of speech analogous to that seen in manic adults. Unless prompted by the interviewer (or parent or teacher)

---

[2] Although they report these figures as nonsignificant, a recalculation of their data using a one-tailed exact probability test reveals them to be statistically significant.

they are unable to maintain a cognitive focus; and if left to themselves they demonstrate a more or less typical flight of ideas. Occasionally an older child will complain of a press of thoughts: "I can't stop thinking even when I go to sleep."

Attempts to document a gross increase in motor activity with objective measuring devices have been variably successful. Bell et al. (1969), employing pedometers, were not able to demonstrate increased activity in a subsample of nursery school children rated as hyperactive by observers. Other studies do provide objective documentation for an increase in motor activity in some "hyperactive" children. Hutt et al. (1963) employed a room with a grid-marked floor which permitted the assessment of changes of location over time and the amount of time spent engaged in one activity; they were able to show that the time spent in any one activity was shorter for epileptic hyperactive children and that the mobility of such children was decreased by amphetamine. Sprague et al. (1969) measured movement by means of a stabilimetric cushion (which measured wiggling) and a telemetric device to measure head movement. Using these measures the authors were able to reliably classify retarded children into either high or low activity groups.

The reason that objective measures sometimes fail to document increased activity is probably twofold. First, the techniques employed vary. Gross motor activity (measured by the pedometer) may not be excessive, while fidgeting (measured by Sprague's technique) may indeed be increased. Second, some MBD children are in fact not hyperactive but only appear so. Some give the impression of hyperactivity because of their constant shifting of activities and lack of goal direction. In other children the striking feature is not the total amount of activity but the children's inability to inhibit activity when inhibition is appropriate; these children are no more active than other children on the playground but cannot curtail their activity in the classroom.

Lastly, there are a very few children with other features of the syndrome who are motorically *hypo*active and listless. These children should be included in the MBD group not only because they possess many other characteristics of the syndrome, but also because they respond similarly to drugs.[3]

---

[3] Anderson (1956) and Bender (1949) note that some children have most of the characteristics of the "hyperactive" (MBD) behavioral syndrome but lack one defining attribute: they are hypoactive. This observation jibes with my experience. Recognition of the subgroup is of practical importance, because by virtue of not being designated as hyperactive, such children do not receive appropriate therapy. This is unfortunate, since drug therapy often seems to be effective for the hypoactive subgroup as well as the hyperactive subgroup.

The excessive motor activity of children with the MBD syndrome decreases with age, as does the motor activity of children in general. The subjective concomitants of the syndrome may not disappear so rapidly. In a follow-up study of hyperactive children, Menkes et al. (1966) found that some patients reported persistent feelings of restlessness which lasted up to the age of 30.

Another major motor deviation seen in many, but not all, of these children is incoordination. Some MBD children have histories of advanced motor development, of having attained developmental landmarks at an early age, and of always having been good at athletics. More common is the history which describes a clumsy, inept child. He may have walked at an early age but he always had "two left feet" and constantly tripped over himself. He may have had difficulty with balance and may not have been able to ride a two-wheel bicycle until he was 9 or 10. He may have poor fine motor coordination: his handwriting is described as unusually poor, and he has had difficulty in learning to button buttons, tie shoelaces, and cut with scissors. (An example in point is that of a boy with a WISC I.Q. of 140 who could not learn to tie shoelaces until he was 10 years old.) Many of the children have poor visual-motor coordination and have great difficulty in learning to throw and catch a ball. This area of disability in particular is psychologically painful to boys, who may report that they are picked eighteenth when baseball teams are "choosing up" sides. As will be discussed later, the characteristic psychological defense of boys takes the form of: "I don't care, I don't like baseball, basketball, ..." This may sometimes lead to feminine identification and/or rejection by the peer group.

Attentional and Perceptual-Cognitive Function

The most striking and constant perceptual-cognitive abnormality of the MBD child is shortness of attention span and poor concentration ability. Parents report that the child never plays at one game for a long period of time and rushes from one activity to another. As a toddler or a nursery school student the child pulls every toy from the shelf, plays with each desultorily, and then seems at a loss for further things to do. When he reaches school age, his teacher is likely to report: "You can't get him to pay attention for long . . . he won't finish his work . . . he doesn't do well on his own—even though he functions well on a one-to-one basis." Both parent and teacher report: "He doesn't listen [for long], doesn't mind . . . doesn't remember."

In describing the perceptual-cognitive problems of the MBD child, Strauss and Kephart (1955) observe that distractibility is "often the most obvious of [the MBD child's] difficulties. He finds it impossible to engage in any activity in a concentrated fashion but is always being led aside from any task at hand by stimuli which should remain extraneous but do not. In extreme cases his activity may appear to be an aimless pursuit of stimulus after stimulus as one after another of the elements in his perceptual environment attracts his attention. If we make the structuring problem easier for him . . . [by reducing extraneous stimuli and/or simplifying the task] his distractibility decreases" (p. 135). The last observation is reflected in the frequently heard assertion that the child functions quite normally "on a one-to-one basis."

Objective documentation of the attentional deficit is sparse. Hutt et al. (1963) were able to show not only that brain-damaged children had a shorter attention span for playing with one object at a time but that they were less able to experience distractions without disruption of their task. Non-brain-damaged children were more readily able to visually fixate on activities other than their main activity, that is, they were better able to direct their attention elsewhere without disrupting their ongoing task.

The quality of "forced responsiveness" to environmental stimuli is often present and reflected in an interest in and attraction to minute details. This concern with the irrelevant seems to reflect an inability to organize hierarchically, so that all aspects—of a percept or an idea—are of equal importance; as much attention is directed to the peripheral as to the essential. This approach may sometimes lend an obsessive quality to the child's actions. The obsessive quality may be strengthened by perseveration, which is another behavior manifestation seen among some MBD children. When both occur together (the repetitive performance of the trivial) the behavior is apt to be labeled "compulsive." The repetitive, stereotyped nature of the behavior is sometimes overlooked because observers focus on its interpersonal consequences and ignore its style. Much of the attention-seeking and demanding behavior of these children has a stereotyped, compulsive flavor.

It is worth mentioning that the classroom inattentiveness of these children is sometimes labeled "daydreaming." Since the rich inner life seems to be more the privilege of the schizoid than the MBD child, the report of such "daydreaming" may erroneously militate against a diagnosis of MBD. Asking a few questions of the child will usually resolve the differential diagnostic problem: whereas the schizoid child is likely to have involved and fantastical reveries, the MBD child who is "daydreaming" is apt to report that he is anticipating his afternoon post-liberation pleasures.

Cognitively, these children manifest varied patterns of defects. Many children show both noncognitive difficulties (which have already been and will be further discussed) and cognitive problems; many children have hyperactivity and other aspects of the MBD syndrome without having any specific perceptual-cognitive problems; finally, many children identified on the basis of "special learning difficulties" that are the major causes of concern manifest other MBD characteristics (including "hyperactivity") only minimally or not at all.

Whether problems of attention or "special learning problems" contribute more to the MBD child's academic troubles is hard to say, since either would be sufficient to cause difficulties. In any event, school underachievement (which is discussed below) is almost a hallmark of this syndrome. The etiological problem is compounded by the psychological consequences of early underachievement; a vicious circle is produced in which poor performance generates criticism and a poor self-image, both of which tend to decrease motivation.[4]

As with hyperactivity, the outward signs of distractibility and inattentiveness tend to disappear with age, but the problems may tend to remain in more muted form. Older MBD subjects tend to report continued difficulty in concentration. It is my impression that such individuals also manifest an absence of sustained interest in nonacademic areas: recreational activities, hobbies, jobs, initially attract the attention of these persons but (like the toys of childhood) fail to keep it.

Learning Difficulties

One complex form of psychological performance in the MBD child that should be commented on especially is school learning performance. The determinants of academic performance are numerous and complex. Capacity, motivation, and adequacy of teaching all contribute to how well a child will learn, and consequently poor school performance is not a specific diagnostic sign. Bearing this in mind, it is of considerable practical consequence to be aware that a substantial fraction of MBD children (of the order of magnitude of one-half to two-thirds) manifest learning difficulties in school, and that *among children with normal intelligence and with good school experience MBD is a very frequent source of academic difficulty.* The most serious manifestation is difficulty in learning to read (although problems in writing—generally sloppiness—and problems in comprehension and arithmetic may be present as well). The terms "reading disability," "learning disability," and "dyslexia" designate the difficulties of an heterogeneous group of children. Included are neurotics, dysphasics, and retarded children. Probably the single most common subgroup, however, consists of children with the MBD syndrome. MBD has been implicated by several

---

[4] For an elaboration of the mechanism of such cycles, "deviation amplifying feedbacks," see Wender (1968).

studies of adolescents with academic problems. Reviewing a successive sample of 20 MBD children over the age of 12, Laufer (1962) found the only characteristic common to all was "poor school performance despite adequate intellect" (p. 505). Working with Swedish teen-age dyslexics of normal intelligence, Frisk et al. (1967) found that approximately one-third to one-half showed current distractibility and restlessness, sleep disturbance, or impaired motor abilities, and that as children they had had an increased prevalence of speech difficulties, clumsiness, and enuresis (an aspect of poor impulse control that will be discussed below). Studying a nonselected group of "adolescent underachievers," Hammar (1967) found that approximately one-half consisted of MBD children "grown up"; when children with undiscovered retardation were eliminated, 67% of the underachievers were MBD.

From a practical standpoint it is important to be aware that not only do many MBD children present as "underachievers" or "dyslexics," but that many children referred for nonspecified "emotional problems" have reading problems together with other MBD problems. The description of Frisk et al. of such a group is consonant with my own clinical experience: approximately one-third of their series of dyslexic children were referred for "physical or neurotic symptoms, although poor adjustment and vaguely described school problems also were indicated" (p. 338). These "neurotic" symptoms were found—and this again is in keeping with my experience— to be appreciably aggravated by the unmet pressures of school and home and the child's sense of guilt and inadequacy regarding his own substandard academic performance.

From the vantage point of the clinician, considerable care must be exerted in sorting out causes and effects: he is apt to be presented with a confusing array of personal and academic problems which overlie and may even conceal the MBD difficulties which are their nidus.

Impulse Control

A very frequently described characteristic of MBD children is poor "impulse control," a decreased ability to inhibit. The principal dysfunctions included under this rather general term include: low frustration tolerance, antisocial behavior (destructiveness, stealing, lying, firesetting, sexual "acting out"), and impaired sphincter control (enuresis, encopresis). Hyperreactivity could also be included but will be discussed under emotional dysfunctions.

Low frustration tolerance, the inability to delay gratification and "impulsivity" have similar behavioral referents. The child in question is described as having little stick-to-itiveness or perseverance; he gives up readily. He rapidly becomes upset when things or people fail to behave as he would have them. He is the opposite of the child who will sit quietly in the corner attempting to solve a puzzle and brooking no interruption. The MBD child may function better when given constant adult attention, praise, and reinforcement—hence the frequent (and already cited) comment of teachers that such a child seems to function well with "one-to-one attention."

Defective impulse control is also manifested in poor planning and judgment. Foresight and organizational ability are qualities which develop, if at all, with age. MBD children manifest less of these attributes than would be age appropriate. They are more likely than most children to run off in several directions at once and to fail to see the future consequences of their action. An attribute which might be placed either under impulsivity or inattentiveness is these children's marked lack of attention to detail. This is manifested at home as disorderliness and a general lack of organization. Parents complain of untidy rooms and failure to dress neatly: unbuttoned buttons, unzipped zippers, untied shoelaces. At school it is seen in their sloppy work, their failure to finish tasks, and their approximations in reading and writing.

MBD children are often reckless and manifest no concern for bodily safety—they act without thinking, are frequently injured, and often seem to be accident prone. The reports of injuries, including head injuries, so often elicited in the histories of these children are often a manifestation of the child's illness and not a primary cause of it.[5]

Social impulsivity—antisocial behavior—is often prominent and tends to dominate the clinical picture: many of these children are wanton destroyers, compulsive stealers, and firesetters. Destructiveness is usually the sign manifested earliest in their development: the children are not malicious but are surprised breakers of toys and wearers-out of clothing—no item seems to remain intact in their possession. Stealing, a ubiquitous and multidetermined behavior of young children, tends to persist in a few MBD children for years. It may have a constant and compulsive quality (continually taking money from the household), or it may appear reactively and in a seemingly understandable way (e.g., as retaliation or in order to win the affection of other children). What is striking is the low threshold for the appearance of such behavior and its failure to respond to social controls. Similar comments apply to lying, firesetting, and sexual

[5] Bond and Appel (1931) reported that many of the postencephalitic children they studied had suffered head injuries, usually from being struck by automobiles as they impulsively rushed into the street. In several instances the children had incurred these injuries following their recovery from encephalitis and their development of MBD symptoms.

"acting out." Very young children are honest and the appearance of lying may be considered a developmental milestone. In the normal course of events, indiscriminate lying is followed by modulated honesty. Not so with some MBD children, in whom compulsive lying persists through adolescence. Fire fascinates primitive man and children alike, but both are generally able to curtail their attraction to it. For a few MBD children this is not the case and in them compulsive firesetting may dominate the clinical picture. "Sexual acting out," sexual promiscuity, is seen in some adolescent girls. Again, obviously, sexual drives are ubiquitous and it is only the failure of inhibition that is pathological. [This last symptom (sign, to be exact) is particularly dependent on cultural definition and may currently be in the process of being legislated out of existence.]

In MBD children in whom "antisocial" behavior is prominent, this behavior usually begins to attract increasing social and professional attention so that the other MBD abnormalities are ignored; in such instances the children are often diagnosed as "psychopathic." Although an appreciable fraction of antisocial and delinquent children may have MBD characteristics, only a small fraction of the children seen with other manifestations of the MBD syndrome conspicuously display "antisocial" characteristics as well. Even so, it may be that the association between the MBD syndrome and antisocial behavior is less than it appears to be; it is likely that hyperactive and distractible children who are otherwise agreeable are not referred to child guidance clinics and that their more distressing fellows are overrepresented.

Another common characteristic of MBD children is defective sphincter control: many of these children are enuretic or encopretic. Whether these problems should be catalogued as problems of negativism, inattentiveness, or impulse control is problematic. Some children are reported as having been unusually obstinate about learning these skills; supposedly they fully understood the demands, but refused to comply with them.[6] Other children apparently have failed to heed internal cues and have wet themselves while playing—they forgot. Nocturnal enuresis is common and might have been listed under motoric hyperactivity since there is some evidence that it is a direct manifestation of problems in the regulation of arousal (Broughton, 1968). True encopresis—a much less common problem—may have similar causes. Generally, however, the encopresis is of the "false" variety; some of the children (generally the more severely disturbed ones) do have full bowel movements in their pants but usually

---

[6] Such children document the psychoanalytic proposition linking obstinacy and toilet-training problems but suggest an alternative explanation: difficult toilet training is the first sign—not the cause—of the later stubbornness.

the complaint refers to another manifestation of the MBD child's neglect of detail—in this instance a nonfastidious inattention to wiping which produces slight staining.

Interpersonal Relations

The most prominent types of MBD alterations in interpersonal relations are a considerable resistance to social demands, increased independence, and extroversion. The MBD child tends to show these patterns in his relations to his parents, parent surrogates, and peers. Probably the single most disturbing feature of these children's behavior, and the one most responsible for their referral for treatment, is their unresponsiveness to social demands. They may appear almost impossible to acculturate. In the area of response to external controls most MBD children are similarly described. They are perennial 2-year-olds. They are obstinate, stubborn, negativistic, bossy, disobedient, sassy, and impervious. All disciplinary measures seem unsuccessful: rewards, deprivation of privileges, physical punishment. "He wants his own way . . . he never learns by his own mistakes. . . . You can't reach him . . . he's almost immune to punishment." The manifestations of noncompliance change as the child grows older. During adolescence his noncompliance is apt to take the form of "passive-aggressiveness" or disengagement and ignoring of his parents. He does not oppose so much as he does not listen.

The child's peer relations are also predictable. With adults he resists controls—with peers he attempts to be controlling. He may be described as having no friends, but closer inspection reveals a pattern much different from that of the schizoid or withdrawn child. The MBD child is usually quite aggressive socially and initiates friendships successfully, but his "bossiness" and insistence that all games be played according to his own rules drive other children away.[7] He is apt to report that he is talked about, rejected, and, perhaps, bullied; these reports are not paranoid but are accurate reflections of what his own behavior compels others to do. He "makes friends easily but can't keep them." As a result he is often found to be playing with younger children, and, if a boy, with girls. A superficial report of the child's peer relations may convey the impression that he is introverted and fearful but closer inspection will usually reveal him to be an unsuccessful extrovert.

The least constant—and most perplexing—aspect of the MBD child's behavior is in the area of affection and dependence. MBD children tend

---

[7] Excessive timidity is occasionally seen. This is more characteristic of the most immature, most physically inept children, who are rejected by their peers and unable to defend themselves.

to polarize along this dimension, and I suspect that their numerical distribution would be bimodal. Many are described as having been infant "touch-me-nots," who did not enjoy being cuddled, who avoided physical contact, and who wiggled off their mother's lap. As toddlers these children wandered away from home and at school age showed no separation anxiety. In another MBD subgroup, the children appear to be excessively dependent or to be vacillating between excessive dependency and independence. They may be insatiably demanding of affection, or they may alternate between such a position and one of complete indifference (in a manner similar to that seen in many institutionalized children). These children are (Bond and Appel, 1931) "mawkishly affectionate, eager to paw strangers, anxious for notice" (p. 15). Whether the polarities of dependence and independence represent "intrinsic" variance or varying psychological responses to the same underlying tendencies is uncertain. In some children the independence seems to be "pure," having been present from an early age and having been unsullied by much affectionateness (the lack of affectionateness may, in fact, be a parental complaint). Even these children are often excessively dependent instrumentally, since poor motor skills combined with poor frustration tolerance favor parental intercession. In other children the independence seems to be reaction formation or a form of bravado. These children are reminiscent of the monkeys studied by Harlow (1958) who would venture into the more open and frightening room only after having "charged themselves" with bravery by first cuddling cloth mothers made available to them.

Emotion

The emotionality of MBD children shows four major types of dysfunction: increased lability, altered reactivity, increased aggressiveness, and dysphoria.

These children's behavior tends to be predictably unpredictable. Their spontaneous lability is reflected in statements such as: "He's happy one minute, impossible to get along with the next . . . . He's got his good days and bad days and it's hard to understand why."

Reactivity to both internal and external stimuli is often altered and may take the form of either hyporeactivity or hyperreactivity: responses are normal in kind but abnormal in degree. Pain responses are often diminished. The children seem unusually undaunted and stoical regarding the frequent bumps, falls, and scrapes to which young flesh is heir. (This may be obscured by the increased attention-seeking some of them manifest —when observed they tend to squeeze every last drop of secondary gain from minor traumata.) As already mentioned with regard to social demands, parents report that physical punishment goes unnoticed. Similarly, psychological punishment—deprivation of privileges, criticism, disapprobation—is also unheeded. "You can't get through to him at all . . . punishment just rolls off his back." It may be noted that in both of the above respects, MBD children are at an opposite pole from many borderline schizophrenic children, who may have catastrophic reactions in response to mild physical injury and who are excessively sensitive to any form of punishment.

The "hyperreactivity" might have been just as logically discussed under the heading of impulse control because it is not clear if the MBD child's abnormal behavior is a manifestation of abnormal emotional reactivity or the inability to modulate normal reactivity. In any event, situations that most children would regard as pleasurable result in excessive excitement, while unpleasurable ones produce excessive anger or temper outbursts. Most young children will become excited at the supermarket or the circus; MBD children tend to become very overexcited and to lose what few controls they do have with brief and/or less intense exposure to such situations. Similarly, most children do not tolerate frustration or disappointment well; such stoical equanimity as they may acquire comes with age. But the MBD child not only has a much lower threshold for such frustration, he also has a more violent reaction to it. When things do not go his way, an MBD child is subject to temper tantrums, angry outbursts, or sullen displeasure—the type of reaction varying, among other things, with the child's age. Such loss of control can also occur in reaction to inner stimuli. Most young children become irritable and regress when fatigued or hungry—MBD children, again, appear to have a lower tolerance for such stresses and a lower threshold for such regression. Under the influence of excitement, MBD children manifest still further disorganization and decreased responsiveness to external controls. This lack of responsiveness to others *is* similar in many respects to that seen in the abrupt "catastrophic" reactions of some schizophrenic children.

Although many parents characterize their MBD children as "angry," they usually describe irritability rather than hostility. Unmodulated reactivity is the referent: "He's got a low boiling point . . . when he gets angry he can't control himself. . . ." Many children are described as being "good-natured" except for infrequent angry outbursts. In others, anger or sadism seems to have been present from an early age, and does not seem entirely reactive to the unusually severe punishment which such behavior generally engenders from parents. Among those MBD children preoccupied with injury, violence and death, one is apt to find a larger fraction of children in whom the MBD syndrome exists concurrently with a borderline schizophrenic process. Sadism, too, directed toward either other children or animals, is *not* characteristic and its presence suggests more serious—schizophrenic—pathology. Again, the bias produced by clinic selection tends to increase the apparent prevalence of children with difficulties in control of anger, which is a socially disturbing symptom. It is less likely that unaggressive children with MBD characteristics will be referred to the child guidance clinic or the psychiatrist.

The major dysphoric characteristics are anhedonia, depression, low self-esteem, and anxiety.

Anhedonia—the inability (or reduced ability) to experience pleasure— is not always conspicuous but it is usually present: "He never gets a kick out of anything . . . he can't be bothered to do much, nothing really seems to give him pleasure . . . you can never satisfy him." The insatiability implied by the foregoing phrases is often considered to be a product of "spoiling" or excessive gratification. Many MBD children do not have a history of being excessively indulged; their insatiability seems more a sign of their lifelong nongratifiability than an effect of cultivated excessive demands. This diminished pleasure sensitivity has not been commented on in previous description of the syndrome. I would like to call the reader's attention to the anhedonia since I believe—rightly or wrongly —that it is a characteristic critically related to the etiology of the syndrome.

Many of the children are said to have "masked depression" or to have "depressive equivalents."[8] The behavioral referents of these statements include: expressions of concern about possible injury and death for their parents and themselves, expressed low self-esteem, feelings of guilt or unworthiness, and lack of zest and initiative.

A characteristic that is far from unique to MBD children but is seen in virtually all such children is low self-esteem. In older children and adolescents the self-evaluations may be concealed by bravado, but parents or teachers will report that the children often describe themselves as defective, bad, inadequate, or different. This low opinion of themselves generally occurs in the absence of any other signs or sadness or depression.

Lastly, excess anxiety is seen in a few children. The children in question usually appear to be "neurotic," that is, overconstricted or compulsive. In some, the compulsiveness appears "defensive" in function—the children's anxiety may increase considerably when their compulsive habits are interfered with. (An alternative explanation is simply that anxiety is

[8] These phrases sometimes contain an implicit assertion about the etiology of the MBD syndrome. In view of the considerable controversy concerning the etiology of depression itself, the explanation by implicit identity is not as clarifying as it first seems.

generated by attempts to alter any fixed habit patterns.) In other instances, the compulsiveness appears to be a familial pattern and seems to have been fostered by the child's parents (who are often over-organized and rigid people themselves.) When nonfamilial, the compulsiveness may have been "hit upon" spontaneously, becoming ingrained in those children who have markedly rigid needs and demands for constancy and sameness. These latter children seem to have difficulties similar to those Goldstein (1942) has described in brain-damaged adults: in both children and adults the compulsiveness appears to prevent the anxiety that some people experience in new or different or unexpected situations. However, although the children may react quite violently to alteration of such prescribed patterns, they do not react in the "catastrophic" fashion Goldstein described in his patients.

Pervasive and prolonged anxiety is not common among MBD children. As a chronic symptom it is more common in the seriously disturbed, borderline schizophrenic children. As an acute symptom it is seen in those children whose impulsivity has momentarily gotten them into difficulty; it is frequently and appropriately seen in children who have recently been suspended from school or called before the juvenile court.

CHANGING MANIFESTATIONS OF THE SYNDROME WITH AGE

A characteristic feature of the MBD syndrome, and one that tends to conceal its diagnosis, is the change in its manifestations as the child grows. The behavior that is salient in a toddler is different from that which is salient in an adolescent.

The reasons for these changes are several. First, there seem to be genuine physiological alterations with maturation—for example, motoric hyperactivity and enuresis apparently decrease with age. Second, there are learned psychological alterations—a child is more hostile after his tenth year of peer rejection than he is after one or 2 years of such treatment. Third, "problems" are socially defined and depend on social expectations: a fidgety nursery school child is expected (and tolerable), while a restless second grader is not; reading difficulty (learning with effort) is expected of first graders, but it may be called "dyslexia" in the third grade.

The most typical patterns during the various stages of maturation would be approximately as follows.

As an infant, the MBD child's most conspicuous problem would be physiological functioning: he is apt to be hyperalert and irritable; he is apt to have "colic," crying frequently and being difficult to soothe; he is

apt to have sleep disturbances (which may be his most prominent abnormality)—he may have difficulty in falling or staying asleep, or he
may awaken frequently and early.

At the toddler stage (2–4 years), the child's behavioral repertoire
mushrooms, and in the case of the MBD child, the capacities for wrong-
doing expand similarly. The most disturbing—and hence most frequently
reported characteristics—are destructiveness (usually inadvertent) and
an inability to "listen," that is, to respond to parental discipline. If un-
attended, the MBD child is "into everything," pulling pots and pans from
cupboards, ashtrays from tables. Unless he is firmly supervised he will
wander away from home, into the street, into a cleverly varied group of
dangerous situations. Parental prohibitions are useless. The instant his
mother's back is turned the child repeats the prohibited activity. Consistency and firmness are relatively ineffectual. The child's "affectionate"
behavior is characteristic: he is a noncuddler, but at the same time that
he is wiggling off laps, he is simultaneously demanding attention. He stands,
so to speak, at arm's length, prodding his parent with a pole. Motoric
abnormalities may or may not be present: he is likely to have some speech
difficulties (immature, "babyish" speech) and is likely to trip over himself
in his destructive sorties. In summary, the MBD toddler is an exaggerated
2-year-old: undisciplinable, strong-willed, demanding, and—most important from the parents' standpoint—singularly ungratifying.

As the MBD child reaches preschool age, most of the above characteristics persist, but at this age the attentional and social problems become
more conspicuous. The short attention span, low frustration tolerance,
and temper tantrums make sustained play and nursery school participation difficult. Indicative peer relations soon appear: the MBD child
teases, dominates, annoys; in more extreme instances his aggressiveness
is more direct. These attributes endear him neither to his teacher nor to
his fellows, and in some instances result in his beginning his academic
career as a kindergarten dropout.

When the MBD child begins the first grade, the motoric restlessness
becomes salient: his teacher complains that he cannot sit still, gets up
and walks around, whistles, and shuffles. Academic problems—though
often present—tend to be ignored. First-graders are not expected to
learn to read. Enuresis may "now" appear. Although it may have been
continually present it is defined as a problem only when the child reaches
an age when it is expected to disappear (usually about 6), or when he
stays overnight at camp or with friends. His other nonendearing traits
at home (noncompliance, tantrums, etc.) are likely to persist but to be
overshadowed by his school difficulties.

At about the third grade, when the child is 9 or 10, academic and antisocial problems assume the limelight. Until that time slowness in reading could be attributed to "immaturity" or academic unreadiness. By the third grade the diagnosis is changed to that of a learning problem, or learning disorder. Reading difficulty causes the greatest concern but the child may also display problems with writing (messiness) and arithmetic. Outside of school, antisocial behavior is likely to command attention. Stealing, lying, and firesetting were tolerable in the 6-year-old but are not tolerable in the 10-year-old. When these behaviors persist—and particularly if they are severe—they make the loudest claim for intervention. In many of these young social transgressors, concurrent academic problems may be overlooked at first. When they are discovered later, after a full evaluation, the child's behavior, his "acting out," is sometimes explained as a reaction to his learning problems.

During preadolescence and early adolescence, social (antisocial) problems become the most common causes for referral. While the academic ones remain, they may now be taken for granted. This is *not* to say that the *same* child who has a reading problem predictably develops social problems. Rather, antisocial problems are among the most common problems for this age group, and MBD children constitute an appreciable fraction of these "antisocial" children. By about age 10 the child is likely to have fallen several grade levels behind in reading. Since adequate performance on most other subjects demands competent reading, the child's academic level tends to be generally retarded. Rejected by the adult establishment and the "proper" boys and girls, the MBD child may take up with other outcasts. Depending on his social class and the era, his group of delinquents will fight, steal cars, or take drugs. Even if the serious antisocial problems are not present, the persistence of the other problems constructs a common and distressing personality structure: an academically underachieving, self-centered, negativistic adolescent.

The *post*adolescent fate of the MBD child is uncertain and his clinical picture cannot be drawn. Some of the possible outcomes are discussed in the chapter on prognosis. It should be emphasized that not every MBD child progresses through each of the presented patterns. Some children manifest difficulties in all developmental stages, some in only a few. As mentioned, not all MBD children have difficulties in all areas at any one stage: some will have academic problems, some will have social problems, and some will have neither. Lastly, MBD children tend to "outgrow" not only their motoric problems but their other difficulties as well. Any given MBD child may follow the developmental sequence listed and "drop out" at one particular stage. In fact, it is usual for the problems to abate at or around the time of puberty. Certainly the developmental stages do not constitute a fatalistic timetable of childhood behavior disorder.

CLINICAL SIGNS

Neurological Signs

There is an increased prevalence of minor or "soft" neurological signs in MBD children, while the prevalence of "hard" (classical) neurological signs is approximately normal. The deviances include poor fine motor coordination, impaired visual motor coordination, poor balance, clumsiness, strabismus, choreiform movements, and "poor speech" [e.g., Prechtl and Stemmer (1962); Stewart et al. (1966)]. Such signs are referred to as "soft" because—unlike the "hard" signs of classical neurology, paresis and paralysis, anesthesia, and reflex changes—the "soft" signs are slight, inconsistently present, and not clearly associated with localized neuroanatomical lesions. Dysfunctions such as clumsiness may represent "normal" variation and be totally unassociated with central nervous system pathology. It is of practical importance that the neurologist who has been trained with adults may neither look for such dysfunctions nor report them when found. Many children diagnosed as neurologically normal by adult neurologists are designated as having "soft impairments" by child neurologists. The teacher or the parent often provides useful information when reporting that the child is clumsy or poorly coordinated; the skilled child neurologist will employ similar behavioral referents and base his judgments on the ease and finesse with which a child performs ordinary tasks. The prevalence of soft neurological signs as defined above is approximately 50% in MBD children referred for psychiatric consultation. Obviously, the percentage of children with such signs is much higher in series reported by neurologists, since in general they see children in whom the presence of neurological abnormalities has served as the basis of referral. The diagnostic usefulness of such signs is limited by the fact that, unlike "hard" signs, soft signs occur in a moderate number of apparently normal persons. Kennard (1966) studied the prevalence of 18 minor neurological signs in two groups of adolescents, hospitalized "organic" patients, and high school students with better-than-average adjustment. Although 100% of the patients and 70% of the controls had at least one sign, the average number of such signs was five and one, respectively. Representative frequencies for particular signs include: extra-ocular muscle dysfunction, 44% versus 12%; tremor, 42% versus 17%; athetoid movements, 32% versus 5%; dysdiadochokinesia, 29% versus 15%; Babinski sign, 20% versus 9%.

The prevalence of abnormal electroencephalograms in MBD children is problematic. Electroencephalographic abnormalities are considered relevant but few authors report their prevalence in a blindly rated control group (e.g., Burks, 1965). An example of a well-designed study is that of Capute et al. (1968). This group studied a sample of children with "minimal cerebral dysfunction." The defining criteria of the sample included the presence of soft neurological signs and thus made the sample a special one (since only about half of nonselected MBD children have such signs). Of 106 children who were evaluated blindly, 8% had marked and 43% had mild-to-moderate EEG abnormalities; the comparable figure for a control group of "physically and mentally healthy children" was 17% mild-to-moderate abnormalities. Since the results refer to a special sample, one cannot generalize from it.[9] An example of the ambiguity of EEG findings in a nonselected sample of MBD children is provided by a study of Eisenberg (personal communication) who found that 70% of a blindly rated sample of "hyperactive" children had abnormal EEG's; the significance of this finding was considerably reduced when the EEG's of the children of the psychiatry department faculty were examined and found to contain a 70% prevalence of the same abnormalities. A provocative—but unfortunately unreplicated—abnormality is reported by Laufer et al. (1957b). This study was based upon Gastaut's photo-metrazol technique in which stroboscopic stimulation is provided while metrazol is slowly injected intravenously. The end point (threshold) is determined by the amount of metrazol necessary to produce a myoclonic jerk or photic driving of the EEG. Laufer et al. reported that "hyperkinetic" children, whether or not they had a history of possible insult to their central nervous systems, had a significantly lower photo-metrazol threshold than controls (with a moderate amount of overlap). Interestingly, amphetamine raised the photo-metrazol threshold.

It is important to emphasize that many MBD children (approximately one-half) are neurologically intact: there is no doubt that the syndrome can appear with the total absence of neurological signs or symptoms or EEG abnormalities.

---

[9] There is a "significant" difference in the prevalence of abnormal EEG's between the two groups, but the degree of overlap is considerable. The general prevalence of MBD with and without soft neurological signs is about 5% and if 43% represents the fraction of MBD children with and without soft neurological signs who have abnormal EEG's, one can calculate the fraction of children with abnormal EEG's who have MBD (Wender, 1967). The figure is very small. A group of 1000 children would contain about 170 with mildly to moderately abnormal EEG's and no MBD and 50 children with MBD, of whom 22 (43%) would have mildly to moderately abnormal EEG's. Thus only 22/190 or about 12% of children with mildly to moderately abnormal EEG's have MBD.

Physical Stigmata

There are some data suggesting a higher than expected prevalence of minor physiognomic abnormalities in MBD children. The detailed description of the abnormalities (and a discussion of their etiological relevance) is included in the chapter on etiology. In general, the stigmata are similar to those described by Goldfarb and Botstein (summarized in Waldrop et al., 1968) in schizophrenic children, and overlap those seen in mongolism: anomalies of the epicanthus and ears; high arched palate; short incurving fifth finger; single palmar crease; abnormally long third toe; syndactylism of the toes; strabismus; and, perhaps, abnormally shaped skulls. Although the discriminative cues may be difficult to specify, it is my impression that a small fraction of MBD children fall into an unscientific but accurately described pediatric subgroup, that of the "FLK" or "funny looking kid."

Psychological Test Performance

As might be expected from the discussion of perceptual and cognitive dysfunction, MBD children show no consistent patterns of dysfunction on perceptual and cognitive tests. In their early study of children with exogenous brain damage (many of whom have many MBD attributes) Strauss and Lehtinen (1947) did find certain characteristic patterns of psychological test performance. In this sample—whose impairment was fairly severe—the children displayed difficulties in organizing percepts and concepts: They found it difficult to replicate arrangements of marbles on a board; they found it difficult to draw patterns they had only felt; they had difficulty in object sorting tests in which objects were to be grouped according to abstract concepts.[10] Unfortunately such consistent results are not found across different samples. Reviewing the area of psychological test dysfunction in children with the MBD syndrome, Conners (1968) concluded that evaluations of children with documented cerebral *lesions* fail to show a single pattern of dysfunction on intelligence tests. The same is true of children *without* documented lesions. Nonetheless, a number of unsubstantiated beliefs are widely held. For example, it is sometimes thought that MBD children have a characteristic pattern

[10] On such a test the subject is presented with a group of objects—for example, real tools, toy tools, and a few toys. Some of the objects might be meaningfully grouped together as "tools," "toys," or "toy tools." A disorganized or poorly abstracted grouping might consist of a real pliers, a toy hammer, and a rubber ball, placed together as "objects you can throw."

of subtest performance on the Wechsler Intelligence Scale for Children (WISC), with performance I.Q. being higher than verbal I.Q. (e.g., Clements and Peters, 1962), but studies have failed to document this belief. In a study of MBD children (who had been referred for neurological evaluation) Paine et al. (1968) found no greater incidence of discrepancy between performance I.Q. and verbal I.Q. than is seen in normal children. Performance on perceptual tests—although sometimes regarded as characteristic—is only variably affected: the Bender-Gestalt Test and tests of figure-ground discrimination (visual and auditory) are often but not inevitably impaired. It is my impression that reversals are particularly common both in the reading and the writing of children with this syndrome. These reversals may be another manifestation of a defect which is revealed in the rotation of figures on the Bender-Gestalt Test and problems with spatial (right-left) orientation. Another function that is sometimes impaired is memory. Teachers frequently comment (Strauss and Lehtinen, 1947) that material apparently well learned one day is completely forgotten the next. Sometimes the children's "forgetting" seems to reflect a genuine impairment in recall and neither a defect in acquisition (through inattention) nor a defensive inability to remember.

CLINICAL SUBTYPES OF THE MBD SYNDROME

The vignettes presented at the beginning of this chapter illustrated several of the "subsyndromes" of abnormal behavior seen in "MBD children." The recognition of these "subsyndromes" is of considerable practical importance. The classically "hyperactive child" or "brain-injured child" presents no diagnostic problems, but the other manifestations of the syndrome do present such problems, as is evidenced by their being called by other names. Here a trivial problem in nomenclature requires some attention. An example was presented of a MBD child whose most salient symptoms were delinquent. Should such a child be called "pseudo-psychopathic"? Or, similarly, should MBD children with "neurotic" symptoms be referred to as "pseudoneurotic" (as has been suggested by Kurlander and Colodny, 1965)? I would suggest not. Neurotic, psychopathic, and schizophrenic children and adults are undoubtedly etiologically heterogeneous groups. To designate a patient as "pseudo-something or other" implies that in his instance the syndrome does not have its usual and "true" etiology. In the absence of information detailing those fractions of neurotic, psychopathic, and schizophrenic children whose difficulties are secondary to the MBD syndrome it would seem premature to call MBD children with these patterns pseudoneurotic, pesudopsychopathic, or pseudoschizophrenic.

The etiological situation may perhaps be clarified by borrowing a model from genetics. There it is recognized that one anatomical attribute may be generated by differing genetic constitutions. In cases in which an alternative genotype produces the same phenotypic manifestation as does the usual genotype, the alternative is said to be producing a "phenocopy." Until the other etiologies of these syndromes are delineated or until the MBD defects are shown to be the most usual cause of these syndromes, the MBD-induced neuroses, delinquencies, and schizophrenias may conservatively be regarded as phenocopies. It may later be shown that for some of these syndromes the MBD syndrome is the usual and not the occasional etiology; in that instance the other etiologies would be producing phenocopies. The meaningfulness of the association between the MBD syndrome and these other nosological entities will be discussed in the chapter on prognosis. It will be argued then that the fundamental defects which generate the "classical" manifestations of this syndrome can be quite easily seen, given other circumstances, to lead to the above subsyndromes.

The major phenomenological subvariants of the MBD syndrome are as follows: (1) the classic hyperactive syndrome, (2) the neurotic, (3) the psychopathic, (4) the schizophrenic, and (5) the "special learning disorder." That the syndrome occurs in conjunction with—and *possibly* as the basis of—*virtually* all nosological categories of childhood behavior disturbances is embarrassing but true. Although the exact fraction of each of these syndromes in which it occurs remains to be established, clinical experience would indicate that it is most common among delinquents, less common among psychotics, and least common among neurotics. In the latter two categories it is seen most frequently among the impulsive extroverted character types (e.g., the "schizopath") and least frequently among the overconstricted, overinhibited children. Case histories vividly illustrating the various subsyndromes and their treatments are presented in the Appendix. The reader should probably postpone their inspection, however, until he has concluded the chapter on management.

That such diverse and seemingly different behavioral psychiatric entities are linked under one rubric might seem to militate against the usefulness of the categorization. A logical set or class that includes unicorns, pebbles, and sounds does not seem to have a central common attribute. Nonetheless, a psychiatric precedent does exist: comparable results have been obtained in a number of recent studies of schizophrenia (Heston, 1966; Kety et al., 1968). These authors discovered an increased prevalence of nonschizophrenic disorders among the separately raised biological relatives of schizophenic patients. In a similar vein, it seems *tenable* that the heterogeneous group of diagnoses associated with the MBD syndrome might share a common biological basis.

As will be discussed in the section on prevalence, the MBD syndrome is far more common in boys than in girls. Since it is later argued that the MBD syndrome is a forerunner or early manifestation of certain psychiatric disorders (e.g., schizophrenia) of later life, *some* of which are *not* sex-linked, its contribution to such pathology in females is problematic. There are several logical solutions to this dilemma. First, one may postulate that in women these adult psychiatric disorders more commonly stem from other sources. Second, one must note that some of the syndromes of which the MBD syndrome is an antecedent (e.g., impulsive and aggressive character disorders) *are* less common in women. Third, one may speculate that the manifestation of the MBD syndrome in girls is different from that seen in boys.[11] Huessy (1967) has observed that the syndrome probably takes a different form in girls, with the symptom of motor hyperactivity more frequently being absent. Since motor hyperactivity is sometimes used as the pathognomonic symptom or defining attribute of the MBD syndrome, normally active girls who are distractible, inattentive, anhedonic, or difficult to discipline would not be identified as "hyperactive" and thus would be excluded as candidates in the prevalence studies. If motorically "normoactive" girls with suggestive symptoms were included in the category of "hyperactive" or MBD children, I feel that the proportion of girls among children with the MBD syndrome would increase. This is an assertion capable of empirical test.

THE SYNDROME AS A "DISEASE": ITS SOCIAL CONTEXT

What has been discussed in this chapter is a variety of more or less quantifiable behavioral attributes. I hope I have made it clear that most of these characteristics are qualitatively normal; they are "signs" or "symptoms" only in that they are excessive or insufficient in degree. This is worth emphasizing since the identification of the child as "deviant" depends very heavily on social norms and expectations. It is a truism of cultural relativism that what is deviant (and what, therefore, may constitute a sign

---

[11] Of interest is a finding of Bell et al. (1969) that for boys "hyperactive" behavior patterns are not seen in conjunction with withdrawn patterns. A boy tends to show one or the other—if he is hyperactive he tends not to be withdrawn and vice versa. The same is not true for girls, who may exhibit hyperactive patterns at one time and withdrawn patterns shortly thereafter. Thus the clinical picture in girls would tend to be mixed.

or symptom) is dependent on cultural, subcultural, and familial norms. If there are some societies which tolerate or encourage symptoms as deviant as hallucinations, it is not surprising that various groups have differing views regarding MBD characteristics such as activity, stubbornness, and aggressiveness. Only when such qualities exceed culturally tolerated norms (which vary considerably) are they regarded as "symptoms," or manifestations of a disease.[12]

To begin with, consider the expectations of parents, particularly fathers, and of primary schools (whose values are disproportionately feminine in origin) with regard to the dimension of activity level. A 7-year-old boy, vigorously engaged in physical activity at the playground, is behaving in a manner which is usually as gratifying to his parents as the same activity in a classroom is distressing to his teacher. A quiet child, sitting motionlessly at (usually) her desk, attentively riveting her eyes on the teacher, is a disciplinarian's delight. The same child, listlessly looking around at the circus may very well be disappointing to exuberant parents and may be considered abnormal. The discrepancy between home and school norms is paralleled by the discrepancy that is sometimes found between the norms of a child's father and mother, with the father perceiving the child as "all boy" while the mother views him as a hellion. A comparable situation, *mutatis mutandis,* will exist in the family of a slightly rambunctious child with two compulsive parents.

Similarly, "compliance" or "stubbornness" are attributes whose desirability varies with the taste of the beholder; discussion about these characteristics often tells one as much about the reporter as about the child. A stubborn, negative, thick-skinned child will be deemed a "severe behavior problem" by his upwardly mobile ex-lower-class teacher. A less conforming teacher might find such behavior a useful manifestation of an inquiring attitude.

Cultural expectations of appropriate sex-role behavior contribute to the definition of a child as "deviant." Certain MBD-like characteristics are highly esteemed in our culture in boys while the same attributes are con-

---

[12] Excessive quantitative variations can be regarded as illnesses whether they are produced by pathological processes or are extreme variants of the normal. Borrowing an example from medicine, consider pathologies in height (the variable being one that occurs along a graduated continuum). Certain extreme instances with documented pathological causes, for example, pituitary giants or achondroplastic dwarfs, are considered to represent "diseases"; while normally proportioned people who are between 5'8" and 6'6" are considered to be variants of the normal. Whether perfectly proportioned "seven-footers" or "four-footers" have "diseases" is problematical: socially and psychologically one may anticipate that they will encounter difficulties similar to those experienced by their dwarfed and gianted brethren.

sidered pathological in girls. An active, tough, strong-willed tomboy may be considered "pathological" even if she possesses the identifying attributes to a lesser degree than her average male playmate. (Whether or not her possession of these characteristics reflects abnormal neurophysiological functioning is moot.)

The discrepancy between children's biologically determined psychological characteristics and society's demands can be considerable. In a study that will be described in more detail later, a large sample of grammar school teachers rated one-fifth of their charges as having problems with attention span. Obviously, when the magnitude of the problem reaches this proportion, it is easier, and perhaps more meaningful, to define the problem as the teachers': they want (and hence expect) more than many of the children can deliver. Such discrepant expectations can play a role—as will be discussed in the chapter on etiology—in determining the severity of MBD problems. Behavior defined as deviant may stimulate patterns of behavior reactions that aggravate the difficulties, thus instituting a self-sustaining "vicious circle."

Finally, and at the risk of some repetition, general cultural characteristics exert an obvious effect on diagnosis. The archetypical all-American (or Australian) boy, independent, stubborn, self-willed, other-directed, would be a miserable failure as a traditional Japanese child. If a child has MBD proclivities, he is well advised to be born as a male, and as the son of a nineteenth century frontiersman with past prison sentences. The child would have a far more difficult time if born as a girl, as the daughter of parents with rigid academic and behavioral demands, and if confined in an urban china shop.

DIAGRAMMATIC REPRESENTATION OF SIGNS AND SYMPTOMS

A simple and useful method of representing the various combinations of clinical symptoms and signs in syndromes is by the use of Venn diagrams. The diagrammatic method, named after its nineteenth-century inventor, is employed in logic to represent various combinations of attributes. In the accompanying diagram, Figure 1, the area included within the circle A represents all those things having the attribute A, for example, "furriness"; and the circle B represents all those things having the attribute B, for example, being an animal. The area marked 1 consists of all those things that are neither furry nor animal (both not-A *and* not-B), for example, plants. The area marked 2 consists of all those things that are A but not B, that is, all furry nonanimals—for example, imitation fur coats.

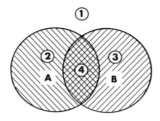

Example: A — furriness; B — being an animal
1. All things neither furry nor animals, e.g., plants
2. All furry nonanimals, e.g., fake fur coats
3. All nonfurry animals, e.g., fish
4. All furry animals

Figure 1. *The Venn diagram.*

The area marked 3 consists of all those things that are B but not A, that is, all nonfurry animals—for example, fish. The area marked 4, in which A and B overlap, is their "intersect" and represents all those things that have both attributes A and B, that is, all furry animals.

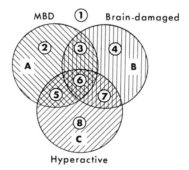

The numbers indicate children who are:
1. Not MBD, nor hyperactive, nor brain-damaged
2. MBD, but not brain-damaged nor hyperactive
3. MBD and brain-damaged, but not hyperactive
4. Brain-damaged, but not MBD nor hyperactive
5. MBD and hyperactive, but not brain-damaged
6. MBD, hyperactive, and brain-damaged
7. Hyperactive and brain-damaged, but not MBD
8. Hyperactive, but not brain-damaged nor MBD

Figure 2. *Venn diagram: MBD, brain damage, and hyperactivity.*

The method can be expanded to include more than two attributes. The accompanying example, Figure 2, deals with one of the attributes of MBD, motoric hyperactivity, and demonstrable brain damage. The numbers and their significance are as follows:

1. All children who are neither MBD nor hyperactive nor brain-damaged.

2. All children who are MBD but neither brain-damaged nor hyperactive.

3. All children who are MBD and brain-damaged but not hyperactive.

4. All children who are brain-damaged but neither MBD nor hyperactive.

5. All children who are both MBD and hyperactive but are not brain-damaged.

6. All children who are MBD and hyperactive and brain-damaged.

7. All children who are hyperactive and brain-damaged but have no MBD characteristics (other than hyperactivity).

8. All children who are hyperactive but have neither brain-damage nor any MBD characteristics (other than hyperactivity).

This method allows an easy pictorial representation of a rather complicated symptomatic potpourri. Utilization of Venn diagrams or their graphical equivalents is a helpful way of discriminating between (and communicating about) the intermixed subgroups.[13]

[13] For a thorough elaboration of the technique as applied to several problems of syndromes of clinical medicine, see Feinstein, 1967.

CHAPTER 2

Etiology of the MBD Syndrome

There is considerable evidence—of varying degrees of convincingness—that the MBD syndrome has several distinct and separate etiologies. The syndrome may be produced by the following: (1) organic brain damage, (2) genetic transmission as (a) a probably polygenetic abnormality, or (b) an extreme placement on the normal distribution curve, (3) intrauterine "random" variation in biological development, (4) fetal maldevelopment, (5) psychogenetic determinants (deviant psychological experience). In addition, the MBD syndrome can accompany other childhood disorders. Possibly most importantly, it also seems to result from the interaction of subthreshold amounts of the etiological components.

ORGANIC BRAIN DAMAGE

The earliest descriptions of the syndrome were found in children who had developed the behavioral abnormalities after injury or infection of the brain, so that a causal relationship was assumed. These early descriptions are reflected in terms such as the following: "postencephalitic behavior disorder" (Hohman, 1922); "organic drivenness" (Kahn and Cohen, 1934); "minimal brain injury" (Strauss and Lehtinen, 1947). Following the World War I epidemic of von Economo's encephalitis, reports appeared describing behavioral sequelae of the illness in children. Hohman (1922) reported that after recovery from the acute phase of the illness, some children underwent "profound changes in character and behavior" and became "irritable . . . restless . . . quarrelsome . . . teased other children unmercifully . . . disobedient . . . no longer amenable to discipline . . . emotionally quite unstable . . . capriciously moody" (pp. 372–373). To these characteristics Bond (1932) added "truancy, lying, stealing, fears and recklessness combined . . . returns to infantile habits . . . and mawkish affection" (p. 311). During the 1920s several reports appeared describing the development of the syndrome following recovery from head injury [Strecker and Ebaugh, 1924; Kasanin, 1929]. Later, Blau (1937) presented a detailed clinical report of the psychological change in 12 cases: "The essential characteristic of the syndrome was a complete reversal of personality from that of a previously normal child to that of one who was asocial, unmanageable, and unyielding to any form of training. . . . Hyperkinesis was an outstanding symptom. . . . At home they were disobedient and disrespectful. . . . Emotionally they were unstable and easily irritated . . . [other characteristics included] unrestrained aggressiveness, destructiveness . . . cruelty . . . lying and stealing . . . . They were essentially egocentric and behaved like young children bereft of any form of social training" (p. 748). Later studies have associated the syndrome with a variety of other noxae to the brain—for example, pertussis (Lurie and Levy, 1942), and lead poisoning (Thurston et al., 1955).

A large number of studies conducted by Knobloch and Pasamanick (1965) have demonstrated the association between prematurity, prenatal difficulties, and paranatal medical complications, and a variety of psychological, behavioral and neurological abnormalities in children (including cerebral palsy, epilepsy, mental deficiency, behavior disorders, and reading disabilities). These reproductive complications are: (1) associated with fetal and neonatal deaths, usually as a result of brain injury, (2) associated with clear-cut neurological disease. There is, therefore, strong circumstantial evidence that behavioral abnormalities seen in children with such histories of prenatal or paranatal difficulties are caused by lesser degrees of brain injury. The highest association between "reproductive casualty" and behavioral deviance was found for the subgroup of children who were "hyperactive, confused, and disorganized," a group obviously resembling and/or overlapping the MBD syndrome.

These studies are only one group from a large number of studies in this area. The influence of prematurity and complications of pregnancy and birth, on early development, and, in turn, the relations between these early difficulties and later development, are complicated and not fully understood; they prompted Montagu (1962) to observe that the material on the subject "is so abundant that a score of volumes the size of this [over 600 pages] would scarcely be enough to contain it" (p. vii). I will not attempt to deal with this difficult topic and wish only to point out the following: (1) There are well-documented associations between complications of pregnancy and birth and the later appearance of the MBD syndrome. (2) These associations, although statistically significant, leave much unexplained. Infants exposed to such complications have an increased risk of subsequent behavior pathology (including MBD), but most infants at increased risk escape such pathology. What affects some children and allows others to escape remains to be learned.

It is studies such as these which willed the cognomen of "minimal brain damage" to (current) posterity in child psychiatry. It is an unfortunate designation for both logical and empirical reasons. Logically it is incorrect because one cannot argue that since some brain-injured children have the MBD syndrome, all children with MBD are brain injured.[1] Empirically it is misleading because in a large fraction of children with MBD, one can neither obtain a history suggestive of neurological damage nor find signs of neurological impairment. The increased prevalence of soft neurological signs in MBD children has been used as an argument for the role of minimal brain damage in the etiology of the syndrome. This, too, is an unfortunate argument. Although it is known that some children with brain damage have soft neurological signs, in the absence of clinical-pathological correlations one cannot assert that *all* children with soft neurological signs have brain damage. Even the fraction of MBD children with such signs seems to vary as a function of the referral source. Neurologists (e.g., Paine, 1962), to whom patients have been selectively referred, report a large fraction of children with organic signs and/or histories (in this instance 40/41 with neurological signs, 25/41 with neurological histories). On the other hand, beginning with children referred with MBD and school difficulties, Knobel et al. (1958) found that approximately 50% had neurological signs. Starting with routine referrals to a child mental health clinic, Daryn (1960) found that about 50% had "organic" characteristics. Unfortunately neither study contains a control group and we do not know the prevalence of such neurological or organic signs in a psychologically "normal" group of children. Werry (1968b) carefully studied a group of MBD children in a child guidance clinic and reported that 64% had abnormal perinatal histories or abnormal EEG's or abnormal neurological examinations (again with no control group). A factor analytic study of the population revealed two rather clear neurological factors which were uncorrelated with cognitive dysfunction and psychopathology in the child and medical-historical data. Werry concludes that these data refute the existence of a "homogeneous 'brain damage' dimension."

Such evidence as I have reviewed here is only negative—the failure to find correlations or signs of neurological damage may mean only that one is using insensitive or incorrect measures. The data in the next sections show positive evidence for the possible role of other causal factors.

---

[1] Logically equivalent is the argument that since some imaginary animals can fly, all flying animals are imaginary.

GENETIC TRANSMISSION

Probable Polygenetic Abnormality

My attention was called to a possible genetic etiology in some instances by three clinical observations: (1) pronounced clustering—that is, in several instances—within the same family, (2) an apparent increase in the prevalence of severe but mixed (schizophrenic, depressive, sociopathic) psychopathology among the parents of MBD subjects without a history of organic insult, and (3) a few instances of the syndrome in foster children whose biological parents had been psychotic.[2] Suggestive evidence also comes from the clustering of certain MBD characteristics and associated congenital abnormalities, but since they could derive from either genetic transmission or fetal maldevelopment, they will be discussed under the latter category.

There are no studies documenting my clinical observations of either a familial clustering of MBD or the tendency for MBD children to have family histories of other forms of psychopathology. However, there are data showing a familial clustering in specific reading disorder ("dyslexia"), a difficulty often associated with, and apparently overlapping, the MBD syndrome.

Two studies documenting the familial clustering of "dyslexia" are those of Hallgren (1950) and Frisk et al. (1957). Hallgren studied 112 cases of "specific dyslexia" referred for learning problems in school and found that 90% had parents and/or sibs with similar problems; the prevalence among the control cases was estimated at approximately 10%. The overlap with MBD signs is evidenced by the fact that 30% of the dyslexic children and 9% of their sibs without reading problems—were characterized as oppositional and aggressive or as restless, childish, labile, and suffering from concentration difficulties. Similar clustering is reported by Frisk et al., who found dyslexia in 65% of the parents or "near relatives" of

---

[2] For example, in one family the mother had had two brief psychotic episodes, one of which antedated the birth of her four children. Her rearing techniques were overprotective but not markedly deviant. All four of the children showed marked MBD characteristics and all had an excellent response to d-amphetamine. In a second instance a 7-year-old separated from her chronically schizophrenic mother at the time of birth had had severe manifestations of the syndrome from earliest infancy—first poor sleeping and colic, and later, typical and florid manifestations of hyperactivity. See also case history 8, "Carl and Jim," in the Appendix, for an account of family reading problems.

teen-age dyslexics. The overlap with MBD signs is evidenced by the prevalence of clumsiness, enuresis, lability, sleep disturbance, and distractibility among the affected group.

Logically, such data could document either genetic or social transmission. That crazy parents have crazy children has two major alternative explanations: (1) transmission by aberrant rearing techniques (deviant socialization); (2) transmission by organic neurological deficit genetically received by the child and secondary to or associated with the parents' psychopathology. In addition, histories of physical abuse are frequently obtained in disrupted families and the mothers of premature children (who are at greater risk for MBD) are often of lower socioeconomic status and manifest a greater than average prevalence of social and psychiatric pathology (Rosen et al., 1968).

The only logically sound way to disentangle the effects of nature and nurture is to study the sibs (or half-sibs) of MBD children who have been reared separately. One such study has been reported by Safer (1969), who investigated the status of sibs and half-sibs of 14 MBD children, all of whom had been reared in foster homes. This study revealed that approximately 50% of the full siblings versus 14% of the half-sibs were characterized by short attention span, repeated behavior problems, and a diagnosis (by an independent rater) of hyperactivity. These differences were statistically significant and consonant with the hypothesis of genetic transmission. There are two minor faults in this study, neither of which vitiates the results: (1) there was a greater prevalence of low birth weight and perinatal difficulties in the full sibs, which might mediate the increased incidence and obscure the possible influence of genetic factors, and (2) the children were placed in foster homes at a comparatively late age. However, when the low birth weight cases and their sibs' cases were removed, the difference between the groups remained statistically significant. The time of placement varied between 8 months and 8 years, with the median age at placement being approximately 2.3 years for the full siblings and 4.8 years for the half-siblings, so that the half-siblings had a longer exposure to a disrupted home; if psychological factors had been primary, the half-siblings should have been *more* disturbed than the full siblings of the index group but such was not the case. This finding partially obviates the need for another comparison group to control for the effects of foster placement. It is possible that all the children in this study might have been rendered "hyperactive" by the effects of foster placement itself. To control for the effect of placement one would have to determine the frequency of hyperactivity in foster-reared siblings and half-siblings of normal children. Although the half-sibs were exposed to more intrafamilial psychopathology in Safer's study (they were transferred at a later age), one might logically argue that earlier transfer is more pathogenic and accounted for the greater pathology among the full siblings.[3] To meet this argument one would have to employ the control group of foster sibs mentioned above. With the above qualifications, the findings of the Safer study are strongly suggestive of the operation of genetic factors in some variants of the MBD syndrome.

It is generally believed that there is an increased prevalence of behavior problems (probably including the MBD syndrome) among adopted and foster children. One cannot assume that this is due to the psychological concomitants of foster or adoptive placement since the population of parents whose children are placed for adoption probably contains an excess of psychiatrically disturbed people. If Safer's findings are correct, one might expect the population of adoptees to contain an excess of disturbed children, not for psychological reasons, but because of genetic factors.

It was indicated that the putative mode of genetic transmission would probably prove to be polygenetic. The reason for this assertion is that the disorder does not appear to "breed true." Abnormality appears to be transmitted from parent to child but its manifestations vary. In families in which there are multiple occurrences of MBD problems in the offspring, one sometimes sees different patterns in the affected children. One child may be classically "hyperactive," while another may manifest dyslexia, and a third may be only clumsy. Similarly, the parents of MBD children appear to have a heterogeneous group of psychiatric difficulties. The parents of MBD children seem to be not only MBD children "grown up" but schizophrenics, manic-depressives, and with acknowledgment of their diagnostic impurity, impulsive characters and alcoholics. While eventually research may show that these groups' offspring differ appreciably, it is my impression that—with the partial exception of children of schizophrenic[4] and manic-depressive parents—there is more overlap than differentiation among the groups. This apparent failure to breed true, while incompatible with simple classic Mendelian mechanisms, is compatible with mechanisms involving multiple interacting genes, so-called polygenetic transmission. Its introduction to explain the genetics of MBD syndrome transmission is not *ad hoc*. First, as will be mentioned in the discussion of symptoms and prognosis, such a mechanism seems to be involved in

---

[3] However, analysis of Safer's data (personal communication) reveals that there is no correlation between age of transfer from the foster home and the presence or absence of hyperactivity in a given child.

[4] Who, not surprisingly, tend to show more atypical MBD syndromes with accompanying minimal thought disorder.

the genetic transmission of another psychiatric syndrome, schizophrenia. Second, such a mechanism suggests that certain of the behavioral characteristics of the syndrome may be independently transmitted, although statistically associated. The genes controlling attentiveness and those regulating motoric activity might occupy separate chromosomal loci and thus vary independently of each other; only when genes producing dysfunctional versions of both traits were present would a child be designated as MBD. This concept of separate underlying dimensions will be elaborated in Part Two, which discusses "theoretical considerations."

EXTREME PLACEMENT ON NORMAL DISTRIBUTION CURVE

Another probable subgroup of MBD children of genetic etiology consists of those children in whom MBD traits represent an extreme placement on the normal distribution curve. In such children the syndrome would represent a random increase or decrease in the amount of a qualitatively normal attribute. If behavioral traits like attentiveness and extroversion are (like height) graduated characteristics determined by several genes, one would expect to find extreme instances of these traits without the presence of any disease; children possessing such extreme instances would be designated as MBD children and would be the behavioral analogues of very tall or very short people. One would expect, in analogy with the dimension of height in which very tall and short children tend, respectively, to have tall and short parents, that some MBD children's parents might have a history of some MBD-like behavior. As previously noted, clinically it is common for parents to report that they had or still have some characteristics similar to their MBD children: "I was a poor student. . . . I couldn't —and can't really now—sit still. . . . I've always been very stubborn (or) got into a lot of trouble (or) did what I wanted." A longitudinal study of "temperamental characteristics" (Thomas et al., 1968) in a nonpatient population of children revealed graduated distribution of several attributes relevant to the MBD syndrome (activity, approach/withdrawal, intensity, distractibility). Interestingly, the traits tended to cluster (as revealed by factor analysis) in a pattern characteristic of the MBD syndrome: approach, intensity, activity, and distractibility all tended to "move" together. Children with this pattern apparently later tended to develop MBD problems. In the follow-up of the sample, 42 of the 136 children developed "problems" and of these 42 (excluding three with demonstrable brain damage), about 13 (10% of the original sample) were fairly typical instances of the MBD syndrome.[5]

Whether these children represent normal variants or whether the dysfunctional characteristics have been transmitted via genetic abnormalities in their parents is not evident from the authors' data (families' histories are not given); but what is evident is that MBD behavioral characteristics do appear as quantitative variations from the normal.

An answer to the question of whether or not the "extreme placement" category exists cannot now be given although additional useful information would come from detailed population studies. The existence of a graduated continuum would not demonstrate that extreme instances were not diseases but it would be suggestive. Contrariwise, the existence of a distorted continuum would not demonstrate that all extreme instances were the result of disease. Consider height. If diseases producing dwarfism and giantism did not exist, a frequency distribution of the population would look like the curve in Figure 3. But diseases producing rare, nonnormally

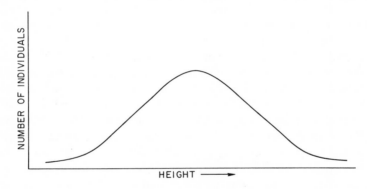

Figure 3. *Normal height frequency curve, without diseases producing dwarf and giantism.*

[5] The early temperamental characteristics of the MBD subgroup would be of interest. The authors have included the probable MBD children among a larger— and perhaps heterogeneous—group of children with "active symptoms," and contrast them with children with "passive symptoms," who were defined as "nonparticipators" who evidenced neither anxiety nor defenses against anxiety. "Active symptoms" referred to children who were aggressive, destructive, and presented discipline problems, and also included nonparticipators who became upset, as manifested by anxiety, crying, somatic symptoms, and so on. The active group—containing probable MBD children, as well as upset nonparticipators and children with other complaints—had been characterized at age 1 to 5 as being more active, intense, distractible, and persistent (stubborn or persevering) than the children who failed to develop problems. Thus it would seem that some children with "normally" excessive behavior traits tend to develop MBD-like symptoms.

distributed extremes do exist, so that the population distribution looks like the "Resultant" curve in Figure 4, with the "blips" at each extreme representing an excessive number of very short and tall people who have genetic diseases, "dwarfism" and "giantism."

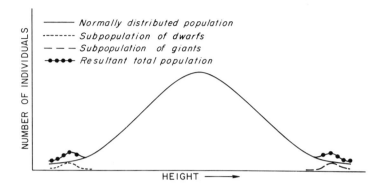

Figure 4. *Height frequency distribution curves: normal, diseased, and resultant.*

Even with the nonsmooth curve, we cannot be certain that some excessively short people are not extremes of normal distribution (Pygmies) and that some excessively tall people are not the opposite extreme of normal distribution (Watusi). Only additional knowledge—dwarfs often have abnormal anatomical structure—allows us, for example, to tell some dwarfs from short normals. Similar knowledge concerning the MBD syndrome is not available so that even if the second distribution is eventually found, we will not, with present knowledge, be sure that *some* MBD children are not a separate nondiseased population of "extremely placed normals."

INTRAUTERINE "RANDOM" VARIATION IN BIOLOGICAL DEVELOPMENT

There are *suggestions* that nongenetic, nontraumatic, prenatal variations can occur and can play a role in the development of behavioral pathology, including minimal brain dysfunction. Such suggestions come from the studies of premature infants and monozygotic twins. In these groups increased MBD pathology is repeatedly seen in the smaller members. This behavior pathology is generally attributed to birth injury, to which a small infant is more susceptible. What is not appreciated is that given a fixed genetic inheritance (genotype), there is still considerable biological phenotypic variation at birth as well as later (such as in size) which itself might contribute to the pathology. In approximately half the instances of schizophrenia in monozygotic twins (for whom the term "identical" is a misnomer) the pairs are discordant for schizophrenia (i.e., one member is ill while the other member is not). Although such results are generally interpreted to indicate the importance of psychological factors, it is important to realize that all that is nongenetic is not necessarily nonbiological. The concordance rate for schizophrenia for monozygotic twins is approximately that of diabetes (Harvald and Hauge, 1965), a disease not generally regarded as primarily psychological in origin. As I shall indicate under the subject of interaction of factors, subthreshold genetic disposition plus other random factors might be operating here.

Considerable nongenetic biological variation at birth has been shown by Williams (1969). Studying the armadillo, an animal which reproduces monozygous quadruplets—and an animal from whom extrapolation to man is admittedly noncompelling—Williams found that at birth brain weights varied by 63%, brain amino acids up to fivefold and brain norepinephrine over sixfold (6.6). Identical gene pools do not produce anatomical and biochemical identicality, at least in the armadillo at birth. The conceptual jump from variations in brain amino acids and amines in the armadillo to MBD in the human child is considerable. It will be argued later that the MBD syndrome may be a manifestation of a diminution in certain brain amines. A finding of congenital nongenetic variations in the chemical precursors of these amines is *suggestive* of a mechanism by which the known association between behavior and birth size might possibly be explained.

Certainly there is an increased prevalence of MBD-like symptoms in small babies. An early longitudinal study of premature children (defined as birth weight less than five pounds) and a comparison of them with their siblings was reported by Shirley (1939). Shirley reported that as infants (at 6 to 24 months) prematures tended to be more attracted to and distracted by sights and sounds, to have more speech and motor difficulties, to have a shorter attention span, and to be more irascible, negativistic, attached to their mothers, attention seeking, and prone to giving up readily.

With regard to activity, "premature babies seem to go to two extremes . . . [being] tense, jumpy, hyperactive or lazy . . . [or] sluggish, clumsy" children (p. 119). As they grew older (2½ to 5 years) these children showed more difficulty achieving sphincter control than did the normal comparison group.

Compared with their siblings in family relationships, the prematures were more jealous, less good to their brothers and sisters, made more demands for parental attention, and were more dependent and less self-reliant.

Comparable results were found in the Edinburgh Longitudinal Study of Drillien (1964). When compared with their larger siblings, the prematures in this sample showed an excess of "restless overactivity" as well as increased classroom maladjustment (see Table 1).

Table 1. Fluctuation of Classroom Behavior with Birth Weight[a]

Classroom Behavior Evaluation	Birth Weight	
	Prematures ($\underline{N} = 50$) 4 lb, 8 oz and under	Siblings ($\underline{N} = 50$) 4 lb, 9 oz and over
Normal	36%	58%
Borderline abnormal	30%	30%
Abnormal	34%	12%

[a]After Drillien (1964), p. 258.

In dealing with the behavior abnormalities of the premature infants, one cannot be certain that the described pathology is a manifestation of the physiological or psychological concomitants of prematurity. Such pathology could conceivably be a product of the mother's reaction to a particularly vulnerable child: overprotectiveness, overindulgence, and diminished demands for performance might contribute to the psychological pictures seen in these infants. That this occurs is likely. Whether it is of particular importance is quite doubtful. More important is the question of whether the syndrome occurs in prematures on the basis of some poorly understood physiological deviation associated with small size or on the basis of actual brain damage—to which prematures are presumably more susceptible. In the latter instance the MBD syndrome associated with prematurity alone might logically be included in that section.

FETAL MALDEVELOPMENT

Several authors have noted the association of MBD and certain congenital abnormalities which could be of genetic derivation but might also result from fetal maldevelopment. Milman (1956) reported congenital abnormalities such as decreased cranial size and strabismus in approximately one-third of 33 MBD children. Daryn (1961) reported that of a nonselected sample of 170 children seen at a child guidance clinic in Israel, 84 were designated as "organic" on the basis of neurological and psychological tests. Of these 84 children only 10 had histories of neurological insult. However, Daryn states that "numerous signs of slight malformation were observed in *most* cases of the organic group, such as epicanthus, malformed ears, underdeveloped palate, hypoplasia of nasion, clinodactyly, syndactyly, the Macacus line in the hands, a large gap between the first and second toes" (p. 301). In addition, 75% of the children had hypoplastic skulls as measured on X-ray (versus 30% in Milman's series).

Waldrop et al. (1968), studying the behavior of 2½-year-olds in nursery school, found that the presence of multiple physical abnormalities was correlated with hyperkinetic, aggressive, impatient, and intractable behavior. The children in this sample had been "observed as newborns and had been considered free from complications of pregnancy and delivery" (p. 393). The anomalies studied were physical characteristics often associated with Mongolism and included anomalies of the epicanthus and ears, high-arched palate, short incurving fifth finger, single palmar crease, abnormally long third toe, and syndactyly of the toes.

What inferences may be drawn from the increased prevalence of anatomical abnormalities among MBD children? Only that these children have a greater likelihood of having chromosomal abnormalities and/or exogenously produced dysplasia during fetal development. Mongoloid abnormalities may be caused by a genetically transmitted tendency toward chromosomal abnormality (the "translocation" subgroup) or by an idiosyncratic but age-related dysfunction in oogenesis (the "trisomy 21" subgroup). No clear inference can be drawn except that one subgroup of the syndrome may be produced by (possibly genetically transmitted) chromosomal abnormalities, or by as yet unknown factors producing fetal maldevelopment.

PSYCHOGENETIC DETERMINANTS

The phrase "psychogenetic determinants" is applied to the putative etiological subgroup in which the MBD syndrome is assumed to be purely a reaction to environmental or inner neurotic stress. "Psychogenetically determined MBD" might logically also be applied to a subgroup in which a deviant early environment has produced a fixed (nonreactive) personality structure with many features of the MBD syndrome. The evidence for the existence of (1) a *purely reactive* form of MBD is doubtful, while there is fair evidence for the existence of (2) a privation-produced form. Unfortunately, the former is named and recognized—as "psychogenic hyperactivity"—while the latter is neither named nor recognized.

To begin with the evidence for the existence of a privation-induced phenotype of MBD, certainly many children with histories of early privation (histories which are unfortunately common among foster children) manifest some signs and symptoms of the MBD syndrome. These children often manifest, in addition, a pattern of weak object relationships, characterized by vacillating excessive affection and total indifference. The latter pattern, called "primary affect hunger" by Levy (1937), was found by him to be associated with early privation. A controlled clinical study suggesting that early privation may induce an MBD-like syndrome was reported by Goldfarb (1943). This study is a psychological and psychiatric evaluation of 15 adolescents (average age 12, range 10–14) who had been placed in a children's institution between the ages of 4 months and 3½ years. The comparison group consisted of children of the same age who had been placed in foster homes. The most striking abnormalities of the institutional group (with comparison figures for the foster home group placed in parentheses) were as follows: "lacks capacity for relationship," 87% (0%); "inability to concentrate," 67% (0%); "restless hyperactive," 60% (7%); "craving for affection," 60% (13%). The institutional group also manifested language disturbances and abstraction difficulties similar to those of some children with MBD. As may be seen, a signal characteristic of the hyperactive institutional group was its lack of capacity for forming relationships. It is important to emphasize that this is an attribute *not* typical of most MBD children. The results of this study must be interpreted with some caution because the family backgrounds of the two groups were not matched and it is possible that the institutional group contained more children who may have been disturbed on a genetic basis.[6]

Another relevant study is that of Pringle and Bossio (1958), who studied the intellectual, emotional, and social development of 188 institutionalized children who were then 8, 11, and 14 years of age. The authors found the following MBD-like behaviors to be common in this group: "educational backwardness," 60%; "restlessness or inability to concentrate," 50%; "depression," 25%. Among this group a correlation was found between educational attainment and psychological adjustment: children with reading disorders were four times as common among children classified as "maladjusted" as among those classified as "stable." Since concentration difficulties contribute both to the judgment of "stability" and to the ability to learn to read, one cannot infer that emotional difficulties which took a form other than that of restlessness and inattentiveness were correlated with learning problems.

---

[6] The mothers of the institutionalized group had a *higher* occupational and educational level than those of the foster group (which should favor higher intellectual achievement among their children), but a much higher percentage of the institutionalized group were born out of wedlock (three-fourths versus one-third). Educated women with illegitimate children may be suspected of being more impulsive than average, and impulsivity (and MBD) may, as has been suggested, be genetically transmitted.

It does not seem untenable that a carefully constructed program of severe psychological traumata and interpersonal privation might generate such behavior patterns; but since not all children placed in miserable environments develop these patterns, one must wonder if the environments are sufficient in themselves to generate the pattern or whether the children placed in such an environment (often, presumably, by neglectful and/or crazy parents) would have been at high risk anyhow.

The evidence for the role of privational factors in humans is suggestive but not certain. Direct evidence that early experience can generate MBD-like abnormalities in animals is reported by Bronfenbrenner (1968). Following a detailed and scholarly review of the effects of early social and sensory deprivation in mammals, Bronfenbrenner concludes that if general *stimulus* deprivation is introduced in early infancy and maintained continuously through later infancy, a number of permanent effects are produced which include the following: "diffuse hyperactivity and a heightened but undifferentiated reactivity to stimuli of any sort . . . impaired cognitive functioning, reflected primarily in shortened attention span, reduced capacity for differentiating perception and response, and retardation in learning ability and problem solving . . . a high level of emotional reactivity . . . but an absence of differential emotional response whether positive (e.g., friendly behavior) or negative (focused aggression or fear)" (p. 754).

The underlying mechanism by which profound stimulus privation produces some MBD-like characteristics in animals is unknown. Krech and Rosenzweig and co-workers (Bennett *et al.,* 1964) have shown that rats who are deprived of both sensory stimulation *and* exercise have altered brain chemistry.

A reactive MBD syndrome, apparently symptomatically similar to "organic hyperactivity," is recognized by some authors (e.g., Chess, 1960). This syndrome, sometimes designated as "neurotic hyperactivity," is characterized by the absence of evidence for brain injury, no evidence of hyperactivity in early infancy, and positive evidence that the behavior pattern represents an attempt to cope with the environment or the child's own neurotic conflicts.[7] If the above criteria are employed individually, the category is a common one: many children with MBD do not have evidence of brain injury (about 50%), many are not reported as excessively active

---

[7] But any behavior may be integrated into a pattern, including organically produced behavior. For example a choreic adult may incorporate his involuntary motion into "meaningful" action: a sudden arm jerk is voluntarily continued into a scratching of the ear. Kahn and Cohen (1934) describe this process in some of their post-encephalitic patients with "organic drivenness."

during the first few years of life (Stewart et al., 1966, reports this is true of approximately 50%) and most behavior—whatever its origin—can be interpreted as at least unconsciously useful or purposive.[8]

A large fraction of these characteristics would have to vary together to provide evidence for the existence of a separate category of "neurotic hyperactivity." Whether they do vary together is not known. As noted, some child psychiatrists label the putative neurotic subgroup as a "depressive equivalent" or a "masked depression." The rationale for this labeling might be that (1) these children develop the MBD behavior in situations that would be expected to provoke depression (e.g., loss of a loved one); (2) some of these children manifest depressive symptoms (low self-esteem, guilt, etc.); or (3) the MBD behavior acts as a defense against depression. I know of no data substantiating the first and third assertions: there is no evidence that the syndrome appears as a sign of object loss nor is there evidence documenting that disappearance of symptoms is accompanied by the appearance of depression. There is evidence that many of these children do have symptoms which may be interpreted as depressive: concern about injury and death, low self-esteem, and so on. The theoretical meaning of these symptoms will be discussed later. In summary, it will be argued that the depressive symptoms are a concomitant of the primary physiological dysfunction and a reaction to the psychological problems that result from this dysfunction.

The positive evidence for the existence of the reactive psychogenic subgroup is twofold: (1) hyperactive behavior can be increased by psychological stress; (2) hyperactive behavior can be reduced by reducing such psychological stress. It is a common clinical experience to see an "unmanageable" hyperactive child behave quite appropriately when placed in a good foster home. Likewise, some formal studies (Bond and Smith, 1935; Hall et al., 1968) have documented the favorable response of MBD children to a well-structured environment. It is also quite common to see school pressures producing "hyperactivity." The MBD child with cognitive and attentional handicaps may work well below his intellectual capacity. If placed in an ordinary "age appropriate" class, he is in a position analogous to that of a retarded child so placed: he cannot do the work, falls behind, and rapidly becomes confused, bored and restless. The contribution of academic stress to the development of the MBD picture may be revealed when the child is entered in a special class and given tasks commensurate

---

[8] Consider that a generation of parents has had to endure guilt as well as a disrupted household because of, say, the interpretation that "colic" derives from the infant's reaction to the tension of the parents.

with his abilities: hyperactivity diminishes as the child is able to master his schoolwork.[9] With regard to etiology such data must be interpreted cautiously. Certainly all but the most disturbed MBD children seem to respond to psychological and environmental variables and it may be most useful—*practically*—to separate out those who can be appreciably benefited by psychological treatment alone.

Since most children do not respond to a particular *current* psychological stress by developing MBD behavior, one cannot attribute such behavior to the psychological stress(es) alone; predisposing characteristics (possibly physiological) must exist. One might then crudely divide children into three groups: those who fail to develop MBD signs under any psychological circumstances; those who will manifest MBD signs under any circumstances; and those in whom MBD signs appear in reaction to psychologically difficult circumstances. This might be represented diagrammatically as in Table 2. In the table the children in the middle row ("Moderate Predis-

Table 2. Interaction of Psychological Environment and Predisposition: MBD Signs[a]

Predisposition	Psychological Environment		
	"Good"	Average	"Bad"
Marked	++	+++	+++
Moderate	+	++	+++
Absent	0	0	0

[a]The symbols in the cells refer to the intensity of MBD signs: 0 = one; + = mild; ++ = moderate; +++ = marked.

position") might be designated as "psychogenic" by some investigators, that is, they are the most sensitive to their psychological environment and most responsive to its change.

It should be emphasized that it *may* be more expedient to alter the psychological conditions rather than the ostensible underlying predisposition. Theoretically it should be obvious that response of a particular dysfunction to a given treatment does not indicate that the dysfunction was due to the absence of the treatment. Rheumatoid arthritis—which benefits from aspirin—and congestive heart failure—which benefits from digitalis—are not diseases due to a congenital failure of the body to produce aspirin or digitalis. Likewise, from the fact that mongoloid children may be operant conditioned to function more adequately, no one would contend that their

[9] An awareness of the possible deleterious effects of school placement is of practical importance, since it suggests an obvious and usually feasible therapeutic maneuver.

deviant behavior had been due to the absence of operant conditioning. Finally, one cannot argue that an MBD child's favorable response to unusually good parenting indicates that the disorder was caused by inadequate parenting.

"SYMPTOMATIC" MBD SYNDROME

Lastly—and not as an etiological category—it should be noted that the MBD syndrome occurs in conjunction with certain other childhood psychiatric disorders, notably mental retardation, borderline states, and schizophrenia. In some instances these disorders (particularly retardation) are associated with etiological factors already listed—such as fetal maldevelopment and brain damage. In other instances (particularly in regard to schizophrenia) our ignorance concerning etiology allows us to draw no additional hints about the etiology of MBD.[10]

INTERACTION OF ETIOLOGICAL FACTORS

That most psychological or social phenomena are "multidetermined," that they are generally the products of the interactions of several forces, not only is widely held but may also be true. If a sufficient "dose" of each of the putative causes (brain damage, genetic abnormality, random variation, fetal maldevelopment, psychological maltreatment) can by itself produce the MBD syndrome, then one might expect that the combination of subthreshold ("inadequate") amounts of each component might do the same. (In the preceding discussion of psychogenic MBD, a model for such an interaction—in that case between environmental difficulties and "predisposition"—was proposed.) Not only does custom sanction a belief in the importance of interactions, but logically one must assume that such interactions are the rule and not the exception. Despite the statistically "significant" association between brain damage or prematurity and later MBD symptoms, only a small fraction of children exposed to such noxae develop MBD symptoms; the statistical relationship obscures the fact that most children who are so exposed do *not* develop symptoms. Accordingly one is forced to assume the operation of other forces[11] and/or the inaccuracy of

---

[10] Except that brain damage may play a role in the etiology of MBD: the prevalence of neurological signs and histories suggestive of neurological damage seems to be higher in schizophrenic children (about 80%, Gittleman and Birch, 1967) than in children with "minimal brain damage" (about 50%).

[11] For a fuller exposition of this generally overlooked point, see Wender, 1967.

the measuring techniques, that is, that there is experimental error. (It might be the case that all children exposed to certain forms of brain damage at birth do in fact develop the MBD syndrome but that methods for assessing the presence or absence of such injuries are only approximate. For example, we may have applied the label "brain damage" where none is present—for example, in children with histories of a difficult birth—or we may have failed to identify nondramatic symptoms as MBD associated. Hence we observe an increased but far from perfect association between the two.)

Logic strongly suggests that the interaction of forces is important. What data substantiate this view—or, to be more accurate, are consonant with it? Two classes of data documenting the effects of interaction will be presented: (1) the interaction between genetic factors and brain damage or birth complications, and (2) the interaction between rearing factors and "biological predisposition."

Interaction of Genetic Factors and Brain Damage or Birth Complications

Animal Data

A study on the rat illustrating interaction between genetic (strain) differences and brain injury is that reported by King (1959). In this animal, lesions of the septal area produce an increase in "emotionality": animals in whom this area is injured demonstrate changes such as increased attack and flight reactions, startle behavior, and resistance to capture. King compared the effect of septal lesions on two strains of rats, one of which was demonstrably more tense, excitable, fearful, and aggressive. Following the production of septal lesions, both groups of animals demonstrated increased "emotionality" but the effects were far greater on the genetically more reactive animals: there was a clear interaction between brain injury and temperament. It appears, the author argues, that (1) the lesions' effect is to release the potential for certain behaviors called "emotional," (2) this potential differs with differing genetic endowment, and hence (3) postoperative behavior differs.

Human Data

Two studies are available, both showing the interaction of genetic and birth complications in the etiology of *schizophrenia*. They can therefore only suggest that similar actions may play a role in the production of the MBD syndrome.

In a study of psychopathology among the offspring of schizophrenic mothers, Mizrahi (1968) showed that those who developed psychiatric illness had a higher proportion of birth "complications" (e.g., uterine dysfunction, prematurity, cord complications) than offspring who did not.[12] However, the schizophrenics' offspring who did become ill had a frequency of complications no greater than that of the healthy offspring of non-schizophrenics (i.e., the schizophrenics' offspring who did *not* become ill had a lower than expected frequency of complications). The sample is very small but the data do suggest that birth problems which are themselves insufficient to produce illness will do so if they occur in a genetically predisposed population.

A study with comparable findings is reported by Pollin et al. (1966). These authors studied 11 monozygotic twin pairs in whom one member was schizophrenic and the other was not. The psychiatric status of the parents is not reported, but since genetic factors have been demonstrated to play a very important role in the etiology of schizophrenia (Wender, 1969) it may be assumed that the parents were at least carriers of the genetic diathesis. Such a diathesis was obviously unable to account for the illness alone since in each of the 11 twin pairs one member was well while the other was ill. In an effort to explain this disparity, the authors examined a number of possible biological and psychological causes. They found several biological differences between the schizophrenic and well co-twin: first, the sick co-twin had a lower birth weight (in all of the 11 pairs); second, the sick co-twin was apt to have had birth difficulties; third, the sick co-twin manifested "soft neurological signs" (in 8 of the 11 pairs); fourth, there was a tendency for the sick twin to have had a number of MBD characteristics including impulsivity, a "high but unsuccessful activity level which led to frequent frustrations," and infant feeding difficulties. These findings are subject to alternative explanations but certainly may reasonably be interpreted to show that factors associated with the genesis of the MBD syndrome (low birth weight, birth difficulties, neurological signs) can interact with a genetic predisposition to "activate" a "latent tendency" to produce schizophrenia.

As observed, these studies deal with the interactions between genetic predispositions to schizophrenia and other biological factors. It is *tenable* that such an interaction occurring between nongenetic biological factors and a genetic predisposition to MBD might favor the development of the MBD syndrome.

---

[12] The author reports her data as insignificant, but a one-tailed exact probability test of her data shows that her results are indeed significant.

Interactions of Child-Rearing Factors and Biological Predisposition

In Drillien's (1964) longitudinal study of premature infants, he evaluated, among other variables, the roles of low birth weight and rearing conditions in physical and psychological development. The dependent variable, behavior, was assessed from teachers' reports and classroom behavior ratings. (These school ratings were subsequently classified by Drillien as normal [0–9], borderline maladjustment [10–19], and obviously maladjusted [20+]. The independent variables were birth weight, social class, and "stress" (parental gross ill health, separation, or death; severe marital discord; hospitalization of the infant, etc.). The fluctuations of classroom behavior with birth weight and stress are shown in Table 3. As one might expect, behavior worsens markedly with the lower weight and the presence of stress.

Table 3. Fluctuation of Classroom Behavior with Birth Weight and Stress[a]

		Birth Weight		
	N	4 lb, 8 oz and under	N	4 lb, 9 oz and over
No Stress	88	%	252	%
Normal		56		72
Borderline		27		22
Maladjusted		17		6
Stress	35	13	86	
Normal		26		46
Borderline		26		31
Maladjusted		48		23

[a]After Drillien (1964), p. 252.

Similar findings, *mutatis mutandis,* were observed for the interrelations between birth weight, "stress," perinatal complications, and classroom behavior as shown in Table 4. The data clearly show the interactions between the three variables and the negative effect on behavior of lower birth weight, stress, and perinatal complications.[13] Several caveats should be observed in interpreting these data. First, the maladjustment rating includes MBD behavior and deviant non-MBD behavior (such as excessive shyness). Second, "stress" does *not* refer to psychological stress alone, but

[13] Interpretation of the perinatal complications is, as usual, impossible. Increased infant illness might be: an early manifestation of "poor protoplasm," the cause or result of brain injury, or reflection of inadequate maternal care (Drillien, 1964).

Table 4. Fluctuation of Classroom Behavior with Birth Weight, Stress, and Perinatal Complications[a]

Stress and Perinatal Complications	Behavior Adjustment by Birth Weight[b]	
	4 lb, 8 oz and under ($\underline{N} = 123$)	4 lb, 9 oz and over ($\underline{N} = 165$)
	Means	
No stress, no complications	6.4	4.9
Stress, no complications	13.1	7.5
No stress, complications	10.5	8.2
Stress, complications	20.0	15.6

[a]After Drillien (1964), p. 254.
[b]Behavior adjustment ratings: 0–9, normal; 10–19, borderline maladjusted; 20+, maladjusted.

includes physical illness in the child, which has been shown (Stott, 1966) to be associated with increased MBD-like behavior in later life.[14] Third, the behavioral abnormalities of the parents may be manifestations of a genetic disorder, genetically as well as psychologically transmitted to the child and contributing to the dispositional part of the interaction.

In a study already referred to, Thomas et al. (1968) conducted a longitudinal study of 136 children whose temperamental characteristics were first evaluated in infancy. These children were followed through early latency and the relationship between infant temperament and parental handling was investigated in the children who developed problems. Of the children in the study, 42 developed difficulties and of these 35 appeared to demonstrate some MBD-like signs and symptoms (about 13 appear to have had enough MBD signs to be considered fairly typical instances). The authors did find that the "difficult infants" tended to become "difficult children;" of the infants in this category (whose symptoms included excessive activity, irritability, unpredictability), 70% developed problems at a later stage of development. A relationship was found, however, be-

[14] Another study illustrating the interaction between perinatal complications and environmental experience (social, psychological, and biological) is reported by Werner et al. (1967). This study had the advantage of being longitudinal, with infants studied at birth, and the disadvantage of a short term follow-up of 2 years. The authors found that the environmental variables—socioeconomic status, familial stability, and maternal intelligence (a variable at least partially genetic)—interacted with perinatal complications to affect infant intelligence. "Environmental" variables had little effect in the absence of perinatal complications, but when perinatal complications were severe, infants from low socioeconomic families or unstable families suffered the greatest impairment (I.Q. differences of approximately 15 points).

tween techniques of parental handling and the appearance of later symptomatology. Parents who were firm and consistent and who managed to
maintain a modicum of equanimity were blessed with the least severely
disturbed of these children. These impressions jibe with my own theory
regarding the source of some behavioral problems in MBD children (as
will be explicated later). MBD children are considerably less susceptible
than normals to parental attempts at socialization but they are not entirely
refractory. As would be expected, those parents who were particularly
persistent in their attempts to socialize their children were apparently much
more effective in doing so.

Thus multidetermination undoubtedly functions in MBD, but a profes-
sion of its importance can act as a screen for ignorance. The causes listed
—brain damage, genetic transmission, intrauterine variation, fetal maldevelopment, psychological experience—cannot fail to interact. Further
knowledge will come only from a detailed consideration of the separate
causes and of the nature of specific interactions, not from an awed con-
templation of the complexity of the interweaving.

CHAPTER 3

Prevalence and Diagnosis of the MBD Syndrome

PREVALENCE

It is atypical to include a discussion of prevalence with a section on "diagnosis." The typical organizational placement is accounted for by the usual view of prevalence, which is largely as an estimate of the public health significance of a disease. However, knowledge of the prevalence of an illness is—or should be—a background factor influencing its diagnosis. This point is generally, if tacitly, recognized. If a disorder is common, one will make the diagnosis readily; similarly, if a disorder is rare, one will hesitate to make the diagnosis even if an individual has pathognomonic symptoms. A physician in North America thinks more than twice before diagnosing a localized anesthesia as leprosy or a recurrent fever as malaria. The major point to be made in this section is that the MBD syndrome is exceedingly common and that in certain circumstances (e.g., appearance at a child guidance clinic with a learning problem) it is an extremely probable diagnosis in the total absence of any other knowledge.

What is the prevalence of this syndrome? Its prevalence is, among other variables, a function of one's demands for diagnostic precision. The MBD syndrome is one that is unusually blurred around the edges and the use of broad or narrow criteria will appreciably influence the reported prevalence figure.[1] "Classical" cases are much less common than atypical ones. With this caveat in mind, we can deal with the question more realistically —if less precisely. It can be answered in two parts: (1) The prevalence

[1] The stringency of diagnostic criteria is an important factor in determining the prevalence of any illness. Consider, for example, schizophrenia, which may appear less prevalent in European than in American clinical centers. In the United States, syndromes such as "acute schizophrenic reaction" and "pseudoneurotic schizophrenia" are included under the same rubric as "chronic undifferentiated schizophrenia," while in Europe the term is apt to be used only for the clearcut "process" manifestations of the disorder.

in the general child population. (2) The prevalence in the child psychiatric population.

Prevalence in General Child Population

A number of relevant surveys of school-age children have been conducted. Prechtl and Stemmer (1962) reported on the prevalence in the Netherlands of the "choreiform syndrome," which was defined by the presence of minimal choreiform movements together with "behavioral problems." They found this syndrome to be present in 20% of elementary school-age boys and "severe" in 5% of them; its prevalence in girls was 10%, with less than 1% having "severe" symptoms. Of children with this syndrome, 90% had more or less severe reading difficulties. Stewart et al. (1966) reported the prevalence of the "hyperactivity syndrome" to be approximately 4% in a population of St. Louis grade-school children between the ages of 5 and 11. In a survey of a second-grade school population in Vermont, Huessy (1967) found the prevalence of "hyperkinesis" to be 10%; he also found that 80% of the children who teachers felt had serious problems fell into this category. The above authors used different diagnostic criteria: Prechtl employed a minor neurological sign, Stewart relied on teachers' reports of overactivity and short attention span, and Huessy depended on school questionnaires. It is of interest therefore that the three authors arrive at approximately the same figures for serious symptomatic involvement: 5% to 10%.

Another pertinent study investigated the prevalence of behavioral and psychological disturbance in Montgomery County, Maryland. Reporting on a stratified sample of 20% of the population of elementary school children (approximately 24,000 out of a total of 120,000 children), teacher ratings indicated that restlessness was a "problem" in approximately 15% of the children in grades one to six and that "problems of attention span" were present in approximately 22% of the children in those grades. "Problems" is a rather vague referent. It implies that the children were more restless and less attentive than their teachers would have them be. Nonetheless, it indicates again that one-fifth to one-tenth of grade-school children had MBD-like problems to some (perhaps minor) degree.

The syndrome—at least when largely defined by the presence of hyperactivity—has a clear sex linkage: the male-to-female ratios range from three or four to one (Paine et al., 1968) to nine to one (Werry, 1968b). These ratios roughly parallel those for other child psychiatric disorders.

Prevalence in Child Psychiatric Population

The frequency with which MBD children are found among populations referred for psychiatric treatment is obviously a function of the referral source and, again, the stringency of the diagnostic criteria. Psychologically unsophisticated parents and school personnel refer children with gross behavioral problems—not schizoid, untroublesome children—and hence one would expect clinics and private psychiatrists to see a disproportionately large fraction of hyperactive children.

I cannot find published statistics reporting the prevalence of the syndrome among children referred to either private practitioners or psychiatric clinics. The experience of a private institution, the Sheppard and Enoch Pratt Hospital (Pats, 1969) may be informative. Diagnostic labels in child psychiatry are vague, and it is difficult to assess others' reports. Of the children seen in this clinic (mean age 9), only 8% were diagnosed as "chronic brain syndrome"; but of the remainder, a large fraction had symptom pictures strongly suggestive of MBD: 34% had failed at least one grade in school, 45% were school underachievers, 34% were behavior problems in school, 68% had symptoms in school, and 73% were "control problems of the parents." In my personal experience in a university clinic, 50% of the latency-age children fell into the MBD category; in a county clinic receiving a large fraction of school referrals, approximately one-half to two-thirds fell into this category.

I draw two pragmatic conclusions from the prevalence data: (1) The MBD syndrome should be a major target for "secondary prevention" (i.e., treatment) in the school-age population, as it apparently constitutes the major fraction of psychiatrically disturbed children. (2) With no further knowledge, any preadolescent child admitted to a child guidance clinic is most probably in the category until proven otherwise. If, in addition, one knows that a child is not bizarre or retarded and has not been recently disturbed by a presumably noxious environment, one can make the diagnosis with some certainty. This diagnostic technique lacks subtle nicety but is quite effective.[2]

DIAGNOSIS

The major thrust of the material presented under diagnosis will be an analysis of the usefulness of the common psychiatric diagnostic techniques with regard to the MBD syndrome. Before approaching these practical considerations, however, I would like to explain my reasons for including diverse symptoms under one syndrome.

[2] It is comparable to a technique of adult psychiatric diagnosis attributed to William Alanson White: when a patient is admitted to a hospital, determine his age. If he is less than 40, he is probably schizophrenic; if he is between 40 and 60 he is probably manic-depressive; if he is over 60 he is probably senile.

Rationale for Grouping Diverse Clinical Manifestations in One Syndrome

The preceding pages have described a complex, heterogeneous, and sometimes mutually contradictory group of behavioral characteristics which have been asserted to be characteristic of a single syndrome. The behavioral manifestations are so diverse that the following questions immediately arise: Is there a "justification" for grouping these characteristics together? Is it "meaningful" or "useful" to place in one category the heterogeneous persons manifesting these characteristics? Let me waive the epistemological question of whether meaning or utility is the best measure of truth, and turn to historical precedent: medicine—at least in its early stages—has found the syndrome concept both meaningful and useful. Medicine has used the word "syndrome" to assert the existence of a state with certain defining attributes and with an indeterminate but presumably small number of underlying causes. A few early examples might include dropsy, rheumatic fever, and consumption. The identification—or construction—of syndromes has proved meaningful when it has pointed to commonalities in etiology, and useful when it has suggested similar modes of treatment. The reasons for placing a certain group of signs and symptoms together in a syndrome are several. In the case of the MBD syndrome they include manifest characteristics, apparent underlying "primary" psychological disabilities, probable biochemical and anatomical lesions, and response to treatment.[3]

With regard to manifest characteristics, the symptoms are grouped together in a syndrome simply because they are associated with one another on a greater than chance basis. Such groupings pose no problems in the "classical" instance in which almost all symptoms are present in a given individual. The syndrome was initially described in children who were hyperactive and impulsive, had cognitive defects, and were emotionally labile. As a world-famous professor of medicine observed, "In such cases even the janitor can make the diagnosis." But should the syndrome be said to exist when only a few of these characteristics are present? What of the

---

[3] The order in which the reasons are presented corresponds roughly to the usual order of historical discovery. The most "superficial" manifestations are described first, their simplest underlying mechanism comes next (physiological or psychological), and their ultimate biochemical and anatomical basis last of all. In the case of diabetes mellitus, polydipsia, polyuria, weight loss, and sweet urine were first described. These characteristics were later shown to be associated with a high level of blood sugar, which in turn was shown to be associated with inadequate pancreatic activity, which in turn was shown to be characterized by inadequate islet activity and deficient insulin secretion. The anatomic and genetic bases of the latter defects are now being explored.

child who is hyperactive and distractible, but shows no cognitive defects and is not emotionally labile? Or the child who is impulsive but hypoactive and undistractible? In general it is impossible, *a priori,* to specify meaningful and exact rules for a syndrome by which one may decide whether a particular individual is to be included or excluded. Rules for inclusion can be arbitrarily decided upon but the usefulness of such assignment rules must eventually depend on other criteria for defining the syndrome. A technique's efficacy in diagnosis (i.e., categorization) can ultimately be assessed only against another method of defining the state in question. This method of evaluation poses many fewer problems for medicine than it does for psychiatry. The criterion attributes (those which define and discriminate a condition) may usually be tested against measures utilized by the pathologist, bacteriologist, or biochemist. An adherent breast nodule is found to be cancerous in $X\%$ of cases, using the pathological specimen as the ultimate deciding criterion. Polydipsia, polyuria, and weight loss are found to be diabetic in origin in $Y\%$ of instances, using fasting blood sugar as the defining attribute of diabetes. These are among the simpler and esthetically more pleasing examples of rational classification. Things are not always so simple even in the realm of medicine. Consider the syndrome of rheumatic fever: acute rheumatic fever may manifest itself with carditis alone, chorea alone, nodules alone, and so on. What, therefore, are its "real" boundaries? In studying the syndrome, clinicians decided to *define* acute rheumatic fever as being present whenever any two of five "major" symptoms are present or when one "major" and two "minor" symptoms are present. Whether this definition is *useful* is an empirical matter. If it is found that some patterns of the syndrome have a benign prognosis while others have a more serious prognosis, the *prognostic* usefulness of the undifferentiated syndrome must be designated as poor. Nonetheless, the *etiological* meaningfulness of this syndrome might still be high: all the different manifest patterns might be found to be a response to a particular infection (associated with the hemolytic streptococcus). Since etiological and prognostic knowledge about MBD is in an elementary stage, it is difficult to know which patterns should be defined as criteria of the MBD syndrome. As with acute rheumatic fever or schizophrenia, it is easy to define "core" cases; the important problem exists at the periphery. This problem might be partially avoided if it were possible to use attributes other than overt behavior to define the syndrome.

With respect to underlying "primary" disabilities, in the chapter on psychological theory I will attempt to show that many of the diverse behavioral characteristics of the MBD child can be seen as superficial variations on a more simple psychological theme—that is, that children with the syndrome are characterized by a few underlying psychological abnormalities which are constantly present in all instances of the syndrome, despite the varying outward manifestations. This is directly comparable to Bleuler's method of solving the classification problems of dementia praecox. Bleuler grouped a fairly heterogeneous group of psychiatric disorders by postulating underlying "primary" defects. The analogous technique in the example of acute rheumatic fever would be to argue that the various manifestations of that disease can be attributed to varying forms of allergic reaction— allergic (autoimmune) reactivity precipitated by the streptococcus that is commonly considered the underlying cause of the syndrome.

Similarly, at a later point in this essay I will hypothesize that the postulated underlying psychological defects may in turn be attributed to certain common and specifiable biochemical and anatomical lesions. This is an assertion of etiological—not intermediate mechanistic—commonality.

Response to treatment enjoys the lowest prestige as a classificatory technique—and not without reason. Different diseases may respond to the same remedy or the same disease may respond to very different remedies. Likewise, response to treatment cannot be depended upon to elucidate cause. Tuberculosis may be cured by isoniazid, but the disorder is not regarded as being due to congenital failure of the body to produce that substance. Nonetheless, response to treatment can form a crude basis for grouping seemingly disparate symptomatic pictures together: only bacterial diseases respond to penicillin—schizophrenia and fractures do not. With the weaknesses of this classificatory principle stated, I wish to propose that an important and unifying feature of the MBD syndrome is its response to treatment with the amphetamines. As I will discuss in the section on pharmacological therapy, the seemingly disparate behavior clusters often respond in such a similar manner to these drugs that the syndrome might be referred to as "congenital hypoamphetaminemia."

Diagnosis: Practical Considerations

Continuing to waive the requirements of exact epistemology for the moment, let us now turn to the following practical questions concerning diagnosis: (1) What are the most reliable ways of obtaining accurate knowledge of a child's behavior? (2) What nonbehavioral measures, if any, correlate with the behavior patterns of the syndrome? (3) And perhaps most importantly, what information will predict responsiveness to treatment?

Bearing these questions in mind, let us first turn to what is actually done. Although clinic procedures are changing, a standard pattern of child guidance clinic evaluation does exist. Traditionally, the social worker queries a child's parents and obtains information from his teachers about the child's behavior, and the psychiatrist examines the child in the playroom to measure his behavior. The child is referred for psychological tests and neurological examination to complete the work-up. Such a battery of tests is the hallmark of the "thorough evaluation," is standard operating procedure, and is considered most desirable even if it is not always practically obtainable. Is it, in fact, desirable, and if so, why? I would like to make the mildly heretical assertion that at this stage of understanding of the syndrome the *practical* usefulness of the traditional "thorough diagnostic evaluation" is questionable.[4] That is not to deny that such a battery of examinations is relevant for research purposes. With information so obtained one can make such assertions as the following: "X% of [a particular sample of] MBD children are below the 50th percentile on the Bender-Gestalt Test"; "Y% of MBD children between the ages of 10 and 11 have a diffusely abnormal EEG." It is my contention that most of the extra-historical information is of limited value diagnostically and therapeutically. Psychological test performance and neurological evaluation neither confirm nor rule out the presence of the syndrome, are of doubtful predictive value for drug treatment, and are of no demonstrated value in planning psychological management.

What is the evidence concerning the comparative usefulness of the following techniques of investigation: history; psychiatric interview with the child; psychological test evaluation; neurological evaluation?

The History

In the chapter on characteristics of the syndrome, the "typical" behavioral abnormalities of the MBD child were described. Such information can only be obtained by historical inquiry. As in the case of all medical and psychiatric histories, reliability is an issue. The child is usually brought by his mother or guardian, who is personally involved and may be expected to present a biased account. The effect of such distortions may sometimes be diminished by multiple informants such as the father, other family adults, and the child's teacher. The teacher is apt to be a most useful source of information. If reasonably experienced, she has established norms for that child's age group and has 30 or 40 peers with whom she may compare him. The father's report may not always be helpful. He is frequently absent from the home, does not have to contend with the behavioral obstreperousness of the child, and hence is apt to minimize the child's problems. An added—if expectable—difficulty is that home and

[4] A conclusion to which many child mental health workers have apparently come independently (Truumaa, 1970). In the event that traditional practices are gradually being abandoned, the following argument should be seen as not attacking a straw man but holding him down.

school reports do not always agree. Some children are reported to mis-
behave at home, some in the school, and some in both. The meaning of
such discrepancies is sometimes difficult to ascertain, but it is wasteful of
data and too easy to immediately write off such discrepancies as simply a
manifestation of poor interrater reliability; in many instances the pattern
of discrepancy can be of considerable usefulness in evaluation. Frequently
one finds a history of misbehavior in school and acceptable behavior at
home. Often this indicates that the parents have lower standards of behavior (whether "rightly" or "wrongly"). The mother will report, "I don't
see what they are complaining about—all my other children act that
way. . . ." And she will add, "I acted that way when I was a child." This
kind of comment emerges with surprising regularity from disorganized
mothers running chaotic homes. When this pattern ((well-behaved at home
and not at school) is veridical it usually indicates an unusually well-
structured home and a child who is unable to cope with the academic stress
of schooling. In these instances a careful history usually reveals that minimal signs of the syndrome have appeared under stress in the past. In instances where the mother reports difficulty and the school does not, one
is most likely to find either a disturbed home (often with a child who is
not MBD) or a mother who is unable to set limits. The capacity of the
child to respond to controls provided by the school is a useful prognostic
indicator of the effects of limit-setting at home.

It is well to remember that parents or teachers can neither be depended
upon nor expected to provide an account adequate to serve as the basis
of a diagnosis. Diagnosis of the syndrome requires a detailed behavioral
history, which the informant cannot be expected to volunteer. The parent
should not be expected to recount spontaneously the presence of positive
signs of the syndrome and to deny the presence of signs that are negatively
associated with the syndrome. For this reason, mental health workers (predominantly psychologists and psychiatrists and *not* social workers) who
depend upon associative anamneses often fail to obtain the relevant information. Detailed anamneses are not *fashionable*. Their utility has been
devaluated for multiple reasons: much information traditionally obtained is
irrelevant and/or useless; the age at which weaning took place has—
despite theory—little predictive value; parental reports concerning long-
past events are apt to be inaccurate; information concerning the birthplace
of the patient's grandparents or the mother's age of graduation from high
school may be reliable but of no consequence. The obvious uselessness of
much material obtained with laborious exactitude has led to an abridgment
of the inquiry process; but the boundaries between the baby and the bath
water have concomitantly been blurred, with the usual results. The age of
the child's grandmother may be of little diagnostic assistance, but the age

at which he can tie his shoelaces may have considerable predictive value. To mention a specific example, the fact that a 10-year-old with an I.Q. of 140 could tie his shoes only with great difficulty was of greater value in planning his therapy than a knowledge of the interesting but secondary power struggle he was engaged in with his mother.[5] Similarly, fidgetiness is not generally considered to be an attribute worth inquiring after or spontaneously volunteering information about. A mother whose 8-year-old son had set fire to the living room couch twice in one week neglected to volunteer the information that her son was quite fidgety and became bored rapidly at games.[6] Likewise, a school referring a 10-year-old with a "special learning disorder" failed to report that he hummed, walked around a good deal, and annoyed his classmates. In all these instances such information had to be sought specifically, was supplied with amused tolerance, and was of greater diagnostic value than the rich and fascinating accounts of family interrelations which were so eagerly volunteered.

In order to secure a useful detailed history, the inquirer must know what he is looking for; if he does not, his inquiry will be as awkward and time-consuming as that of the novitiate physician. A medical student requires hours to get an inaccurate history of a heart attack, while an intern, knowing what he needs to know and what he must ask, obtains an accurate account in several minutes. Similarly, the mental health worker must inquire directly about the presence or absence of the characteristic dysfunctions listed earlier. This is in direct contradiction to the tacit assumption of the nondirective interviewer that the interviewee will tell you everything if you don't interrupt. Obviously such direct questioning requires care, since the interviewer must avoid "suggesting" behavior the child does not have or has only to a minimal or "normal" degree.

An experiment documenting the necessity of specific inquiry for accurate evaluation is reported by Graham and Rutter (1968). These authors compared the number of complaints reported spontaneously by parents with those reported on direct inquiry and found that underreporting by parents was the rule rather than the exception. Of 48 children in whom overactivity, fidgetiness, or concentration difficulties were found to be present upon direct inquiry, the parents spontaneously reported their presence in less than 20%; likewise, in less than 40% of cases did the parents spontaneously report the presence of stealing, destructiveness, disobedience, bullying, serious lying, and truancy. The only abnormal child behaviors which parents accurately reported more than half the time were temper tantrums and irritability.

---

[5] See case history 9, "Edward."
[6] See case history 5, "Robert."

The Psychiatric Interview with the Child

Since the child *is* the patient, the playroom interview with the child is traditionally accepted as the most important and useful investigatory technique—either because this is so, the psychiatrist performs it, or because the psychiatrist performs it, it is so. What information is available to *document* its usefulness? Not much.

Rutter and Graham (1968) have investigated the reliability and validity of a direct psychiatric assessment of the child. These authors found some crude correlations between parents' and teachers' reports and psychiatrists' appraisals: 60% of those diagnosed by parents or teachers as severely disturbed were diagnosed by the psychiatrists as such; 70% of those diagnosed by parents or teachers as having a slight psychiatric disorder were rated by the psychiatrist as having a slight or severe disorder. Children with "antisocial" problems—whose problems, like those of many MBD children, were greater problems to others than to themselves—were diagnosed as showing "slight abnormality" in 45% of the cases and as showing "no abnormality" in 30% of the cases. In another study (Zrull, 1964) in which mothers' reports, teachers' reports, social workers' reports, and psychiatrists' playroom evaluations were all intercorrelated, the evaluations that correlated least well with the others were the psychiatrists'.

Rutter and Graham also investigated the ability of the examining psychiatrist to detect specific abnormal behaviors that were reported by other observers and the ability of psychiatrists to agree among themselves. With regard to the first question, they found that when interviewing groups independently diagnosed as having no psychiatric pathology, as "neurotic" or as "antisocial," the psychiatrists could detect no difference between the neurotic and antisocial groups in fidgetiness, poor attention span, or distractibility. Since there were no independent "outside" reports of these traits in these groups, this finding may mean that these characteristics "really" are equally common in the two groups; or that the psychiatric interview is a poor place to measure the presence or absence of these characteristics.[7] With regard to the second question, interrater reliabilities were assessed and found to show variable fair-to-moderate agreement between the different examining psychiatrists. The authors commented that "the reliability of some judgments is too low, and much more investigation is required into the processes involved in inferring anxiety, depression, emotional responsiveness . . . although, in this age group [7–12] antisocial

---

[7] Since the prevalence of these characteristics is higher in both the neurotic and antisocial groups than in the normal group, these presumably MBD signs may be characteristic of a large proportion of all children with problems.

children were differentiated fairly well from children in the general population on the basis of their peer relationships and neurotic traits, the interview offered little opportunity for the expression of their aggression or antisocial tendencies. It is unlikely that the interview would be of much value in differentiating the nonneurotic delinquent child from the normal child" (p. 576). Since the nonneurotic delinquent child and the MBD child have many characteristics in common—and, in fact, they may be the same child—this comment by Rutter and Graham again raises the question of the usefulness of the diagnostic interview with the child. Reliability (agreement) is, of course, not validity ("truth"). Rutter and Graham raise this obvious philosophical question: which blind man is to be believed? If the teacher and parent disagree with the psychiatrist, which is outside Plato's cave? Who is "right," and how can we know? Although it is not the most parsimonious explanation, it is possible that in the instance of disagreement, the psychiatrist might be right and everyone else might be wrong. It is perhaps more likely, however, that a psychiatrist obtains a deviant sample of a child's behavior. It is "normal" for a child to be at school or at home; it is "abnormal" for him to spend an hour playing and talking with a strange adult.[8] To the extent that the child is psychologically responsive, with his behavior influenced by his environment, one would expect an abnormal environment to produce abnormal behavior and one would expect the psychiatrist to obtain an invalid sample of the child's behavior. The question of validity in the interview is generally neglected or, if recognized, is considered to be a problem only in that *no* information may be forthcoming. One practical difficulty is that the interview with the child may provide misleading information. Physicians and psychologists, like teachers, may find that the child "responds well to one-to-one attention" and does not appear hyperactive. The difficulty stems from the unquestioning assumption that the expert examiner cannot but obtain "true" information. It is embarrassingly common to obtain a report from such an examiner stating that the child was not hyperactive at the time of his examination and concluding prematurely that the previous reporters must have been misled.

I do not wish to convey the impression that the interview with the child is never of diagnostic value. The psychiatric evaluation of the child can be extremely useful in one subcategory of MBD children: the borderline schizophrenic child. Many children who are both hyperactive and psychotic

---

[8] After all, which behavioral sample seems, at face value, to lend itself more readily to extrapolation to real life: "adjusts well to strange adult in clinic playroom" or "adjusts well in school and home"?

are not described by other observers as bizarre. It is with this kind of child that the psychiatrist can make a particularly useful contribution— for example, by ascertaining whether the content of the child's "daydreams" runs to routine or pathological fantasy.

In these somewhat heretical views concerning the general usefulness of the *diagnostic* interview, I am expressing an opinion similar to that of Rutter and Graham, who remark that "although the psychiatric interview with the child has been shown to be a fairly reliable and valid instrument (at least with regard to some types of behavior), it might still be questioned whether it adds anything to the diagnostic process that cannot be better obtained from the parents' or teachers' account of the child" (p. 575).[8a] The relevant question here is *only* whether or not a given child falls into the category of the MBD syndrome, *not* how the child is reacting to or with this syndrome. These comments do not apply to the question of the therapeutic usefulness of interviewing the child, which will be discussed later.

Psychological Test Evaluation

Intelligence and achievement measurements and certain special educational tests may be helpful in determining the appropriate education placement for MBD children with learning problems. Until recently, educational testing procedures have been relatively crude and, although capable of assessing general aptitude and achievement, could only roughly identify areas of perceptual and cognitive dysfunction. Recent research in children with special learning disorders (Chalfant and Scheffelin, 1969) has been directed at specifying and assessing the exact nature of the varied perceptual and cognitive dysfunctions found in such children. Perceptual dysfunctions, for example, may be subdivided into those affecting a given sense (or senses), those affecting a particular aspect of a given sense (e.g., auditory discrimination, visual perception of spacial relationships), or those affecting integration of two or more senses (e.g., sight and hearing). Such diagnostic specification may have important consequences for remedial education. Remedial techniques might employ carefully graduated training in the area of deficit (e.g., training in auditory discrimination) or attempt to teach the child by circumventing the area of deficit (e.g., teaching a child with auditory perceptual problems by employing techniques used with the blind). The questions of which educational techniques are most effective with children with which deficits remain to be answered.

[8a] Although the authors qualify this statement by adding that "Our findings so far can only provide a very tentative answer to this question, but it does seem that certain aspects of behavior (. . . . the child's emotional responsiveness and inter-personal relationships . . . .) can be better evaluated by an interview with the child" (p. 575-576).

If educational placement is not at stake, the usefulness of psychological testing is questionable. The factor analytic studies that I discussed in relation to characteristics of the syndrome indicate that there is no correlation between performance on routinely administered psychological measures and the behavioral or neurological attributes of the syndrome; the presence or absence of abnormal test performance tells us nothing about the child's behavioral status. Furthermore, there is no evidence that performance on such tests predicts response to drug or other therapy. There is, however, one important exception to the uselessness of routine psychological testing: the Rorschach test can be useful in recognizing a borderline psychotic child. Identifying the subgroup is of some importance since the borderline psychotic child's response to drug therapy may be qualitatively different from that of other categories of MBD children. How the Rorschach's discriminating value compares with that of a skilled clinician is problematic.

At this juncture a hypothetical psychodiagnostician might protest: Cannot the CAT, TAT, Draw-a-Man, and Rorschach inform us about the psychodynamics of a particular child? Whether they can do this in many cases is moot; a more realistic claim would be that they might be informative in *some* cases. All such tests are still subject to the questions of whether the desired information can be reliably obtained, whether it is valid, and whether it is useful, most combinations of these three attributes being possible.[9] Until such questions can consistently be answered affirmatively, it is reasonable to ask whether one should *routinely* expend the time, effort, and money to occasionally elucidate that which may be largely epiphenomenal.

Neurological Evaluation

In many clinics, neurological evaluation and an EEG[10] are routinely obtained. In the factor analytic studies mentioned previously, the following results were found: (1) *Abnormalities of neurological functioning bear no relationship to other characteristics of the MBD syndrome.* (2) *They are of no predictive value with regard to therapy.* Obviously, neurological evaluation is necessary for the child with concurrent neurological disease or in the child in whom one suspects a progressive neurological lesion. In the few hundred MBD children I have seen during the past several years —with the exception of those with epilepsy and known cerebral palsy— I have not seen a single child in whom the presence of progressive neurological disorder has been detected. Obviously such disorders exist. The

---

[9] For example, such testing might be reliable, invalid, and useless; or unreliable, valid (in a particular instance), and useful; or reliable, valid, and useless.

[10] The EEG is of such limited value in the work-up of the average MBD child that one waggish neurologist has observed that more good can be done for the family if the mother spends $35 (the cost of an EEG) on a hat for herself.

point is that they are seen uncommonly and that, accordingly, routine neurological evaluation would not seem to be indicated.[11]

Certainly, one must rule out the presence of any medical disorder which might cause signs attributed to MBD. Many children who see or hear poorly do not "pay attention." Sight and hearing disorders must always be ruled out.

What then may be concluded about the usefulness of routine evaluation techniques in the diagnosis of the syndrome? For treatment—not for research—I hope the answer is obvious. The history is the most important diagnostic tool (and is usually relegated to a junior member of the mental health team). The psychiatric evaluation of the child is generally of limited value (and is assigned to the most experienced member of the team). Psychological evaluation *may* be helpful: the psychological evaluation can be of use for educational placement and is sometimes helpful in identifying borderline psychotic children. Neurological evaluation is almost irrelevant.

At the expense of being tedious I want to reemphasize that in the practical management—the diagnosis and treatment—of children with suspected MBD, the traditional diagnostic measures are of little help. From the standpoint of cost utility they are of even less value: not only do they contribute little, but also they sap limited resources—both professional time and family or community money. The continuing use of such studies is perpetuated largely through force of custom: they are part of the team diagnostic *ritual*. They are useful for research; they are expensive and generally useless for practice.

Diagnostic Decision Making: An Addendum

In many psychiatric circles diagnosis is considered to be an anachronistic activity confined to either the recent immigrant from internal medicine or the obsessive character, fearful of close human contact and defensively banding together with a small and vanishing group of Kraepelinians. With regard to the MBD syndrome, diagnosis is not a sterile exercise in classification but a prescription for action. As will be seen in the section on treatment, classification of a given child as having the MBD syndrome

---

[11] Although neurological and psychological testing are of limited value in confirming the diagnosis of MBD, they are sometimes of value in suggesting the diagnosis. Pediatricians and psychologists who are aware of the syndrome sometimes discover suggestive evidence of MBD in children who are referred for seemingly different problems. The pediatrician may be alerted to the problem by discovering signs of motor difficulty and the psychologist may suspect MBD when he finds impairments of attention, concentration, abstract thinking, or problems of perceptual-motor coordination.

should result in a trial of drug treatment. Since there is no way of making a 100% accurate diagnosis and since there are no absolute criteria against which one may check, one can decide to employ criteria that are either too loose or too stringent: one can be prepared to either overdiagnose or underdiagnose.[12] This is rational behavior. Since diagnosis is a basis for action, and since such action has both advantageous and disadvantageous consequences, one's preparedness to under- or overdiagnose should be dependent on the probabilities and strengths of these consequences. If a treatment is never dangerous there is no harm in overdiagnosing. If a treatment is very dangerous and a diagnosis leads to such treatment, one must diagnose with caution. To misdiagnose someone as having a strep throat when in fact he has a cold is to commit oneself to a therapeutic regimen involving antibiotics and perhaps aspirin; this regimen will probably provide symptomatic relief although it will also expose the patient to a small (but measurable) risk of a harmful reaction.[13] To misdiagnose a child as having leukemia when he does not will result in his treatment with dangerous and possibly life-threatening medication. In this equation one must also consider the consequences of failure to make a correct diagnosis followed by a failure to administer correct treatment. To fail to diagnose the child as having acute leukemia when he does in fact have that disease is to doom him to death within 2 or 3 months.

Diagnosis, then, is not simply the mechanical assignment of a term on the basis of the presence or absence of certain clear-cut characteristics, but is an act based on an expectation of error—error that will itself have consequences in action. I am here tacitly referring to a concept that will be explicitly dealt with in the section on treatment—the concept of the "payoff matrix." At this juncture I merely wish to emphasize a factor in diagnosis that is not usually considered—that one of the criteria that determine diagnosis is the practical consequences of diagnosing. To err is likely but to err planfully is human.

[12] It is generally felt that errors in diagnosis are (or should be) random and that it would be foolish to introduce systematic deviations. I would argue that systematic diagnostic bias (always a pejorative phrase) must always be present (given the nature of man and our present knowledge of psychiatry) and, that this being the case, the practical question is how to make a virtue of a necessity.

[13] This calculation is unconsciously made by the sloppy doctor who gives antibiotics with the formula, "It can't do any [much] harm and it might do some good."

CHAPTER 4

Prognosis of the MBD Syndrome

It is a widely held belief among child psychiatrists that the MBD syndrome first improves and later disappears as a child grows older. The belief is supported by the rather obvious diminution of certain MBD signs with age: enuresis, hyperactivity, immature speech, and "childish" behavior. This apparent tendency for improvement with increasing age forms the basis for one diagnostic synonym, "maturational lag." It does *seem* that many children do get appreciably better at or around the time of puberty. The problem is the following: of how many is this true? This is the core question involved in the prognosis of the MBD syndrome.

As has been discussed, there are probably several etiologically distinct groups comprising the MBD syndrome. Although it is *conceivable* that all etiologically distinct subgroups have a common (physiological and/or psychological) final pathway and hence a similar natural history—as I shall later attempt to show—it would be more cautious to assume first that this is not necessarily so. Accordingly, it would be desirable to discuss prognosis as a function of a specific subtype. Unfortunately, with the exception of MBD linked to clear neurological insult (brain injury, encephalitis) there are no documented etiological subtypes.

The two techniques available for assessing prognosis scientifically are anterospective (longitudinal) studies and retrospective (cross-sectional) studies. In the former instance, one inspects the fate of children diagnosed as MBD; in the latter, one investigates the history of MBD in various clinical populations (e.g., healthy adults, "neurotics," schizophrenics). Each method has advantages and disadvantages. Anterospective studies in general involve the practical problem of attrition over time. Retrospective studies involve the difficulty of the reliability of the old data and also certain interpretative problems, which will be discussed later. A third source of prognostic hypotheses—not data—is anecdotal reports. These may suggest outcomes, and hence dimensions to be evaluated in future studies. They can demonstrate nothing about frequency of outcome.

The contributions of all three sources of prognostic information will be discussed in this chapter.

ANTEROSPECTIVE (LONGITUDINAL) STUDIES

There are two additional problems peculiar to the evaluation of anterospective studies in MBD children. First, the difficulties in delineating the syndrome aggravate the perennial problem of comparability of studies. The only samples of whose homogeneity and comparability one can be reasonably certain are those composed of children with certain or probable neurological injury (Bond and Smith, 1935; Menkes et al., 1966). To confine one's attention to this subgroup is to exclude a large fraction of MBD children. A second complication is that the diagnosis of the MBD syndrome in the absence of suspected brain injury is of comparatively recent origin, and the boundaries of the syndrome are unclear. There are as yet no anterospective studies available in terms of current MBD diagnoses, and such anterospective data as are used have been culled via an awkward retrospective process. Looking at old and perhaps inadequate records, one must decide which children would fall into the group that *now* would be designated as MBD and select them as the sample to evaluate. Obviously the characteristics of such a group cannot be specified as accurately as those of a group diagnosed contemporaneously. Thus, in two of the reports discussed in this section—Morris et al.(1956) and Robins (1966)—I and not the original authors have made the judgment that the follow-up studies are of samples which *probably* included a substantial fraction of children with the MBD syndrome. Whether I am correct in my judgment is certainly open to debate. Since it is difficult to be certain of the similarity of such variously obtained samples, quantitative differences in outcome are difficult to interpret meaningfully. The samples presented here are heterogeneous both in regard to the severity of illness (inpatient vs. outpatient) and subtype of the syndrome (with signs of neurological impairment versus without such signs); it seems plausible that the differences in outcome may be attributed to such sample differences. There are no published follow-up reports of the variant of the MBD syndrome most frequently seen: a hyperactive child of roughly normal intelligence, referred for learning problems or mild behavioral difficulties, showing no signs of neurological impairment, who responds favorably to treatment with amphetamine, and for whom hospitalization is never considered. This review is therefore biased. The anterospective studies it reports are of the most seriously disturbed MBD-like children. Their prognoses, as will be seen, are not good; but their prognoses may be unrepresentative. The anterospective studies which follow should therefore be read with particular caution.

In a study of a severely ill population, Bond and Smith (1935) followed the histories of 85 children who had been diagnosed as "postencephalitic" following recovery from von Economo's encephalitis or head injury and had been treated as inpatients at the Franklin School. Following illness, these children had been described as having changes in their behavior in the direction of "restlessness, disobedience, aggressiveness, loss of fear of punishment, truancy, stealing. . . . The children [had become] intolerable at home and at school and in foster homes" (p. 18). At the time of admission the children's ages ranged from 4 to 10. The length of residence is not given but apparently was generally greater than 6 months. The period of follow-up varied (exact figures are not given) but seems to range from one to 9 years. Of 76 children who had been discharged from the school, 20 "recovered the position which they had held before their illness" (p. 26). Although the remaining 56 had evidenced a "moderate to extreme improvement" (p. 29) in the school, most did poorly: 33 out of the 56 "were later taken to state hospitals, schools for feebleminded, or reformatory institutions" (p. 30).

Morris et al. (1956) reported a 21- to 31-year follow-up of the fate of 90 children, ages 4 to 15, *admitted* to the psychiatric unit of a Pennsylvania hospital. The sample followed—which represented approximately 40% of the total population of the psychiatric unit—was characterized by the following criteria: (1) positive criteria—repeated truancy, stealing and lying, cruelty, destructiveness, and "severe tantrums when crossed"; (2) Negative criteria—I.Q. greater than 80, *no signs of brain damage,* no psychosis. Virtually the entire sample is described as disobedient and markedly restless. This sample would seem to be a severely disturbed (hospitalized) "antisocial" group of MBD children without known brain damage. Of 68 children followed until age 18 or older, 12 had become psychotic, 34 had "never adjusted," 10 had been diagnosed as "borderline," 7 had acquired a criminal record, and 14 had been described as "doing well." (The sum is greater than 68 because some individuals were placed in more than one category.)

Menkes et al. (1966) studied the outcome of 14 children evaluated at the Johns Hopkins Child Psychiatric Service outpatient clinic 25 years previously. The positive criteria for inclusion in the sample were as follows: hyperactivity, learning disorders, and one or more nonbehavioral criteria of brain dysfunction—clumsiness, visual motor deficits, impaired or delayed speech. "Hyperactivity" included distractibility, short attention span, emotional lability, impulsivity, and low frustration threshold. All patients were free of seizures and had I.Q.'s above 70. What fraction of the total outpatient population this sample of children constituted is not stated. It should be noted that this sample consists of one of the proposed etiological subgroups: those with neurological concomitants and probable organic brain injury. At the time of reexamination, four of the patients were institutionalized psychotics, and two were retarded and non-self-supporting; eight were self-supporting, and of these, four had been institutionalized for some time. Three of the subjects, then about 30 years of age, complained that they still felt restless; in the others, restlessness had generally disappeared between the ages of 12 and 14, although in some it was delayed until as late as twenty-one years. Low I.Q. and brain damage (definite rather than probable) correlated with later lack of social self-sufficiency.

Robins (1966) has reported a 30- to 40-year follow-up of 524 children seen at the St. Louis Municipal Psychiatric Clinic between 1924 and 1929. This population was heavily biased toward children with acting-out problems. The proportion of juvenile court referrals was 45%; the proportion of "antisocial" problems varied in the years covered between 55% and 85%; the mean age of the population at the time of first contact was 10–12; the socioeconomic class tended to be low and the backgrounds were, in general, seriously disrupted. The original clinical data did not always specifically deny the presence of particular symptoms; accordingly, failure to find such a symptom in the record might mean either its absence or a failure to inquire about its presence. Thus, absence of particular kinds of data relating to the MBD syndrome is impossible to interpret. With these qualifications in mind, an inspection of the data reveals that "enuresis" and "impulsivity"—symptoms *associated with* the MBD syndrome—were predictive of a later diagnosis of sociopathic personality: approximately 25% of the children in the study were described as "enuretic" or "impulsive," and 35% of those who were characterized as "impulsive" and 29% of those over age 6 who were described as "enuretic" were diagnosed as sociopaths as adults.[1] Likewise, other antisocial symptoms—pathological lying, lack of guilt, sexual perversions—which are also seen in *some* MBD children were associated with a diagnosis of sociopathic personality in later life. In this rather special "acting-out" sample, shyness, seclusive fears, and hypersensitivity—characteristics often thought to be predictive of schizophrenia—were not associated with adult psychopathology; instead, one-half of the schizophrenics in the adult follow-up population had histories of theft, "incorrigibility," and truancy. The conclusion would seem to be

---

[1] For normative figures regarding enuresis, McFarlane et al.'s (1954) data on the Berkeley growth study may be employed. They found that approximately 10% of the 13-year-old boys were persistently enuretic.

that "acting-out" problems are predictive of a spectrum of later psycho-pathological conditions. I most definitely do not wish to suggest that the index population in this study was predominantly children with MBD. The relevance to the MBD syndrome is suggestive: in this sample many children having symptoms which overlap those seen in the MBD syndrome developed a variety of serious psychiatric disorders, while children with symptoms unlike those seen in MBD children apparently did not develop such disorders.

RETROSPECTIVE STUDIES

The studies in this category begin by choosing a heterogeneous or homogeneous group of psychiatric patients and a comparison group, and then determining the earlier and/or current prevalence of certain signs and symptoms considered diagnostic of the presence of the MBD syndrome. In general, such studies document an increased prevalence of minimal brain damage or MBD signs and symptoms in a number of clinical groups. For example, Goldfarb (1961) has reported that 65% of schizophrenic children seen at the Ittelson Treatment Center had or had once had at least minimal signs or symptoms of neurological damage.

Beginning in the 1930's, Michaels (1955) called attention to the association of persistent enuresis and "a particular and compulsive psychopathic type of character . . . immature, relatively primitive, and undifferentiated in a psychopathological sense" (p. 116). Healy (1936), comparing the prevalence of a variety of characteristics in delinquents and sibling controls, found the following variables (all of which have been reported as being more frequent in the MBD syndrome) to be significantly more common among the histories of delinquents: cross and fussy babyhood (14% versus 5%); enuresis (21% versus 4%); *hyperactivity, restlessness, great impulsiveness* (44% versus 0%); "ascendant tendencies" (27% versus 6%); expressed marked feelings of inferiority (36% versus 4%). That characteristics seen in the MBD syndrome are also seen in the history of delinquents logically proves nothing. From the assertions that some MBD children are impulsive and some delinquents give histories of impulsivity one *cannot* conclude that "some MBD children become delinquent." That conclusion is *compatible* with the premises, not derivable from them. These data can only be suggestive.

Working with a clinically less disturbed population, a successive sample of adolescent underachievers admitted to the University of Washington Adolescent Clinic, Hammar (1967) reported that approximately one-half of these children had signs of "minimal brain dysfunction." The youngsters in this group, whose ages ranged from 12 to 18, were or had been characterized behaviorally as having: poor memory retention, a short attention span, distractibility, and impulsive behavior; however, hyperactivity was not a problem. This sample seemed to contain a large fraction of MBD children "grown up" and leads to the inference that some MBD children become "underachieving adolescents." These data also suggest that hyperactivity itself may disappear with increasing age while other of the temperamental characteristics associated with the MBD syndrome may not. Further suggestive information comes from some uncontrolled drug studies by Splitter (1966), who reports that the tricyclic antidepressants, which seem to be effective in hyperactive *children* (Krakowski, 1965), are highly effective in underachieving adolescents. The fact that the two groups respond to the same medication hardly documents that they have the same etiology, but considered with the retrospective study it lends credence to the view that some MBD children do become "underachieving adolescents."

Various studies of psychiatric inpatients reveal an increased prevalence of signs and/or histories of MBD-like problems in earlier life. Hertzig and Birch (1968), reporting on a sample of hospitalized adolescents (ages 11–16), stated that they found "soft" neurological signs in 30% of their patients and 5% of a control population. Pollack et al. (1968) found "suggestive" or "strongly suspicious" evidence of a history of "early minimal brain damage" in 47% of 74 hospitalized schizophrenic patients; such histories were correlated with poor prognosis. Hartocollis (1968) examined the childhood characteristics of a group of adult psychiatric inpatients who were selected as possibly organically impaired on the basis of neuropsychological tests, and found histories with suggestive evidence of MBD. He chose "only patients whose difficulties did not immediately establish the presence of cerebral dysfunction" (p. 103). Of 54 patients between the ages of 15 and 25 who met this criterion, 15 patients whose test scores revealed moderate "cerebral dysfunction" were selected for further study. The early histories of these patients were reviewed and tended to reveal the following characteristics: difficult gestation and/or birth, feeding difficulties, clumsiness, hyperactivity, temper tantrums, and aggressiveness. Although their presenting adult clinical pictures differed, "all subjects" had had varied degrees of "abnormal manifestations in the motor sphere" (overactivity), in intellectual performance (concreteness, reading difficulty), and in the "emotional sphere (extreme lability of mood, irritability, excitability, and sometimes violent outbursts and attempts at suicide)" (pp. 109–110). Latency behavior was clearly MBD-like and adolescent behavior included "lying, petty thievery . . . truancy . . . and quarrelsome aggressive behavior" (p. 111). These patients in adulthood comprised a number of personality types, primarily "infantile" (8/15) but also impulsive, schizoid, emotionally unstable, phobic, and hysteric. Diagnoses included schizophrenia (8/15), depression (4/15), infantile personality (2/15), and adjustment reaction of adolescence.

Another retrospective study linking MBD problems in childhood with psychiatric disorders of later life is that of Quitkin and Klein (1969). The authors examined 105 psychiatric inpatients under the age of 25 for histories of soft neurological signs during childhood and early adulthood. Such signs included difficult birth history with early developmental abnormality, hyperkinesis, impulsivity, marked clumsiness or athletic inability, speech difficulties, learning problems, and temper tantrums. Forty-two patients (40%) had such signs; in 11 they were "borderline" and in 31 (30%) definite. Using anamnestic data it was possible to divide the 31 subjects with definite signs into two distinct, relatively homogeneous, behavioral syndromes. The first, the "socially awkward, withdrawn" group (12 individuals), manifested "obvious intellectual defects, thought disorder, lack of social skills, social withdrawal, and marked inability to organize their life" (p. 133). The second, the "impulsive-destructive" group (19 individuals), manifested relatively good intellectual functions and little thought disorder, but were characterized by "destructive-impulsive behavior, low frustration tolerance, apparently endogenous mood swings, overreactive emotionality, and temper tantrums" (p. 133).

The two groups, who had some MBD characteristics in common, differed significantly from patients without soft signs and from each other in behavior in the hospital and in the diagnoses which they received. Both groups tended to act more on sudden inclination and to alienate others by their egocentricity more than the group without soft signs. Compared with the group without soft signs, the "impulsive-destructive" patients were significantly more manipulative while the "awkward-withdrawn" patients tended to somatize, lie, and seek attention. Diagnostically, the 19 "impulsive-destructive" patients were characterized as follows: character disorder (17)—mainly "emotionally unstable;" schizophrenia with childhood asociality (1); schizo-affective, manic (1). The 12 'awkward-withdrawn" patients received the following diagnoses: schizophrenia with childhood asociality (7); character disorder (5)—mainly schizoid and passive-dependent.

This study, in addition to providing further corroboration of the relationship between MBD characteristics in childhood and psychiatric pathology in later life, is useful in clarifying certain developmental trends. It suggests that MBD children with cognitive defects and asociality are more inclined to become schizophrenic or schizoid, while those whose MBD picture is dominated by impulsivity, overreactivity, and mood swings are more apt to develop characterological problems, probably of the emotionally unstable variety. The implication of these studies taken together is that an appreciable fraction of adult psychiatric patients give a history of having manifested the symptoms of MBD during childhood. These studies do *not* imply that a large fraction of MBD children become adult psychiatric patients.

ANECDOTAL (CASE HISTORY) REPORTS

In 1941, Greenacre, on the basis of her experience in the psychoanalysis of severe neuroses and borderline states, hypothesized that patients with these conditions had undergone "severe suffering and frustration [during] the antenatal and early postnatal months" (p. 610). These patients demonstrated "a genuine physiological sensitivity" which "heighten[ed] the anxiety potential," "an increase in narcissism," "an insecure and easily slipping sense of reality," "an increase in the sense of omnipotence," "libidinal attachments [which] are urgent but shallow . . . and ego drives not well directed towards satisfactory goals" (pp. 610–611). The following were among the characteristics these patients had had as children: severe temper tantrums, inability to concentrate, fretfulness, and prolonged enuresis. Greenacre argued that the organic traumata attendant on difficult labor and delivery might produce a "heightened organic stamp on the make-up of the child" which was "so assimilated into his organization as to be almost entirely indistinguishable from the inherited constitutional factors" (p. 610), and that the principal manifestation of this "organic stamp" was an increased susceptibility to the development of anxiety; this heightened anxiety then predisposed the individual to the formation of the personality characteristics already listed. Without considering Greenacre's theoretical arguments, I wish to point out that she has described the apparent correlation between increased risk of neurological damage and/or the MBD syndrome and certain later features of adult psychopathology.

Anderson and Plymate (1962) have reported that in their clinical experience with MBD children they have seen "definite continuing intellectual and emotional characteristics which are expressed in the behavior patterns [of these MBD children] at any age level" (p. 493). This group of patients, which is referred to as having "Association Deficit Pathology," apparently may include individuals with minimal schizophrenic psychopathology as well as the "pure" MBD syndrome. Unfortunately the authors did not specify precisely the population considered, but they are the only source for a fairly fine-grained clinical description of the natural history of some MBD children. It may be useful to present their impressions in some detail. As adolescents such children are described as having "disciplinary problems, being repetitively defiant and unmanageable . . . have little capacity for appraising situations except in a stereotyped fashion, [show] impulsivity and explosive behavior [as] the rule . . . sexual drives and activities may be delayed or they are perseverative . . . expressed plans for the future are unrealistic and poorly conceived . . ." (p. 493). As adults "they have become more or less comfortably settled into a groove but are particularly vulnerable to the stress of change. Even marriage is not especially disturbing; it is the spouse who suffers! The latter finds himself or herself confused and bewildered, living with a person who is assumed to be normal but who consistently uses poor judgment, is shallow, has little capacity for interpersonal relationships, for realistic planning, or tolerance for frustration. Immature sexual patterns tend to be preferred and there is little sensitivity to the nuance of feeling that normally exists in interpersonal relations. . . . Although there are innumerable variations, salient characteristics at any age are immaturity, poor interpersonal relationships, impulsivity, difficulty with change or the unstructured, and low frustration or stress tolerance which is manifested in incongruous worries, temper tantrums, rages, panics, or major catastrophic reactions often indistinguishable from schizophrenic episodes" (p. 494).[2]

Several points should be made about these various kinds of prognostic studies. First, the increased prevalence of neurological signs in a psychiatrically disturbed population or the increased prevalence of neurological signs among people who later become psychiatrically disturbed does *not* document that neurological impairment causes psychiatric illness. All that has been noted is a correlation between the two. It is entirely possible that both the neurological signs and the psychological problems might be common manifestations of an underlying disease process. A concrete example of this would be Huntington's chorea: neurological abnormalities might be the early signs of general malfunction of the brain. Second, retrospective studies are all subject to a common type of misinterpretation. The increased prevalence of neurological signs or MBD histories among psychiatric patients does *not imply that most—or even many—minimally neurologically impaired children (MBD children) become psychiatrically disturbed adults.* In the Hertzig and Birch (1968) study of psychiatrically disturbed adolescents, 30% were found to have some neurological abnormality as compared with about 5% of the control population. If it is

---

[2] These remarks jibe with the author's limited experience with adults who appear to be "MBD children grown up." Several of these patients have expressed and/or revealed their "inability to communicate" and understand others. It is worth emphasizing that these patients were *not* schizoid or borderline individuals. They were, and apparently always had been, socially assertive and manifested no signs of schizophrenic cognitive disorder.

assumed that approximately 1% of the total adolescent population are as psychiatrically disturbed as the samples, it can easily be shown (Wender, 1967) that only about 6% of the neurologically impaired population subsequently develops this degree of psychiatric impairment.

The studies cited deal with heterogeneous populations and have a number of methodological deficiencies. Nonetheless, they have three rather important implications. First, the usual complacency with which the prognosis of the hyperactive child is regarded in the child psychiatric literature may not be justified. It is commonly asserted that such children "will grow out of it" at the time of puberty. From the evidence that is available (e.g., Menkes et al.), it seems that hyperactivity itself may disappear at this time but that the other and perhaps more serious features of the syndrome may not. Whether the persistence of these behavioral abnormalities is due to the persistence of the putative underlying physiological abnormalities or due to characterological traits which have been learned and ingrained on the basis of those physiological abnormalities cannot be determined. It makes good intuitive sense that a feeling of inferiority originally based on an accurate perception of such inferiority might persist long after the initiating causes had disappeared. This is an assumption consistent with beliefs about the primacy of early learning. Plausibility is, however, a far cry from certainty.

A second implication of these studies is not only that the psychological abnormalities associated with MBD may persist, but that these abnormalities may change their form. The MBD syndrome may be an early manifestation or precursor of psychiatric and social disorders of adolescence and adulthood that are more likely to be recognized. These may include academic underachievement (a numerically important but formally unrecognized syndrome), infantile and impulsive character disorders, sociopathy, and schizophrenia. From Hartocollis' study, one may see an analogical relationship between the MBD symptoms of childhood and the diagnoses of adult life. These later diagnoses may depend on which early symptoms were most prominent and which are most persistent: if impulsivity and poor susceptibility to social controls are salient, the adult is apt to be diagnosed as "sociopathic;" if volatility, demandingness, and concrete thinking are prominent, the adult is apt to be diagnosed as an "hysteric," "infantile," or "emotionally unstable" character; if cognitive abnormalities dominate the picture—and particularly if this occurs in association with increasingly poor social functioning—the adult MBD patient may be diagnosed as "schizophrenic."

A third implication of these studies is that future investigators would be wise to include some relatively subtle follow-up measures. If Anderson and Plymate's impressions are correct, gross measures of "adjustment" (e.g., formal psychiatric diagnosis) might reveal psychological "health"— and tend to support the belief that "the MBD syndrome . . . disappears"— while a more detailed investigation would reveal continuing and important areas of psychological dysfunction.

The question asked at the beginning of this chapter—the question of how many children "outgrow" the MBD syndrome—remains unanswered. From the studies reviewed it *seems* that children with definite brain injury and serious antisocial symptoms do not have a good prognosis. The fate of the more common and less seriously afflicted, the hyperactive, inattentive child who is difficult to discipline and has minor learning difficulties, is problematic. On a short-term basis, the latter children usually respond well to treatment with medication; the relevance of such response to long-term prognosis is unknown. Clinically, it is common to have one parent of such a child report that he or she had similar characteristics in childhood and has since made a good psychological and social adjustment. Apparently some MBD children do outgrow the syndrome. The question of which children develop in what ways and how often requires further research.

CHAPTER 5

Management of the MBD Syndrome

The treatment—and treatability—of the MBD syndrome is an issue of both theoretical and practical importance. Both are in turn related to a common factor: the response of the afflicted children to the stimulant drugs.[1] Psychological intervention with the children is far from irrelevant but it is clearly of secondary importance both theoretically and practically. Accordingly, drug management will be discussed first and psychological management second; after an examination of the two types of management, several comparative questions regarding treatment as a whole will be explored.

The correct treatment of the MBD syndrome is generally brief, specific, and highly effective. Too often, children with the syndrome are misdiagnosed; and when properly diagnosed, they are frequently inadequately treated. At the present stage of knowledge this is unforgivable.

The recommendations for management that follow are, I hope, explicit. Accordingly they may be accused of being "cookbookish." Why this term is pejorative I do not know. Specification is not a sin. The novitiate cook must learn that bread requires *yeast;* she may later adjust *salt* to taste. That I can be specific is a reflection, of course, of the fact that the syndrome is probably largely physiological in origin. For that reason, like the internist, and unlike the poet and psychiatrist, I can hope to communicate by instruction rather than by evocation.

DRUG MANAGEMENT

The discussion of drug management of the MBD syndrome must be overwhelmingly concerned with the stimulant drugs—with general

---

[1] The major stimulant drugs are the amphetamines and methylphenidate (Ritalin). Since the amphetamines were first employed and since the effects of both are very similar, "amphetamine" will be used in the text for both agents.

considerations of responsiveness and with the practical aspects of administration. These agents are, however, not always effective. Following a discussion of their use, I will present a summary of secondarily useful agents which are sometimes effective when stimulant drugs are not; I will also indicate the limits of medication.

Responsiveness to the Stimulant Drugs: General Considerations

In 1937, Bradley described the rather striking therapeutic effects of benzedrine (*dl*-amphetamine) on an heterogeneous group of children in a residential treatment center. He found that the children, whose "behavior disorders" included specific educational disabilities, schizoid problems, and aggressive problems, responded quite dramatically to the administration of this drug. There was a "spectacular improvement in school performance of half of the children. A large proportion of the children became emotionally subdued without, however, losing interest in their surroundings" (p. 584). Bradley noted the surprising and "paradoxical" effect of benzedrine: that a drug with a stimulating effect on adults had a sedating effect on children. The paradoxical response of MBD children to the amphetamines has been repeatedly noted since and appears to remain in the category of an unexamined familiar oddity.

The importance of the amphetamines in child psychiatry is threefold. It relates to the drugs' efficacy, specificity, and paradoxical effect. These agents are often of dramatic effectiveness in reversing the signs and symptoms of psychiatric disturbance in a group of children with *seemingly* diverse diagnoses. It is my argument that upon closer inspection it is common to find that such children often share "incidental" psychological characteristics. The characteristics are those that have been described as defining the MBD syndrome. It was the common responsiveness to amphetamines which constituted one of the reasons for grouping this seemingly heterogeneous group of children together under the cognomen "minimal brain dysfunction." (It also suggested the only semi-facetious name, "congenital hypoamphetaminemia.")

Little has been made of the specific paradoxical effect: whereas in adults the amphetamines[2] produce increased activity, tension, and often euphoria, in MBD children the action of the amphetamines is generally to decrease

---

[2] Although both racemic (*dl*-) amphetamine and dextro (*d*-) amphetamine are effective in the treatment of the disorder, *d*-amphetamine may afford a greater "therapeutic ratio" of useful actions to side effects. Although the word "amphetamines" is used in this chapter, the *d*-isomer is the agent which is usually therapeutically employed.

motor activity and to produce sedation and, often, depression. Of perhaps even greater interest is an effect rarely commented upon: in a moderate number of MBD children (perhaps one-fourth) amphetamines have a virtually specific therapeutic effect. This effect is comparable to that of electroshock therapy on involutional depressives or that of lithium on some manic patients. Its action seems to be more "fundamental" than that of being a simple chemical sledgehammer or straitjacket. In such instances the drug appears to alter "basic" psychological functions in a most striking way, not simply reversing difficulties but promoting psychological growth. It is this specific responsivity which suggests a chemical and psychological mechanism of action for the drug and a chemical and psychological model for the etiology of the dysfunction in these children.

When effective, the drug has a profound influence on the activity level, impulsivity, social behavior and cognition of MBD children. These and related behavioral and psychological areas are discussed below.

Activity Level and Attention

In those MBD children who are "hyperactive," the drug often has a quieting effect, usually without producing drowsiness or "grogginess"; occasionally the sedative effect is more extreme, and in rare instances children may even be put to sleep. A sedative action is one that is shared by many agents, and this effect of amphetamine is surprising only in that it is produced by an agent which is always excitatory in adults. The drug's effects on attention are more specific: parents and teachers, and the children themselves when older, are apt to report increased attentiveness and per-sistence, and decreased distractibility. This is sometimes accompanied by a subjective feeling of increased "tension." Such increased attentiveness may be dose-responsive and may reach excessive proportions. For example, one very hyperactive and distractible 9-year-old, who, before drug treat-ment could be neither induced nor terrified into studying for more than 15 minutes at a time, proved unusually responsive to medication. A few weeks after having been started on a small dose of *d*-amphetamine she unfortunately misheard her teacher, and thought that the class assignment was to write the Roman numerals from one to one thousand, rather than those from one to one hundred. *Five* hours after supper her flabbergasted parents discovered her in her room patiently plodding away. Such pathologi-cal perseverance is rare but striking. Another illustrative case concerns a 9-year-old boy whose mother reported he was "unable to learn to read." The child's "block" existed before his placement in a children's residential treatment center, persisted throughout his stay, and continued after his return despite continuing psychotherapy. With one-to-one supervision he would read one page in an hour to an hour and a half; five repetitions were insufficient to enable him to learn a new word. While under medication he was able to read four pages in a half-hour by himself and retain new words after one or two repetitions. These illustrations are somewhat dramatic examples, but such changes do occur moderately often; they illustrate that the increased persistence is more than the simple absence of abnormal distractibility.

Another manifestation of decreased inattentiveness is diminished "daydreaming." Daydreaming, from the teacher's standpoint, is synonymous with inattention. The kind of daydreaming that, for example, consists of desultory considerations of the joys of baseball is apt to "respond" to treatment with amphetamines; prolonged autistic reveries are likely to be aggravated.

An occasional child may respond to the drug by becoming increasingly active, distractible, and fidgety. Such an adult response is also apt to occur as a child "outgrows" the syndrome, at which time the paradoxical effect of the amphetamines is reversed.

Impulsivity and Response to Controls

It is common for parents to report a generalized improvement in behavior. Amphetamines produce one unique change in children, however, which to the best of my knowledge is unparalled by that of any other drug in any other psychiatric syndrome.

The effect in question is that of increasing the child's sensitivity to reward and punishment. Parents are more sensitive to the changes in response to punishment than to the changes in response to rewards and hence are more likely to report them. Whereas formerly a child may have failed to respond to the mailed fist, parents report that he is now apt to burst into tears at the sight of a mild parental frown (for which reason it is often necessary to counsel parents to be less severe). This increased sensitivity to punishment seems often to be accompanied by an increased concern with past transgressions. In some instances past misdeeds are exhumed spontaneously and may be ruminated about at some length. This effect usually appears only during the first few days of treatment. It bears a striking phenomenological resemblance to the self-criticism seen in some adult depressions. As in the case of adult depression, the child's observations are apt to be accurate: he will justly criticize himself for defects whose presence he previously denied. This effect can be most striking when a previously guarded, evasive, and denying child seeks confessive absolution from his parents. In addition to the superego hypertrophy, one often sees a similar hypertrophy of the ego-ideal. Children often begin to talk about and behave in a manner consonant with their parents' formerly unheeded "oughts" and "shoulds." More insightful and communicative children are aware of this. One bright 8-year-old referred to *d*-amphetamine as his "magic pills which make me into a good boy and makes everybody like me."[3]

The other effect of the drug on reinforcement—the changed responsiveness to rewards—is usually not recounted spontaneously but may frequently be discovered when inquired after. Children who hitherto appeared to act as if their central nervous systems were unaware of the theory of operant conditioning are now apt to respond positively to rewards.

Parents of MBD children have often abandoned the use of rewards, privileges, deprivation of privileges, and praise because of their ineffectiveness, and it may be diagnostically necessary and therapeutically useful to have them reinstitute such measures.[4]

The increased responsiveness to social controls is generally accompanied by greater "self-controls," controls from within. The drug often decreases impulsivity, excitability, and tantrums, increases planfulness and stick-to-itiveness, and turns a butterfly into a bulldog. An implication of this transformation is that similar mechanisms (or structures) are responsible for responsiveness to external controls and self-direction: factors that affect one seem to affect the other.[5]

Social Behavior

As noted in the section on symptomatology, many MBD children are reported by parents and teachers to be marked extroverts. They are often reported as lacking friends, but this is because of their heavy-handed and domineering manner. Their social vector is definitely directed outward: they generally bound back from social rebuff to antagonize others again.

The general effect of amphetamines is to decrease social assertiveness and sometimes increase social avoidance. The effect can be quite pronounced and in some instances a Rotarian may become a "loner." In some children it is necessary to titrate the dosage of amphetamine with particular accuracy; in others it is necessary to decide which target symptoms are most important to resolve. A difficult case in point was that of a young firesetter[6] in whom stealing could be curtailed only at the expense of marked social withdrawal: whenever his dose of amphetamine was reduced to

---

[3] See case history 1, "Michael."

[4] The obvious implication is that the drug response described would greatly facilitate a child's responsiveness to "operant therapy." Such indeed does seem to be the case. See " 'Structuring' the Environment" under the section on psychological management.

[5] This parallel development of internal and external controls is reflected in a commonly observed phenomenon, that of the 2-year-old angrily adjuring himself: "No, no, Billy, don't touch the plug."

[6] See case history 5, "Robert."

below a certain threshold level the child became extroverted and light-fingered, and whenever the dose was increased above the level the child became law-abiding and withdrawn.

The increased introversion may be manifested not only in social behavior but in the direction of a child's interests. Parents sometimes report that while treated with amphetamines a child not only avoids his peers but reads compulsively and resents interruptions.

Possibly related to the changes in sociability—and to the changes in response to controls as well—are the changes sometimes produced along the axis of independence-dependence. Many, though not all, MBD children are reported to be excessively independent *affectionately*. They include those who were not cuddly as infants, who wandered away frequently as toddlers, and who were unusually unaffected by discipline techniques involving the withholding and granting of affection. Amphetamines often affect spontaneous affectional behavior as well as response to parental approval and disapproval. Children sometimes appear to develop—or reveal—increased dependency needs: they become more expressive of affection and seek it more directly. The important question of whether such needs are latent and uncovered by amphetamines or developed (engendered) by the drug is at present phenomenologically unanswerable.

Cognition and Learning

The increased attention span manifested in many MBD children treated with amphetamines may appreciably affect academic performance. In his initial report on the effect of the drug, Bradley (1937) stated that "possibly the most spectacular change in behavior brought about by the use of benzedrine was the remarkably improved school performance of approximately half the children. This is the more striking when we note that these patients were of good intelligence and that they were receiving adequate attention for any personality disorders which might affect their school progress. Moreover they were already in a school where specially trained, sympathetic teachers dealt with their pupils either on an individual basis or in a very small group. To see a single dose of benzedrine produce a greater improvement in school performance than the combined efforts of a capable staff working in a most favorable setting would have been all the more demoralizing to the teachers had not the improvement been so gratifying from a practical viewpoint" (p. 582). Bradley went on to add the following: "As far as improvement in the individual school subjects was concerned the teachers were most impressed by changes in the arithmetic performance, since speed of comprehension, degree of accuracy, and quantity of output were all favorably affected" (p. 582). Employing more sophisticated methodology that included a double-blind crossover design,

Conners et al. (1967) have reconfirmed Bradley's initial finding. They evaluated their results by means of a factor analysis of children's performance levels before and after medication. They, too, found increased performance, which they attributed to greater assertiveness and drive and not to improved intellectual ability.

Whether "cognitive abilities" *per se* are affected by amphetamines is problematic: performance on most tests is such a complex resultant of motivation and information-processing behavior that only precise specification and measurement at a "molecular level" could hope to answer the question. Whether amphetamines affect the specific learning disabilities (e.g., reversals, difficulties with discriminations) which are seen in some children with the MBD syndrome has not yet been fully evaluated.

Whatever underlying changes account for the behavior differences, it is very common to obtain reports indicating the following sorts of changes in children's academic behavior: (1) an increased compulsivity, as manifested by neater handwriting, a tendency to finish assignments, and a tendency to check work; (2) greater perseverance and frustration tolerance—a child is more apt to wrestle with a task until he solves it; (3) improved memory—children are reported as retaining learned material better. Whether the improved memory is secondary to motivation is again uncertain; even without medication, if sufficiently motivated, the child might be able to remember as well, but whatever the cause the effect is often grossly noticeable.

The effects of the amphetamines are remarkable not only in the variety and psychological complexity of their manifestations but also in the fact that they are not "antiregressive," although often described in that way. The improved behavior is induced even when it has never before been present. For the duration of their action the amphetamines institute psychological growth. It is this growth-promoting action of the amphetamines that suggests the mechanism of the underlying physiological and psychological deficit in the syndrome, which is explored in the two chapters on theoretical considerations.

Amphetamine Administration: Practical Aspects

The stimulant drugs are of the greatest practical use in the treatment of the MBD syndrome. The following discussion will elaborate on their effectiveness, predictors of response, the placebo effect, the mechanics of treatment, side effects, and the discontinuation of treatment.

Effectiveness of Amphetamine Treatment

Thirteen years after his first report of the utility of benzedrine (*dl*-amphetamine) in the treatment of behavior disorders in children, Bradley

(1950) published an excellent clinical review summarizing his twelve years of experience with amphetamine treatment. The population discussed consisted of more than 350 children between the ages of 6 (a few were younger) and 11, of normal or above-average intelligence, who had been placed in residential treatment with a variety of behavioral problems. The problems were categorized as psychopathic personality, schizoid personality, and "behavior problems." From the accounts given, the latter group seems to have overlapped with the kind of children I am including in the MBD group. Bradley found that between 50% and 85% of children in these categories improved symptomatically with amphetamine treatment. His report suffers from a failure to satisfy the precise canons of modern psychopharmacological research—placebo controls were not employed and evaluation was not blind. Such techniques are useful in separating out the effects of placebo response and rater bias. With regard to placebo effects, it is useful to remember that the children had already received the non-specific benefits of removal from the home and placement in a presumably therapeutic institution. With regard to rater bias, there is no doubt that blind ratings are necessary in the judging of equivocal responses; and the more doubtful and less interesting the response, the greater the need for objectivity. In the instance of amphetamine response, evaluation is made easier by the very dramatic nature of the good response and the brief latency of response. A child will serve as his own control while off medication one day and on the next: it requires no nicety of design to detect drug effects when a child is a constantly negativistic, whirling dervish while off medicine and a quiet, compliant child the next day while on medication. Although the failure to use placebos and blind ratings does diminish the certitude with which Bradley's findings can be compared with other results, the article still remains a useful source for qualitative descriptions of patterns of response.

Since 1950, a number of studies have appeared describing the effectiveness of amphetamine in "behavior disorders" in children. Some representative studies are as follows: Eisenberg et al. (1963, 1967), Zrull et al. (1964, 1963), Knobel (1962), Burks (1964), Nichamin and Comly (1964), and Conrad and Insel (1967).

The study by Conners et al. (1967), mentioned earlier, is a methodologically sound study of a diagnostically related group. These authors evaluated the effects of d-amphetamine on a miscellaneous group of grammar-school children referred for academic and behavior problems. Inspection of their data reveals that approximately 65% (37/52) would fall into the MBD category. The double-blind crossover design included a placebo, and demonstrated that d-amphetamine improved class behavior, group participation, and "attitude to authority."

In general, the published studies tend to confirm Bradley's findings: the studies using more precise methodology than his report improvement rates varying between 44% and 70%.

Predictors of Treatment Response

There are no good predictors of response to drug treatment. "Organicity" has been considered by some to be a variable with predictive value, but one can find studies in which organicity predicts a favorable response, studies in which it predicts an unfavorable response and studies in which it is not a predictor.

Conrad and Insel (1967) reported the effectiveness of *d*-amphetamine in 31 MBD children seen as outpatients. Without knowledge of treatment response, the children were classified *post hoc* as primarily organic (O), primarily "emotional" (E), or mixed (OE). The "emotional" group seems to have included a putative genetic group and might possibly have included some borderline children. Using global improvement ratings, the study showed that 10/16 (61%) of the O group as compared with 1/6 (17%) of the E group showed definite improvement with treatment.

Epstein et al. (1968) studied the metabolic and psychological effects of *d*-amphetamine on five "organic" and five "nonorganic" hyperactive children. Using global behavioral ratings, the study concluded that the organic group showed somewhat greater behavioral improvement and less intense side effects. Interestingly, the nonorganic group had several non-paradoxical responders—that is, children who became worse ("with excessive crying and irritability" [p. 96]) when treated with *d*-amphetamine.

In a study with an opposite outcome, Burks (1964) reported the effects of benzedrine on 43 children with school problems, 33 of whom had abnormal electroencephalograms. Outcome measures were teacher ratings on a 28-point scale. Children with normal EEG's improved to a significantly greater degree on perceptual-discrimination, social-emotional, and "vegetative-autonomic" (activity level, variability measures) scales.

Two studies failed to find any relationship between organicity and response to *d*-amphetamine. The first is that of Zrull et al. (1966) who employed a double-blind crossover design utilizing a placebo, *d*-amphetamine, and either chlordiazepoxide or diazepam. They found little difference between the responding and nonresponding groups in several respects, including neurological findings, although there was a greater (nonsignificant) proportion of "organic" children in the group that responded.

Werry (1968b), in a factor analytic study, found that response to drug therapy failed to correlate with any factors including the following: poor environment (which Conrad and Insel found correlated negatively); and neurological factors, including historical and current indicators of neurological impairment.

Is it possible to rationalize the above discrepant findings? Possibly, at least to some extent. Very simply, one can question the criteria by which "organic" and "nonorganic" categories are defined. It is quite possible that many MBD children whose problems are not organic in etiology have organic signs and symptoms: Werry (1964) found that 21% of a control population of children had abnormal pregnancy or birth histories as compared with 42% of hyperactive children; he also found an approximately equal prevalence of abnormal EEG's in the two groups. Probably, therefore, any group designated as "organic" on the basis of a neurological history and/or an abnormal EEG would be likely to contain children whose behavioral abnormalities were unrelated to these neurological deviations. Similarly, the group defined as "nonorganic" is a mixed one. In the Conrad and Insel study it probably contained "upset" children who were not afflicted with the MBD syndrome; since the group was defined by emotional illness in the parents, the group members may have been biased toward a genetic variant of the disorder whose responsiveness to drugs has not been investigated. From a practical standpoint, such a group might well contain an excess of borderline and schizophrenic children, whose condition would be expected to worsen on amphetamine therapy (see below).

Rationalization of discrepant studies—here and elsewhere—is possible, but probably not worthwhile. There are two reasons for this judgment, one theoretical and one practical. In terms of theory, one should expect the reported studies to differ in their findings because most of the studies do not report drug response as a function of age, sex, and I.Q. of the patient, the dose of medication received, or the exact diagnostic characteristics of the child. Totally unreported are the unconscious sampling biases introduced by the location of the investigator and his source of referral. Unless psychiatric problems are as unresponsive to environmental status as is cyanide poisoning, one would expect, for example, a population from a ghetto school to respond differently from a population of private patients. The major difficulty is that in most instances the investigator, through no fault of his own, is unaware of the biased sample on which he is reporting. Unless the nature of the relevant variables can be specified precisely, it is fairly meaningless to report results to two or three significant figures. It is scientifically meaningless to report one variable to a high degree of precision when another one cannot be specified exactly; and it is questionable whether the variables specifying the population can be defined precisely at all.

In practical terms, the value of rationalizing discrepant studies relates

to the question of how useful it is to be able to specify outcomes exactly—
that is, to the question of how differences of X% in various studies will
differentially affect the physician's behavior in deciding to institute treatment. This issue will be discussed later in the context of the payoff matrix.

The Placebo Effect

Psychopharmacological research in children is still relatively primitive
and not all of the studies cited employed control groups. In order to obtain
a more refined idea of the usefulness of these agents it would be helpful
to have a rough idea of the amount of improvement to be expected on the
basis of the nonspecific effects of intervention, that is, the placebo effect.
Some data are available. Cytryn et al. (1960) investigated the effects
of short-term psychotherapy combined with double-blind drug therapy in
outpatients. They found that 40% of the "hyperactive" group, as compared
with 70% of the neurotic group, showed "significant" improvement[7] with
either meprobamate, prochlorperazine, or placebo (amphetamine was not
employed)—that is, the "constitutionally restless" group showed considerably less improvement than did those children in whom it was felt "hyperkinesis might be secondary to anxiety." Antisocial behavior problems—
which may overlap the MBD syndrome—improved significantly in only
10% of the cases. Thus, the groups least responsive to the "placebo effect"
included those groups most like the MBD group. An 18-month follow-up
study of the original patients (Eisenberg et al., 1961) showed "maintenance
of improvement in the neurotic group but a gradual loss of even the lesser
gains obtained by the hyperkinetic group" (p. 1089). Another study by
Eisenberg et al. (1967) showed that after 8 weeks only 4% of "hyperkinetic" children receiving placebo demonstrated "marked improvement."
A follow-up of a comparable group of hyperkinetic children who received
"conventional outpatient psychotherapy" found an improvement rate of
only 15%.[8] No additional studies of the natural history of the disorder
are available, but one conclusion can be drawn: the MBD child differs

---

[7] Since the groups of subjects were small, the "true" population values for improvement of the hyperactive children range from approximately 10% to 75%, with 95%
confidence. The reported figure is not discrepant with the 15% figure cited by Eisenberg et al. (1967).

[8] The duration of the placebo response is unknown. Since MBD is a chronic disorder, the placebo response would be expected to be only temporary. The author has
seen follow-ups of several MBD children erroneously diagnosed and treated with
psychotherapy at a university hospital. They did indeed enjoy transient benefit and
would have been counted as psychotherapy cures at the time of discharge from the
clinic. Following their relapses, which occurred within a few months, their parents
had failed to recontact the clinic, anticipating that further therapy would be of no
further help since the first course had failed.

from the usual child psychiatric referral in that the latter has a high spontaneous recovery rate and the MBD syndrome does not. Precise figures for the spontaneous placebo recovery rate in non-MBD children are not available but rough estimates are. Perez-Reyes (1967) found on a follow-up of a heterogeneous population of disturbed children "treated" by diagnostic study alone, that "from 76% to 93% had improved, with half being well, and half fairly well" (p. 619). Levitt (1963) found an overall improvement rate among "defectors" from child psychiatric clinics of approximately 70%. Clearly, then, any ostensibly effective treatment for MBD children will be easier to evaluate than one for neurotic children since the base rate of recovery is so low.[9] Reports—such as Bradley's—of 50% to 70% substantial improvement in children already receiving residential care for MBD-like disorders are very impressive.

Mechanics of Drug Treatment

The mechanics of drug treatment is a subject of no great theoretical importance but of considerable practical importance; especially since the correct usage of these drugs is not widely understood. In his large review, Bradley (1950) reported that most children who responded to benzedrine (dl-amphetamine) did so at doses no greater than 40 mg/day. He found the median useful dose of d-amphetamine was 10 mg, with approximately 25% of his sample receiving 20 mg/day and 5% receiving 30 mg/day. In my experience with d-amphetamine, many children do respond effectively to doses of 10 to 20 mg, but for many other children there seems to be a positive dose response curve, with gradual improvement in behavior (with or without the appearance of side effects) as the dose is increased to 20 or 30 mg/day and in a very few instances to 40 mg/day or beyond.

The most common failure in amphetamine treatment results from the use of inadequate amounts of medication for too short a period of time.[10] It has been fairly common in my experience to see children who had received insufficient doses referred to as "unresponsive" to amphetamine; they responded satisfactorily when given adequate amounts of medication.

In general, the racemic form of the drug appears to be approximately one-half as potent on a weight basis as in the d-isomer. There may be more side effects with racemic amphetamine and hence the d-form is generally preferred. Bradley did report that some children did respond better to

[9] Similarly, it is easier to evaluate the results of drug treatment on tuberculous meningitis than pulmonary tuberculosis, since the untreated mortality rates of the two disorders are 100% and less than 1%, respectively.

[10] A recent review article (Pincus and Glaser, 1966) recommends a dose of d-amphetamine beginning at 2.5 mg/day followed by "gradual increments." Such amounts of medication (5 to 10 mg/day) are often totally inadequate.

benzedrine. Whether this was due to change in dose or to a differential action is unclear. The *dl*-form *may* have a different central effect. Accordingly it might occasionally be worthwhile to try it when *d*-amphetamine is not completely effective.

d-amphetamine may be administered in several daily divided doses or may be given in the form of a long-acting capsule. The tablets are more bothersome for all concerned but permit more accurate adjustment and regulation of treatment response. The latency of onset of action for the medication appears to be approximately one-half hour, and its effects last for 3 to 6 hours. The prolonged-action capsule's duration of action appears to be between 6 and 18 hours. It is important to be aware of the duration of action—not only because the child's behavior reverts when the medication wears off, but because there is often a behavioral "rebound" as the medication loses effect. Since this is apt to occur at the end of the day when the parents first see the child after he has returned from school, they are apt to report that the medicine is of no effect or has been detrimental. It is therefore useful to inquire when a child's "bad behavior" occurs. In some of the cases I have seen in which medication was reported to be ineffective, my first thought was to discontinue it; however, when continued inquiry revealed that the bad response occurred late in the day, I suggested, instead, an additional dose, with beneficial results.

The technique of administration I employ is as follows: children over the age of 6[11] are begun on 5 mg of *d*-amphetamine before breakfast and at lunch. If the drug is effective but its action wears off in the late afternoon, a third dose is added in the mid-afternoon. If the twice-a-day schedule produces insomnia, the total dose is given in the morning. The drug is then increased every 3 days in small amounts (e.g., 2.5-mg dose on the twice-a-day schedule) until either satisfactory behavioral effects are produced or side effects (particularly anorexia and insomnia) become troublesome. The importance of this last step must be emphasized: like digitalis, the amphetamine dosage should be increased until therapeutic benefit is obtained or toxicity is produced. Many young children need—and tolerate—doses that are extremely large compared with those employed in treating adult patients. Some young children (6–10 years) manifest increasing symptomatic improvement when the medication is increased to 40 mg/day. Some of these children tolerate such doses with no sign of side effects. The usual dose necessary to produce therapeutic results ranges from 10 to 40 mg/day; the median dose appears to lie around 20 mg/day.

[11] In my experience, the stimulant drugs are much less effective in children under the age of 6. When giving these younger children a trial of medication, I start with a dose of 2.5 mg of *d*-amphetamine twice a day.

If multiple daily doses are required, once the therapeutic dose of *d*-amphetamine has been established, I attempt to give the full dose each morning in long-acting form (e.g., [TM] Dexedrine spansules). This is more convenient but less flexible. Often the duration of action is either too brief or too long; in the former instance, the behavioral problems reappear in the afternoon when the drug effect wears off, while in the latter instance insomnia may be produced.

If therapeutically effective doses of *d*-amphetamine produce disturbing side effects, I employ a trial of methylphenidate (q.v.).

A substantial number of children, perhaps one-third to one-half, manifest a "neutral" response to treatment—that is, no response other than the appearance of side effects.

Among the children who do respond, there are several qualitatively different patterns of drug response, the "good," the "bad," and the "tolerant," as follows:

1. The "good" response. In my experience, approximately one-third to one-half of outpatient MBD patients fall into the category of immediate and excellent response. In such children the results of treatment are prompt and dramatic. These are the children in whom thorough behavioral changes —of the sort detailed earlier in this chapter—occur. On days when a child fails to receive his medicine, his parents and the surprised teacher are apt to report an unexpected behavioral reversal.

It is the response of such children which makes a physician feel that he is dealing with a specific remedy for a metabolic abnormality and not with a psychological illness. Such a response to treatment can constitute an experience that is both unusual and gratifying for a psychiatrist: he can "cure" a patient. Some children, perhaps 10% to 20%, display an unequivocal but moderate degree of therapeutic response. The total number of children thus evincing immediate response would seem to be in the order of magnitude of 50% to 70%.

There are also, I have found, a few children who respond initially with increased activity or irritability, but upon persistent administration of the drug manifest a good response. This discovery was serendipitous. It occurred when a mother who was more dutiful than intelligent followed what she thought were the doctor's instructions and persisted in giving her son *d*-amphetamine for 2 weeks although "for the first week, Doctor, it was terrible." During the second week of treatment the child gradually became subdued and manifested a good, "obedient" type of response.

The delayed response to treatment is of both practical and theoretical interest. It is of practical interest because to the best of my knowledge it has not been previously described. I had previously dutifully followed the prescriptions of my elders and discontinued amphetamine treatment whenever a child's initial response was that of excitation. Since many MBD children do not respond effectively to other medications and since in some the initial response is misleading, the correct inference would seem to be that, in the absence of medical contraindications, amphetamine treatment should be given a trial of a week or two before it is discontinued as ineffective.

The theoretical importance of the delayed response is that it implies that some metabolic change is taking place over the period in which a child changes his responsiveness. It has been suggested[12] that in such instances the mechanism of drug action may be that of drug-induced production of a "false neurotransmitter." The theoretical model—which might be testable—is that the chronic administration of amphetamine might result in the production of a neurohormone(s) which does not normally occur, which in turn would interfere with or react with the neurotransmitters customarily present in the particular child.

2. The "bad" or negative response. A "bad" response occurs in a small fraction of the children receiving amphetamine, possibly of the order of magnitude of 10%. There are three major forms. In the first, which is the most common, a child's hyperactivity increases and his symptoms are aggravated, and these effects do not disappear with continued administration. In the second, schizoid characteristics may appear or, if present, be intensified; the child becomes asocial, withdrawn, and preoccupied. In the third, which is extremely rare, the child develops an acute psychotic reaction. I have seen only three such reactions in several hundred children (ages 5–16) treated with this medication. All occurred in MBD children with fairly conspicuous schizoid characteristics, in all instances the children were young (less than aged 10), and in all instances the response occurred with a comparatively small dose of medication (approximately 10 mg of *d*-amphetamine). In all three instances the symptoms disappeared within 12 hours of the last dose of medication.

3. The "tolerant" response. I have seen three or four cases in which a child had the dramatic "good" response on initial treatment but developed a rapid degree of tolerance within a relatively brief period of time. All instances occurred in borderline psychotic MBD children. The first, a boy, obsessively preoccupied with somewhat bizarre science-fiction matters, settled down and became relatively unpsychotic on a dose of 10 mg of *d*-amphetamine. Within a few days this response disappeared but similar improvement was noted for 2- or 3-day periods when the dose was increased by 10 mg. In the second instance, a 12-year-old girl of normal intelligence had been frenetically hyperactive from infancy and was developing an intense and dangerous interest in fire. On an initial dose of 10 mg of *d*-amphetamine

---

[12] Probably p-hydroxynorephedrine.

her lifelong enuresis stopped, she became calm, she abstained from setting her wastepaper basket on fire, and she became compliant. Two days later she had reverted to her previous ways but again responded when the dose was increased to 20 mg. She continued to have transient dramatic responses to increased doses until I reached *my* ceiling for drug administration— which in this instance was 60 mg/day of *d*-amphetamine.

Another form of drug tolerance is the gradual form. I have seen many children who had an initial dramatic response and who then became mildly tolerant to the medication; in almost all instances the children became fully responsive to increased dosage. For example, a 7-year-old boy, one of a pair of hyperactive sibs, presented with behavioral difficulties and reading reversal problems. His stubbornness, negativism, and academic difficulties all lysed on a dosage of 20 mg/day of *d*-amphetamine but reappeared over a period of three months. A favorable response reoccurred and was maintained (with a follow-up of one year) on a dosage of 40 mg/day.

Lastly, there are some children who develop a slow tolerance in a manner similar to that seen in adults. I have seen such cases only among adolescents.

Side Effects

Side effects occur in an appreciable fraction of children and are dose-related. The most common side effects of amphetamine treatment are insomnia and anorexia. Other side effects, which occur less frequently, include mild stomach aches and headaches (of the sort that an adult might associate with prolonged hunger), a mild tremor of the extremities, and increased "tension" behaviors including nail-biting, eye-blinking, nose-picking, skin-picking, and other mannerisms. Other children may develop a sunken-cheeked, dark-eyed, somewhat sallow, pale look which is understandably disquieting to their parents. Both the anorexia and the insomnia tend to disappear with continued administration of the drug. In many children these effects are not present, and, as noted, in some, an increase in the dose of amphetamine actually produces drowsiness. A parent's anxiety can be substantially allayed by anticipating these responses and explaining their course over time. I have seen many children lose a moderate amount of weight (a phenomenon also observed by Bradley), but I have never seen a child in whom the drug had to be discontinued on that account. As already mentioned, increased schizoid behavior does develop in some children; it is uncommon but of theoretical interest. A similar effect that bears repetition is that in which minor variations in dose will push a child from one extreme to the other of the extroversion—introversion spectrum; as indicated, careful titration is required to produce a child who is reasonably well adjusted socially.

In addition to the acute manifestations of toxicity—that is, the side effects—what of other toxic effects? Interestingly—and in contradistinction to almost all other drugs—there appear to be no reports in the literature of idiosyncratic or allergic responses to the amphetamines. In particular, there are no descriptions of blood dyscrasias. There is no evidence *to date* that there are chronic toxic effects of the amphetamines when employed in the range suggested. Several authors (Bradley, 1950; Laufer et al., 1957a) have claimed that they have employed the drug on a continual basis, without demonstrable ill effects, for periods up to 5 years. We do know that the drug may possibly result in central nervous system damage when taken in much larger amounts (of the order of 1000 mg/day) for periods of months.[13] With current practices of underreporting drugs' toxicity, one cannot be as certain as one would like that chronic administration of the drug in amounts of less than 40 mg/day over periods of several years is entirely safe for children. Nonetheless, since the agents have been used for over 30 years, one can have a reasonable degree of certainty about their safety.

Several authors suggest the use of "rest periods," that is, drug-free periods, to prevent the development of tolerance to medication. I follow that practice, not because I have seen any evidence or had any experience that it does prevent the development of such tolerance, but because I attempt to minimize the amount of medication administered. The reason is obvious: although there is no *evidence* that the amphetamines have cumulative toxicity in this dose range, there is no reason to believe that they are biochemically health-promoting, and therefore their use (and that of all drugs) should be avoided whenever they are unnecessary. Accordingly, I attempt to diminish or discontinue their administration in less stressful periods of the year, particularly vacations. Practically, I have found this laudable intention generally unworkable until the child has outgrown any further need for medication.

Discontinuing Drug Treatment

To the question "How long should treatment be continued?" the obvious answer is "As long as a child needs it and benefits from it." This may be a period of several years. I have seen many children in whom amphetamine successfully controlled all behavior problems for 2 to 3 years and in whom

[13] And that very high doses may produce impaired cognitive functioning. Kramer et al. (1967) write that one-third of adult amphetamine addicts, following discontinuation of the drug, reported that their memory or their ability to concentrate had been impaired since experience with high doses of amphetamines (100–300 mg every 2 hours for 5- or 6-day "runs" over a period of months). The duration of these effects is not reported.

problems promptly reappeared on the first day medication was discontinued.

It was suggested above that children should receive "rest periods" to prevent the development of tolerance and/or decrease the possibility of chronic toxic reactions. Such drug-free intervals may serve as trials to determine if a child has "outgrown" his need for medication. Sometimes a child who has begun to reach this stage can, for example, go without medication during a less stressful vacation period without a recurrence of symptoms, but has a recurrence of symptoms upon return to school. In such children intermittent drug therapy (medication during the school year only) has been successful.

In some cases a comparatively long trial of treatment (several months) may be followed by a long, perhaps permanent, period of improvement without medication. I have seen this in several cases in whom the behavioral problems had existed for many years and in whom a placebo response seemed unlikely. The most plausible interpretation of the drug's effect was that it had terminated a self-perpetuating vicious cycle. Medication had improved the child's academic performance, changed his peer relations and his relations to his parents, and increased his self-esteem. It had allowed him to develop new and presumably self-reinforcing patterns of behavior.

In those children for whom chronic treatment is necessary to maintain benefit, the physician is faced with the alternatives of a known benefit and a low but possible danger of chronic toxicity. Neither logic nor pharmacology provides an answer to this dilemma.

Other Useful Drugs

There are several other groups of drugs which may be effective in children with the MBD syndrome; these agents may be employed when the usual agents are ineffective.

l-amphetamine

Bradley (1950) reported that *dl*-amphetamine (benzedrine) was more effective than *d*-amphetamine in the treatment of some children. If this is so, the differential effect would have to be secondary to the content of *l*-amphetamine. There have been no formal trials of *l*-amphetamine, but I have had *limited* clinical experience with this agent. In a few children who failed to respond to *d*-amphetamine (which had only partially diminished their activity, had increased their irritability, and had produced depression and insomnia), there was a clearcut response to *l*-amphetamine (which in these children was employed in the same dose ranges as the *d*-isomer). Formal clinical trials of *l*-amphetamine would seem to be useful.

Methylphenidate

Methylphenidate (Ritalin) is a drug with an action very similar to that of amphetamine but with a few practical advantages and disadvantages. Methylphenidate's practical advantages are as follows: (1) It sometimes is effective when amphetamine is not; for this there is no formal evidence, only clinical impressions.[14] (2) It has a less intense effect on sleep and appetite than does amphetamine. Its disadvantages are that its duration of action is shorter, it is not available in a long-acting form, it is more expensive, and it must be ingested on an empty stomach since milk interferes with its absorption. It is approximately one-half as potent as *d*-amphetamine on a weight basis and accordingly the daily dosage range is approximately between 20 and 100 mg[15] as opposed to 10 to 40 mg/day of *d*-amphetamine.

The Tricyclic Antidepressants

There have been a few reports (Rapoport, 1965; Krakowski, 1965) suggesting the usefulness of the tricyclic antidepressants in the treatment of the MBD syndrome. The possible effectiveness of these agents in the treatment of this syndrome is of theoretical interest since their mechanism of action and that of amphetamine are believed to be similar. Rapoport summarized his clinical experience (noncontrolled, nonblind) with the use of imipramine (Tofranil) in a variety of behavior disorders which were of the type he had formerly treated with amphetamine. He employed doses of 10 to 40 mg/day in children ranging in age from 5 to 21 years and reported an 80% "improvement rate." Krakowski investigated the effect of amitriptyline (Elavil) in 50 "hyperkinetic" children between the ages of 2 and 18. He employed a double-blind design with a placebo. The etiology of the syndrome was considered to be environmental in 65% of the cases and probably organic in 20%. The duration of illness was over three years in 70% of all the children. One-half of the 50 were initially placed on placebo and the other half were initially placed on amitriptyline. The children who received placebo for three months and who failed to respond (89%) were subsequently also placed on amitriptyline, and the total group (placebo failures and the initial drug group) was then followed. These 47 drug-treated patients were followed for varying periods of time (from less than one month to over one year) and approximately 70% continued to show a good treatment response. Krakowski employed doses of 20 to 75 mg, and

[14] Another clinical impression holds that the reverse is also true: *d*-amphetamine is sometimes useful when methylphenidate is not.

[15] Although one study (Lytton and Knobel, 1958) reports using up to 200 mg/day in some children.

found that serious side effects, necessitating discontinuation of treatment, occurred in only one case (atropine-like effects).

My own experience with these agents has been limited since I have employed them only in MBD children "grown up" in whom amphetamine treatment seemed inadvisable because of the risks of habituation. In two instances these adolescents had taken d-amphetamine in an attempt to become "high;" they reported its effects to be pleasant (perhaps "calming") although apparently not euphoric. In both cases the children, who had failed to respond to prolonged psychotherapy, had a response to imipramine similar to that produced by amphetamine in younger subjects: decreased motor activity, decreased irascibility, greater social compliance, lessened impulsivity, and improved academic performance. Contrariwise, I have also seen two or three instances of younger adolescents in whom imipramine was ineffective but amphetamine was effective.

Lithium

Lithium has been reported (W. Dyson, personal communication; Annell, 1969) to be effective in some "hyperkinetic" children. Again, such a finding, if reliable, is of theoretical importance in view of lithium's hypothesized action on the transportation of cerebral neurohumors.[16]

Phenothiazines

Chlorpromazine and other phenothiazines have been used in the treatment of hyperkinetic children. The effective dosages of chlorpromazine employed have ranged between 30 and 300 mg/day (Freed, 1962). The phenothiazines do seem to produce diminished hyperactivity (Werry, 1966) and diminished aggressiveness (Freed, 1962). As with adults, they have been found particularly useful when there are schizophrenic components to the clinical picture. The piperazine compounds trifluoperazine and perphenazine have been recommended for hypoactive children (or for children whom chlorpromazine made too groggy). Unfortunately, these agents apparently are unusually apt to produce disturbing extra-pyramidal signs such as dystonia.

It has been my experience that many of the children who fail to respond to d-amphetamine either have borderline psychotic characteristics or have borderline or psychotic parents. This finding is in accord with that of Conrad and Insel (1967), who found that children from an "emotionally disturbed background" did not respond as well to d-amphetamine as did "organic hyperactive" children. In my experience, such children do respond

---

[16] At present, lithium occupies the status of an investigational drug and cannot, therefore, be routinely employed in the treatment of this problem.

well to phenothiazines. This finding does not justify Conrad and Insel's interpretation that failure to respond to *d*-amphetamine reveals a psychogenic etiology. My interpretation is different; namely, that the disturbance in the parents may be a manifestation of a biological problem in them *and* in the child, rather than the psychological cause of it in the child. Failure to respond to amphetamine and positive response to phenothiazines may indicate a different metabolic problem, not the presence of a psychological problem.

I wish to emphasize that some children with psychotic characteristics and/or family histories do respond to stimulant drugs. Since these drugs are safer than the phenothiazines, they should first be given a trial even though they are reasonably likely to be ineffective.

With regard to administration, it is useful to note that the phenothiazines can often be given in one daily dose as is the case with adults (Klein and Davis, 1968). In these instances, the entire dose of medication can be given one or 2 hours prior to bedtime. The soporific effect, lasting only several hours, insures a good night's sleep, while the "anti-MBD effect" (like the anti-psychotic effects in adults) lasts all day. In some children the anti-MBD effect lasts less than 24 hours and the medication must be given in daily divided doses.

In my own experience the phenothiazines have not had the general behavioral effects on nonpsychotic MBD children that the amphetamines do: they do not generally facilitate social responsiveness, improve learning, etc. For this reason I have employed these agents only when children have been refractory to amphetamines.[17] Another consideration is that the phenothiazines are not as safe as the amphetamines. There are acute toxic effects (allergic reactions, blood dyscrasias), and there are chronic toxic effects (documented to date only in adults) related to the total amount of drug ingested (e.g., lenticular opacity.) Lastly, these drugs can affect hypothalmic functioning and thus may possibly affect physiological maturation.

Diphenhydramine

Several authors, particularly Fish (1968), have recommended diphenhydramine (Benadryl): it is administered in doses of 2–10 mg/kg/day. Fish states that it is often effective in reducing symptoms without producing drowsiness in young children and that its useful action disappears at pu-

---

[17] In general these have been either MBD children with borderline attributes or very aggressive MBD children whose aggressiveness has not improved with the administration of stimulant drugs. With the very aggressive MBD child, combined amphetamine and phenothiazine therapy has sometimes proved useful: amphetamine has increased attention span and susceptibility to social demands; and phenothiazines have reduced aggressive outbursts.

berty. In my limited experience with this drug children have developed a tolerance to its effects fairly rapidly.

Diphenylhydantoin

Diphenylhydantoin (Dilantin) has at times been reported as an effective agent in the treatment of some behavior disorders, many of which would seem to overlap the MBD syndrome. There are no well-controlled studies documenting its efficacy in MBD children. I have seen four instances in which children failed to respond to amphetamine and did respond rather dramatically to Dilantin. All were in children with periodic rather than continuous MBD symptoms. One was a boy who had participated in a double-blind study of d-amphetamine and had failed to respond to either the placebo or the active agent. His periodic temper outbursts responded very dramatically to Dilantin. The second child was a 10-year-old boy with ego-dystonic rage outbursts which occurred several times a day; the tantrums failed to respond to d-amphetamine and responded promptly to Dilantin. The third instance was that of a child with a rather classical MBD syndrome, most of whose symptoms responded effectively to amphetamine but whose periodic, ostensibly psychogenic, gagging reactions persisted. When directly observed these attacks were seen to be accompanied by a mild clouding of consciousness. The attacks responded entirely to Dilantin, implying that they must have been a "seizure equivalent." The last instance was that of a 5-year-old girl who had intermittent periods of irritability, negativism, low-frustration tolerance, and affectional insatiability. These behaviors were unaffected by stimulant drugs. Following the appearance of occasional minor motor seizures, she was placed on Dilantin. On this agent both the seizures and the MBD-like behavior disappeared.

Phenobarbital

Phenobarbital is contraindicated. It is an effective agent for aggravating the syndrome and further disquieting the adults who must deal with the child (Ingram, 1956).[18]

Mysoline

Ingram (1956) reported that several hyperactive epileptic children who had failed to respond to d-amphetamine did show a useful response to Mysoline; unfortunately the study is no more than provocative because of

---

[18] Eisenberg (1966) reports that "hyperkinetic" children placed on phenobarbital did significantly worse than those on placebo. This is important to note because some physicians tend to diagnose the MBD syndrome as a "seizure equivalent" and treat it with phenobarbital, thus further aggravating the problem.

its small size. There are no controlled studies of the effect of Mysoline in the literature.

Other Agents

As might be expected, a generous fraction of the pharmacopoeia has been employed at one time or another, with varying results, in the treatment of this syndrome. A review of some of the better documented studies may be found in Millichap and Fowler (1967).

The Limitations of Medication

Drug treatment is of great importance, but it must be emphasized that there are several things medication cannot accomplish. Once the syndrome has remained untreated for any length of time, psychological deficits accumulate. Obviously, medication cannot compensate for educational and experiential deficits. Medication can facilitate learning, not provide compensation for several years in which a child may have been severely handicapped in learning. It can help a child learn to read, but it cannot teach him. Drugs can make the child more amenable to discipline and more lovable, but they cannot provide the experience of having been loved, trusted, admired, and accepted in the past. The consequences of these limitations are twofold. First, when indicated, medication should be used promptly in order to prevent the development of secondary problems. Second, when such problems have developed, another modality of management—psychological management—may be necessary. New experience will be necessary for the child to learn that which he has not learned and to experience that which he has been prevented from experiencing.

PSYCHOLOGICAL MANAGEMENT

The evidence for the usefulness of drug therapy is something less than perfect, but that supporting the usefulness of psychological intervention is far less convincing: there are no studies evaluating—much less documenting—the usefulness of psychological intervention. Any rigorous attempt to substantiate the usefulness of what follows would fail miserably. The justification for the techniques outlined is twofold: *a priori* and "clinical." The *a priori* justification refers to techniques that seem to have a face-valid usefulness. In psychiatry the face valid or "obvious" is often deemed superficial and is therefore rejected. To such objections I have no logical recourse and can only suggest that the apparent is not always illusion. The "clinical" justification refers to my own and others' experience, which has been collected without benefit of adequate sampling, double-blind testing, or freedom from bias. Such impressions are, therefore, highly suspect, but a few useful facts may have been garnered—after all, that is the way most human knowledge, such as it is, had been acquired until the last 100 or 200 years.

For purposes of organization the discussion will be divided into two parts: intervention with the family and intervention with the child.

This division obviously eliminates the approach of family therapy, which focuses mainly on the transactions between parent and child. My studied neglect is also twofold in origin: first, an impression, based on a perhaps insufficient number of cases, that the family approach offers no general advantages for the management of these problems; second, a belief that the suggestions proffered may be incorporated, with only slight modifications, into the medium of family therapy. For example, work with the parents involving the setting of limits, the establishment of rules, and the preparation for contingencies may easily be done in the presence of and with the assistance of the patient.[19]

Psychological Intervention with the Family

Psychological intervention with the family can be discussed under six headings: (1) "causes" of the problems: educating the parents; (2) explaining drug management; (3) "structuring" the environment; (4) changing the environment: nonspecific; (5) handling resistance; and (6) assisting in the parent-child relationship.

"Causes" of the Problems: Educating the Parents

As discussed in the section on etiology, the "causes" of the MBD children's problems range from those in which nonpsychological biological factors play a minor role to those in which nonpsychological factors play a major role. Although certainty, as in all human affairs, is impossible to attain, the evaluator can make a reasonably educated guess about the predominant source of the child's problems, particularly when the child lies at a not uncommon extreme. He will not have to guess about the one child

---

[19] There is one pitfall to which the family therapist is prone. The family therapy literature is apt to refer to the child, and here the MBD child, as the "identified patient"—with the implication that his role as patient is more a result of his having been scapegoated than of his psychopathology. (This scapegoating need not have been arbitrary; the family may have pinpointed some real "deviations" in the child. Ostracism, victimization, and blame are more apt to descend upon the exception.) The danger is that the avowed and enthusiastic family therapist may focus—as may the traditional therapist—on the more or less epiphenomenal or secondary family problems and neglect the real and specifically treatable problems of the "identified patient."

in a family of five who is having difficulties, has a history of erythroblastosis fetalis, and has been exceedingly hyperactive from the age of one year, nor will he have problems with the child who has always done well and who has become abruptly "hyperactive" at age 8 in the context of a difficult family situation.

The assignation of responsibility is important from the standpoints of both humanity and tactical utility. Consider the probable beliefs of the parents before they reach "expert" attention. Before such intervention, it can generally be assumed that the parent or parents assume total responsibility for their child's difficulties. The generation raised on Spock and Americanized Freud is largely, if unconsciously, committed to psychological determinism; the parents "know" that there is little biological difference between children in terms of behavior. They believe that a problem in their child signifies their ignorance and incompetence, perhaps even their malevolence. Unfortunately, many mental health workers, who should know better, share and reinforce this view. By unusual skill with logic, such workers reason that the child acts the way he does because of psychological determinism, but that the parents' behavior is the product of free will, and consequently blameworthy. Were this true, it might be, tactically, a poor idea to so inform the parents, but nonetheless they are often so informed, being indicted either explicitly or implicitly. The upshot is increased guilt, confusion, and defensive hostility.[20]

The intervener is therefore in a position to manipulate the parents' guilt. I say "manipulate" to emphasize both the therapist's ability to control the parents' guilt and his responsibility for doing so. His explanation of the problem can predictably minimize or increase guilt to any degree he desires. If he clearly and authoritatively presents the problem as "absolutely typical brain damage," and repeatedly asserts that it would have occurred no matter how the child was raised—*and* succeeds in convincing them—the parents' guilt will decrease. If he portrays the problem as one of "neurosis," the parents may choose to be hoisted on the petard of either heredity *or* environment: they are guilty of bad genes, bad child-rearing practices, or both.

Declaring that the responsibility lies with the child's nervous system serves both humane and tactical purposes. The humane purpose is obvious: the parents need to be absolved from torturing themselves for sins they have never committed. Their gradual acceptance of such absolution (when appropriate) is often accompanied by an appreciable resolution of their

---

[20] One cannot but feel that the attack on the parents frequently stems from the psychiatrist's or social worker's sense of inadequacy in dealing with the child's problem.

own anxiety and depression; as in the case of the retarded child, the psychiatrist can relieve the burden from a family even when he is unable to help the child. The tactical use of correct assignation of responsibility is as follows: our society absolves a "sick" person from certain responsibilities and demands. Defining a child as "mad" rather than "bad" will often decrease parental hostility and permit the parents to behave in more therapeutic ways. Frequently the parents of MBD children become involved in a vicious circle of alternating hostility and guilt. This is behaviorally manifested by an alternation of over- and underpermissiveness which tends to aggravate the child's problems. Diminishing the child's responsibility (he "doesn't mean it" and "can't stop himself") diminishes parental hostility; this in turn diminishes "rebound" guilt. Likewise, diminishing the parents' responsibility diminishes the parents' need to atone for their supposed guilt by overpermissiveness and overindulgence.

Since the therapist may initially be in doubt as to how much of the child's behavior is a function of the parents' misbehavior, he will not want to commit himself at first and assign full responsibility to constitutional factors in the child. Fairly elementary therapeutic tactics will prevent the therapist from painting himself into such a corner—for example, a statement such as, "It's hard beforehand to know where the trouble lies. It may lie largely in the child's physiology or some part may lie in the family. Let's give the medicine for a while and on the basis of your child's reaction to it, we'll have a better idea of how to proceed." If the child responds immediately and dramatically to medication, one can infer that the family's etiological role was not of primary importance; in such cases little or no work with the family will be necessary. If the child fails to respond to medication, introduction of other techniques (other medication or counseling) should not be difficult since such changes in technique have been anticipated. The family may not be responsible, and the initial statement will have allowed enough possibilities to motivate the parents to continue the child in treatment.

The explanation of the problem to the parent, the definition of the child's difficulties, requires a modicum of common sense. Many physicians identify the problem to the parents as being one of "minimal brain damage." Not only is this in many instances incorrect (since there is often no indication of neurological impairment), but it often has a painful and useless connotation to the parent. The layman's fantasies of "minimal brain damage" seem to consist of an image of a brain with many small holes, something like a Swiss cheese. *"Minimal* brain damage" is perceived as a "touch of pregnancy" or a "mild case of leukemia." The problem may be fairly honestly explained (to the child as well as to the parents, as indicated below) as one of congenital variation. For less educated parents I employ the analogy of breeds of dogs, contrasting feisty fox terriers and lethargic St. Bernards; with more educated parents I allude to biochemical differences between children. Such an explanation helps the parents to recognize the existence of a congenital difference for which neither the parent nor the child is blameworthy and which cannot be altered by psychological means alone.[21]

It must be mentioned that it is sometimes extremely difficult to convince the parents that their child's problems are "physiological" and not the product of subtle child abuse. The parent will not hear the explanation, will hear it but not believe it, or will attribute the explanation to the doctor's good will.[22] It is my impression that this is not due to unconscious masochism but is rather a reflection of the common man's solution of the mind-body problem. The average citizen, like the social scientist, finds it almost impossible to believe that products as ethereal as behavior and feelings can have a biological underpinning: gross aberrations perhaps, but subtle deviations never. Animism is persistent. Parenthetically, and ironically, the ubiquity, antiquity, and stability of the belief almost force one to believe the antinomy that psychologizing has a biological basis.

Explaining Drug Management to the Parents

Placing a child on medication also requires an explanation and justification to the parents and the child. The more sophisticated and psychological-minded the parents are, the more difficult such a justification may be. That a chemical could rectify their child's problems—which they persist in perceiving as psychological and interpersonal—seems improbable and perhaps impossible. Given their knowledge, their position is entirely tenable. They have no experience with the action of medication, they are not familiar with the rationale that relates biochemical variations to personality functioning, and, lastly, they have been oversold on psychotherapy as the best treatment that money can buy.

There are additional, even more emotional reasons for their rejection of drug therapy. An acknowledgment that drug treatment is necessary is an acknowledgment that something is *organically wrong* and such organic impairment is seen as due to brain damage, which is irreparable, or to hereditary factors, which are culpable. The organic is felt to be irremediable while something that is "only psychological" can easily be righted. For such multiple reasons these parents regard psychotherapy as the treatment

---

[21] For use at a public clinic dealing with large numbers of such children I have prepared a simple explanatory brochure for parents; it is available to the interested reader on request.

[22] Placing the physician in the role of Dostoevski's Grand Inquisitor.

of choice, and drug therapy as "second-class treatment": "That only smooths over the problems, Doctor, let's go all out and really get to the bottom of them." If their children are to receive drug therapy, parents must sometimes be seduced into accepting it. It is sometimes necessary to obtain full diagnostic batteries and offer brief "psychotherapy" to meet the family's needs. Otherwise, they are apt to withdraw and search for "real therapy" elsewhere. The quintessential episode involved the mother of a "classically" MBD child placed on medication after the second visit and who had a virtually complete recovery; the mother failed to return, stating, "His problems are almost one hundred percent better but I want him to get psychotherapy."

Some parents are delighted to hear that their child's difficulty is not their fault. Such feelings of relief are predictive of a willingness to use medication and sometimes also of an unwillingness to look at possible familial contributions. As has been explained, the parents' sense of responsibility can, and initially should be, maintained at a level adequate to facilitate psychological intervention; this can be accomplished humanely and noncensoriously.

In the treatment of the MBD child the unsophisticated and unpsychologically oriented family may for once be advantaged. Not exposed to psychiatric "oversell," they may retain a child-like belief in the existence of a magic medicine that can solve problems. Since such "primitive fantasies" are often correct for the MBD child, their attitude is pro-therapeutic.

Parental resistance to drug therapy can present a serious impediment to treatment. The psychiatrist must have enough conviction to offer the patient what the patient needs and not what the patient's parents want. If he falls into the latter trap he is abdicating his medical responsibility and is analogous to a surgeon who takes out a gall bladder because the patient feels it is indicated.

"Structuring" the Environment

There seems to be a consensus—and some documentation—that one of the "psychological" modes of intervention that is particularly useful is a specific form of alteration or "structuring" of the MBD child's environment. The observations that form the basis of this consensus are in accordance with the theory I shall later postulate regarding the MBD child's defect (which is not surprising, in that the theory derives, in part, from such observations). A major aspect of the theory, briefly, is that such children condition with difficulty; if the theory is valid, one would expect that unusually consistent and predictable contingencies would facilitate learning.

An excellent anecdotal account of the benefits of structure may be found in Bond and Smith (1935), who reported on the comparative effectiveness of several treatment regimes in 85 institutionalized postencephalitic children. In the first regime, "based somewhat on the assumption that the behavior disorders in the children existed because of undue emotional stress and strain on the child" (p. 19), the staff practiced an "attitude[s] of wide tolerance" (p. 18). This approach produced transient improvement which was followed by a reappearance and persistence of the behavior difficulties. Since these children had not received psychotherapy, arrangements were then made to give each child from one to four hours of individual psychotherapy per week. With this addition, "the situation seemed little different, and all indications pointed to a need for change in the school . . . and a need for special restrictions on certain children" (p. 19). In the last phase a "constructive restrictive tolerant environment" was provided. The environment was "not lax . . . [and] a definite level of confirmation of behavior . . . [was] expected of them" (p. 21). Children were isolated but not censured for impulsive behavior, and their reactions might later be worked with in psychotherapy. Although not evaluated by follow-up studies, the last regime produced the greatest benefit for children while they were in the school.

Clinical experience documenting the usefulness of firm, consistent rules is common. The most common instance occurring naturally is that of the child who is well behaved with a firm teacher at school and unmanageable at home. In such cases, as already noted, it is also common to see the MBD's child's problems occurring in a disruptive unstructured home setting. There are several possible explanations of this observed association. First, it might be that those MBD children with chaotic families are most apt to develop problems and hence form the sample seen at the clinic. Second, many parents—possibly because they are the genetic carriers of the same disorder that is manifested in their children—have always been unplanful, somewhat disorganized people themselves. Third, other parents, relatively organized at first, have gradually become disorganized as they have abandoned one imperfect plan after another. Many have in confusion seen strictness as severity, and have mistakenly chosen weakness, failing to recognize any alternative to a distasteful harshness. Some have been taught—by mental health experts—that *all* disturbed children need increased permissiveness and opportunity for expression, and this has led to the fourth and most distressing explanation: some MBD children have problems that have been iatrogenically exacerbated—that is, their controls have been diminished and their problems have been aggravated by planned release therapy. I have seen several children for whom activity and nondirective therapy have apparently been psychonoxious. Fortunately, this phenomenon is uncommon.

These disorganized parents—and their children—may be helped by a program of old-fashioned guidance in which the parents are helped in the following ways: (1) to establish a hierarchy of importance of rules, distinguishing between misdemeanors and felonies. Many parents—in the last stages of confusion—punish illegal parking with the gas chamber and punish murder with a warning. The parents have never decided what is trivial, what is important, and what is essential. They often have considerable difficulty in making such distinctions and helping them to do so allows them to focus their demands on what is important and allows the child some breathing room. (2) To pre-decide upon a plan for rewards and punishments: help the parents to arrange a hierarchy of inducements—in the *child's* eyes—and teach the parents to assign important rewards and punishments to important behaviors and lesser rewards and punishments to lesser behaviors. A guideline of singular simplicity, neglected by many parents yet easy to teach, is the "one-time principle." This consists of teaching the parents to prescribe or proscribe only once before rewarding or punishing. MBD children—who, like all other children, are congenital lawyers—will soon learn that what their parents say is nonnegotiable. This policy, consistently applied, is not only restful for the parental larynx, but presents the child with an absolutely predictable environment. As a result, limit-testing, if at all susceptible to external variables, will decrease. (3) To pre-decide that both parents shall abide by the prescribed course of action. This policy is not always easy to implement. It is customary for each parent to have devised his own inadequate *modus operandi* in dealing with the child and for each to attribute the child's problems to the other's mismanagement. Such an atmosphere militates against the consistent united front which is a minimal requirement of a predictable structured environment.

The foregoing may appear trivial. It is, after all, primarily educational. The important test of its efficacy is empirical, not theoretical. Those parents who can change their ways in the suggested manner often are rewarded by an improvement in their child. Such a program may meet resistance for dynamic reasons. Sometimes it meets resistance for cognitive ones in parents who equate greater consistency, which is applied on an apparently unreasoning basis, with less love. In such instances, gradual institution of the scheme will often convince the parents, particularly when followed by gradual success. Resistance should not always be assumed. Ignorance is sometimes the cause of noncompliance; and of the relevant means of remedy, education is by far the quickest.

A more formalized mode of structured approach is that of "operant therapy." Its major principles are no different: reinforcing (rewarding) the desirable and punishing the undesirable behaviors. Its most useful subtlety, which otherwise escapes parents, is that attention is rewarding no matter what its guise; thus punishment is more rewarding than ignoring; and discussing a child's problems with him may induce him to commit more misdeeds for further discussion. The operant technique consists of constructing a system of programmed rewards (and perhaps punishments) with which the child is fully acquainted beforehand. The two usual reinforcers are (1) the quiet room (an isolation room) as a punishment for objectionable behaviors, and (2) a system of tokens, later redeemable for more tangible goods, as prompt rewards for desirable behavior. With the first reinforcer, a misbehaving child is summarily dispatched to an isolated quarter of the house to stew until self-controlled. He is sent without discussion and received back with warmth, thus reinforcing desirable behavior (self-control) and not rewarding (no "Tell Mommy what's bothering you") his loss of control. In the token system, the child can accumulate the credits that he earns for desirable behavior and can exchange them for objects (or privileges) that he regards as desirable (if the exchange is for money, the technique is referred to as "capitalism"). I have found both techniques useful, particularly in latency-age children with unresourceful or overly psychodynamic parents. The psychodynamically oriented parent who can be encouraged to use these techniques is less likely to reinforce the child's "insightful" but unhelpful comments. Popular notions of the efficacy of insight tend to equate it with usefulness, but parents may sometimes succeed in reinforcing self-referred comments in the child without affecting the child's maladaptive behavior. The child's accurate description of himself as angry when he hits his baby sister is an interesting instance of the ability to comment on one's own behavior; it is not helpful to one's baby sister. The techniques are also useful for the chaotic parent, relieving him of the need to decide in a particular instance, preventing negotiation with the child (and hence inconsistency), and diminishing the parents' anger—what is nonnegotiable is nonarguable.[23]

Changing the Environment: Nonspecific

As discussed in the section on etiology, in some MBD children the current home environment seems to play a pathogenic role. The homes in

---

[23] Three examples of experiments evaluating operant theory with various kinds of children are as follows: Zeilberger et al. (1968) demonstrated the efficiency of the home use of the quiet room technique for a probably hyperactive child; Hall et al. (1968) illustrated the use of programmed teacher attention in increasing studying and decreasing dawdling in the classroom; Edelson and Sprague (1969) illustrated the use of operant conditioning to reduce activity level (as measured by objective techniques) in hyperactive mental retardates. The duration of conditioning effects following termination of reinforcement may not be long; in the last experiment hyperactive behavior reappeared as soon as reinforcement was discontinued.

question may be variously and nonspecifically noxious, ranging from the chaotic and disrupted to the rigid and punitive. The pathogenic role of such homes is evidenced by the disappearance of *some* of the child's symptoms when his parents' pathology can be reduced or when he is placed in a new setting. In some instances the origins of such changes in the child are clear-cut: they seem related to the fact that the improved parents—or new parent surrogates—are more "reasonable" people who establish firm, sensible limits. In other instances the improvement seems related simply to a more beneficent atmosphere. If anxiety—however produced—offers a synergistic contribution to the symptom picture, an atmosphere that is less anxiety-provoking might be expected to produce less disruptive behavior in the child. That both sorts of changes would foster greater self-control is theoretically sensible in learning theory terms: under the "firmer" surrogates, the predictable environmental contingencies are easier to learn; and in the more "beneficent" atmosphere, the better-loved adults are more powerful reinforcers.

The major reason for altering the deviant home—outside of the tacit value that all should live like the psychiatrist—is humanitarian. We invariably attempt to reduce chaos, mute overpunitiveness, and otherwise ameliorate the sins to which parenting flesh is prone. In some of those instances in which such changes can be accomplished one may find some additional improvement in the MBD child.

Handling Familial Resistance to Improvement in the Child

One important dynamic issue deserves special attention. It concerns the family which is resistant to improvement in the child. In my experience, such families are nowhere near as common as some family therapists would imply.[24] They do exist, however, and recognition of them is important because they can sabotage a child's treatment.

The most frequent indicators of familial resistance are failure to give medication consistently and failure to perceive probable progress. Failure to give medication is sometimes only a reflection of parental intimidation ("He didn't want it, Doctor, so I didn't make him take it."), sometimes another manifestation of parental disorganization, and sometimes a (usually unconscious) reluctance to help the child to improve. A failure to detect improvement is most often due to its absence. There are times when a discrepancy between reporters leads one to believe either that a child's behavior differs widely in different settings or that one set of reporters (here

---

[24] Indiscriminate attribution of the patient's failure to recover to the family's resistance can be dangerous—or at best misleading. It tends to conceal the very real possibility that such failure to improve is a consequence of ineffective therapy.

the parents) cannot accept improvement. When a teacher reports a switch from irascibility to affability, resistance to compliance, peer rejection to peer acceptance, grade improvement from C's and D's to B's and A's, and the parents report "no change," some suspicion is justified. Motivations for refusing to see improvement are varied: the child may serve as a scapegoat, a vehicle for parental opposition, or as a reason for parental separation.

Failure to see improvement may also be another manifestation of an initial reluctance to see a disability. After all, how can a child get better when he was never worse? An understanding of the basis of a family's resistance is obviously necessary in order to work with that resistance. But a failure to ameliorate such resistance need not signify an inability to help the child. Many children can be benefited—by their testimony and that of their teachers—with medicine and without complete family participation. It is much better to have complete family cooperation, but as long as a child ingests effective medication he may receive benefit without parental blessings. The situation is analogous to that of an epileptic child for whom parental empathy and anticonvulsants are preferable to medication alone but for whom Dilantin and Tridione may be helpful by themselves.

The author has seen a disconcerting number of families with an MBD child who family therapists inaccurately described as "unworkable." In many instances they appeared at first to be correct: the families were unworkable. What they failed to perceive is that the children were workable. Administration of medication—often by a public health nurse at school—produced considerable improvement in the child despite lack of cooperation by the parents. In such instances discharge of the parents as "unworkable" is an evasion of responsibility. One would not fail to treat an epileptic child because his family was "unworkable." A failure to treat the MBD child because of his family's difficulties occupies a comparable logical and moral status.

Assisting in the Parents' Personal Relationship with the Child: the Parent as Therapist

Prior to diagnosis of the problem, the MBD child has frequently been the recipient of considerable parental accusation and even abuse. "Why must you be bad, why can't you do what you're told, why must you have tantrums, why don't you behave yourself?" These are representative questions to which the child is frequently exposed.

The disclosure to the parents that their child is not malicious but a subject of deviant physiology is apt to place the parents in the role of tolerant permissive determinists. They are apt to reverse their stance completely and to communicate—either directly or indirectly—the notion, "You can't help yourself, dear." The effects of this approach can be disastrous: determinism—psychological or physiological—can be an impenetrable screen.

Accordingly it is useful to instruct the parents in several basic tactics for tolerable parent-child existence. These include (1) teaching the parent to recognize his child's feelings and communicate his recognition of them without offering either tacit approval or disapproval, and (2) teaching the parent to help the child distinguish between feelings (which are acceptable) and actions (which are not). Parental toleration of the child's feelings may or may not relieve the child's anxiety about having them and may or may not relieve enough "steam" (the economic theory) to preclude their being acted upon. It is reasonable to expect the child to feel less guilty if he knows that bad *thoughts* do not mean he is bad and worthless in his parents' eyes. Since the past he has *acted* in a way deemed most unacceptable, he is apt to regard comparable thoughts as comparably reprehensible. It is therefore useful to instruct the parents that bad thoughts are common, that unacted upon they are harmless, that recognizing and acknowledging them in their child is often helpful to the child, and that such identification of unpleasant emotions does not lead to their being acted upon (loosely, "acting out," or more accurately, "acting up").

Psychological Management of the Child

There are two major aspects of psychological intervention with the child himself: psychological treatment directed at the child as patient, whether in an individual or a group setting; and special educational training for cognitive and motor defects when present.

Psychological Treatment of the Child

As is usual among the psychiatric disorders, there is a paucity of controlled studies of psychotherapeutic intervention in the MBD syndrome. The single study that is available does not document the usefulness of psychotherapy. Eisenberg et al. (1961) reported a small series of "hyperkinetic" children treated with perphenazine plus psychotherapy, with placebo plus psychotherapy, or with psychotherapy alone; none of the groups did significantly better than untreated controls. It is unfortunate that these groups were not compared with a group treated with amphetamine, an agent of known efficacy. Although the data superficially point to no beneficial contribution of psychotherapy, it is possible that this particular population would have been refractory to *any* therapy; had amphetamine been used, which presumably would have led to better results in the group so treated, the conclusion regarding psychotherapy (and the other "treatments") might have been more significant.

As in most studies of psychotherapy, the results may be minimized by the adherent of psychological modes of therapy on two counts: (1) "Psychotherapy" is a single term for numerous varieties of intervention. The fact that a nonspecified type employed by random therapists did not work in this research can obviously not be generalized to include *all* types of therapy conducted by all types of therapists. Different therapists or different techniques *might* produce different results; the studies refer to traditional modes of child psychotherapy and it is *conceivable* that techniques with a different approach, such as operant therapy, might yield different results. (2) The duration of intervention in this study was only five sessions, which is considered very brief. Nonetheless, one is left with data that tend to indicate that psychotherapy is not universally useful. Such data as are available, taken together, indicate that (1) for a heterogeneous group of "disturbed" children the spontaneous recovery rate is very high (Perez-Reyes, 1967; Levitt, 1963); and (2) for hyperkinetic children the spontaneous recovery rate is very low. The single study available (Eisenberg et al., 1961) shows that brief psychotherapy offers no benefit for "hyperkinetic" children, while another study shows that therapy does afford a statistically significant, if inappreciable benefit for "neurotic" children (Eisenberg et al., 1967).[25] In spite of the absence of any data supporting the usefulness of psychotherapy and the presence of data denying its usefulness, many psychiatrists consistently recommend it. As Werry (1968a) observes, "child psychiatrists prescribe individual psychotherapy in the same indiscriminate way that surgeons once removed tonsils, teeth and colons as a cure for all ills and with about as much evidence of efficacy" (p. 592).

Despite the lack of convincing evidence concerning the usefulness of psychotherapy, it is my experience that *some* forms of psychological intervention are useful with *some* MBD children *some* of the time, as in the following concrete examples:

1. Explanation of the child's problem to the child. Even prior to his referral to the child psychiatrist, the usual MBD child has some awareness of his deviance. He is not infrequently labeled by members of his peer group, who are often competent psychiatric diagnosticians, as a "retard" or an "odd ball." He has generally been ostracized by his peers and singled out by his teacher and parents as a miscreant; he is often an inept athlete

---

[25] In this study it was found that brief psychotherapy (five sessions) provided a statistically significant improvement over that provided by diagnostic intake ("consultation") alone; 32% of the psychotherapy group versus 23% of the consultation group showed "marked improvement."

and poor student—and usually aware of these deficiencies; and he is frequently rejected by all. A final confirmation of the child's suspicions is provided by the trip to the psychiatrist, which is often perceived as a documentation of his suspected craziness. However, when he is interviewed by the child psychiatrist, the MBD child almost inevitably denies any problems or awareness of them; like low self-esteem, denial of deviation is a usual concomitant of the syndrome.[26]

I have found it extremely useful to provide an explanation to the child of his abnormality. Such an explanation will necessarily vary as a function of the child's age. Both younger and older children may be told, quite accurately, that people differ at birth in a variety of ways. All children recognize the fact that some people are larger, some are smaller, some are faster, some are slower, some are easier to get along with, some are harder to get along with. It is useful to call this to the child's attention and then inquire whether he has noticed in his class that there are some children who sit quietly and attentively while there are others who are more fidgety and restless. He may be told, again quite accurately, that "some children are this way" (restless), that it provides some disadvantages as he undoubtedly has observed, and that if he is patient, he will eventually outgrow it. The problem in the meantime is how to learn to deal with it. I have found that the child's immediate overt expression of agreement is neither common nor necessary. As in interviews with psychotic patients, the patient knows what the matter is, I know what the matter is, he knows that I know, and he will not—for varying reasons but mainly in order to save face— admit his awareness at the present time. With older and brighter adolescents I have been able to refer, somewhat vaguely to be sure, to differences in brain chemistry; this explanation has been found to be entirely satisfactory. The effect of such a disclosure is to exempt the child from moral blameworthiness. However, some additional remarks to the child are necessary lest the disclosure also seems to exempt him from all responsibility for his actions: "I can't help it—I was made that way." The ethical and moral difficulties of psychological determinism may be avoided by telling the child that children with problems such as his can learn, if they want to, to control their problems—that these differences that some children have need not prevent them from acting like other children.

This sort of education of the child leads directly to the second kind of psychological intervention I have found particularly useful with MBD children—explanation of the use of drugs.

[26] The usual response of the child brought to the psychiatrist is to deny the imputation of deviance fully and to a degree which makes one feel that "taking" the Fifth Amendment is a transcription of an innate idea. For this reason I never anticipate the child's agreement that something might be the matter.

2. *Explanation of drug treatment.* The purpose of explaining the use of drugs to the child is to make him one's ally, not one's opponent, and to allow him to feel that he is the master of the situation. My approach is to tell the child—again, obviously varying the phraseology with the child's age—that medicines often help children to do more sitting down so they can do what they want to. In order to allow the child to save face and to increase his sense of autonomy, I make an assertion which may or may not be true: "Obviously this medicine can only help you to hold your temper (concentrate, etc.—mentioning whatever the child's particular problem is) if you really want to—most of it is up to you." I said that this may be a lie, since I have seen children become "good boys" and good students when the medicine had been virtually forced down their throats, but I cannot help but feel that the face-saving and the increase in the child's sense of autonomy are desirable aims.

Since children rightfully interpret being brought to the child psychiatrist as a sign of "craziness," receiving medicine—"tranquilizers"—sometimes merely provides a further confirmation of this belief. I have seen instances in which an explanation of the purpose of drug administration has decreased the child's anxiety and decreased his hyperactivity. A case in point is that of a Negro ghetto child with an I.Q. of 130 (approximately three standard deviations above his group's mean) who was markedly "hyperactive" and doing poorly in school. He received some benefit from a small dose of d-amphetamine but when this was increased he did worse. Further increases continued to aggravate the child's behavioral problem until the pediatrician supervising his treatment had the unusual common sense to inquire about the child's perception of the situation. The boy replied, with faultless logic, that more medicine meant he must have been even crazier than he had realized. When the rationale was explained to him his increased "hyperactivity" disappeared promptly.

Many older children—particularly adolescents—resist taking the medicine; they cannot take it without acknowledging incomplete control of their actions. My approach, as with psychotic patients, is to acknowledge their discomfort about taking the medicine and then tell them firmly that they will. Many subsequently recognize that the medicine has benefited them. It is not necessary to make the adolescent lose face by openly acknowledging this, and both parties can get along well with the adolescent's passive acceptance.

Most children do, in fact, become quite aware that the medicine is helping them and many remind their parents to give it to them on occasions on which their parents forget. I have referred already to the bright 8-year-old who described d-amphetamine as "my magic pills which make me into a good boy and make everybody like me." Such a response is frequent. Most children use what Bleuler referred to as "a double-entry system of bookkeeping," in which they deny the drug's efficacy but dutifully remember to take it.

3. Psychotherapy narrowly construed. Many MBD children, particularly older ones, have engrafted psychological disabilities upon their temperamental ones. Many of these difficulties are in the interpersonal sphere, and I have received the *impression* that psychotherapy with certain limited goals has proved useful with *some* such children. The goals in question are the following: communicating a consensually valid view of the world; attempting to reshape attitudes and beliefs toward self and others that have been skewed by the child's previous experience; explaining, clarifying, and otherwise giving instruction concerning the whys and wherefores of human interaction. Many of the techniques are similar to those suggested by interpersonal and "ego-oriented" therapists working with schizophrenic patients. I would be unable to prove the utility of such techniques and can only point to their face validity.

Before leaving the subject of psychological treatment of the child, I wish to mention possible psychonoxious effects. It is almost universally believed by psychotherapeutic adherents that psychotherapy enjoys a unique role as a potent treatment modality—that it has the power only to produce good. There are not only observational reasons for thinking this to be false (Bergin, 1966) but theoretical ones as well. As mentioned previously, my own observations agree with those of Eisenberg (1956) who has observed children whose problems appear to have been exacerbated by psychotherapeutic intervention. "Release therapy," whether administered individually or in an activity group, has diminished some of the weak controls in these particular children and thus aggravated their problems. Among theoretical reasons for questioning the desirability of traditional therapy for the child is the possibility that identifying a child as a patient may be demeaning for him; his own culture identifies psychiatrists as doctors for crazy people and not as agents of self-actualization. Such intervention might well be expected to diminish the child's self-esteem. Lastly, looking for causes that may not be there is a frustrating occupation, except, perhaps, for theologists.

Educational Intervention

Remedial education is obviously indicated for those children who are academically disabled. Although medication sometimes eliminates and frequently diminishes learning problems, in many instances special educational intervention is necessary. Even those children whose learning problems abate with medication often need educational assistance. Too often, by the time his disability is recognized and treated, the MBD child has fallen behind in many subjects. Learning problems are cumulative; consequently the child cannot recoup his educational losses, despite improved functioning, unless adequate remedial tutoring is provided in those areas in which he has fallen behind. The problem of cumulative educational deficit is most severe in those MBD children whose difficulties are first identified in adolescence. These children, who often have received repeated "social promotions," are apt to be several grade levels behind in a number of areas. Unfortunately, though medication may still be effective, appropriate educational facilities are often not available, and these children, humiliated by their academic inadequacies, tend to give up. It is my impression that adolescent MBD children constitute more than their share of high school dropouts. Remedial education for children "with special learning disorders" is currently a subject of considerable dispute. If one can generalize from experience in medicine, the presence of considerable dispute probably documents the lack of clear-cut advantages for any of the proposed treatment programs.[27]

It is possible that specific training may help the MBD child to overcome his impulsivity and organize his own behavior more effectively. A provocative study suggesting the possibility of such an approach is that of Palkes et al. (1968). These authors trained "hyperactive" children to incorporate self-directions into the performance of a task. The self-directions were to stop, listen, and think before proceeding, and they resulted in improved performance (decreased impulsivity) on experimental measures of impulsivity. The persistence of this training or its generalization to other tasks has not been studied. One would hypothesize that the effect of such training would interact favorably with medication, with drug treatment favoring retention of the newly taught technique.

---

[27] One approach in particular has acquired enough attention to warrant singling out for explicit rejection. Over the years there has been continuing discussion concerning the relationship between "laterality," motor coordination, and special learning disabilities. Authors have commented on an apparent greater-than-chance association between "mixed handedness" and/or "mixed dominance," poor coordination, and learning problems. Concomitance has been interpreted as cause and the learning difficulties have been seen as a manifestation of the neurological characteristics. On the basis of such soggy theoretical foundations, a number of programs in special motoric reeducation have been proposed and promoted. The rationale has been that since poor motor performance "causes" learning problems, improved motor performance (presumably achieved, for example, by fostering unilateral dominance) should result in better learning. Such techniques are purely speculative, and at present there is no information whatsoever to document their efficacy. This is particularly true of the Doman-Delacato program which has received considerable publicity but for which there is no evidence of specific therapeutic value. [This is a conclusion reached by the American Academies of Neurology and Pediatrics, among others. (See *Develop. Med. Child Neurol.*, **10**:243–246, 1968.)]

A special form of remedial education to which I would like to call attention is that which attempts to improve the child's motor skills by graduated practice. It is my impression that such programs are occasionally useful. Their efficacy is again face valid and not based upon any theoretical preconceptions—it is simply the case that a child trained to throw and catch better is less apt to be rejected as a poor athlete.

In general, it has been my *impression* that remedial techniques, when effective, have favorable consequences in areas other than those treated. For example, clumsy latency-age boys have had an increase in self-esteem and generally improved behavior when they have been coached into being adequate athletes. A similar view is held by Bender in regard to helping children with reading problems. She stated (1956) that "in a follow-up of several hundred schizophrenic and nonschizophrenic children, there was no therapeutic program that could materially or statistically change the course of a child's life. On the positive side there [was] evidence that if problem children have a reading disability regardless of other diagnosis or factors and receive remedial reading tutoring they improve in every respect" (p. 271). Such an assertion is not logically impeccable—only children who show benefit from tutoring may continue to receive it and improvement in reading might be a manifestation of and not the cause of psychological improvement—but, again, the comment makes good intuitive sense. A school-age child's self-esteem is largely dependent on his intellectual—and for a boy, athletic—performance. Anything that improves a child's performance might be expected to raise self-esteem and generally improve his psychological functioning.

THE DECISION TO TREAT WITH MEDICATION: THE PAYOFF MATRIX

At the end of the chapter on diagnosis the issue of choice of treatment was raised. Given the failure of present diagnostic methods to predict drug responsiveness, how should a clinician decide whether or not to give a child a trial of medication? A useful technique, used both in decision and game theory, is the construction of a "payoff matrix." This is nothing more than a listing of the probabilities and consequences of all forms of action and nonaction (i.e., treating with medication or not treating) and the classes of subjects' responses (in this instance, good response, neutral response, and bad response). Thus six possible states exist in the drug treatment matrix, as shown in Table 5. The decision to act, that is, to give or not give medication, could be optimally decided if one knew beforehand whether a given child would be positively or negatively respon-

Table 5. Responsiveness to Medication

Treatment	Response of Children (%)		
	Good	Neutral	Bad
Medication given	50-70[a]	20-30	5-10[b]
Medication not given	4-15	85-96	0

[a] Includes approximately 4–15% placebo effect.

[b] Because of the placebo effect, 4–15% of this fractional group of children (i.e., about 1% of the total receiving medication) might improve if not given medication.

sive or unaffected by drugs. But one only has the crude information indicated in the table—the rough percentage of children falling into each response category. Given this limitation, one can only ask what the consequences of an arbitrary decision to treat or not to treat may be. Since the percentage of children who have a good, neutral, and bad response to treatment is roughly known and since the small fraction who have a favorable placebo response (whose duration is unknown) is known, one can roughly fill in the cells in the table. One may see, for example, that the decision to give medication to all children can result in a 70% improvement rate and at worst a 10% rate of bad responses. The decision not to give medication to a particular child, who has a 5–10% chance of being a negative responder, will result in a 4–15% chance of improvement—that is, when faced with a child of unknown response, one can assume that medication has a 50–70% chance of eliciting a good response and a 5–10% chance of eliciting a bad response and that failure to give medication leaves one with a small chance of seeing improvement and virtually no chance of seeing an immediate worsening. Given the distribution of responders, one may easily determine for oneself that the "greatest good for the greatest number" will be accomplished by giving all children a trial of medication—or so it would seem at first glance. To fully answer the question of whether to treat or not to treat, one must answer a number of questions which are not answered in Table 5.

First, what are the disadvantages of giving medication to a child with a good response to drug treatment? Obviously there may be both psychological and physiological toxicity. As mentioned earlier, there is no evidence to date of serious physiological toxicity with the amphetamines, even when they are employed for several consecutive years. Anyone who does employ this drug, or any other medication, must always have the fear at the back of his mind that ill effects will be discovered at some future date. These probabilities cannot be measured at all accurately and must be weighed against the roughly estimable danger of nontreatment.

With regard to the danger of "psychological toxicity"—that is, the psychonoxious effect of giving the drug to a child—the sequelae include the effect of the drug on the child's self-esteem and the effect on the parents' localization of responsibility. The child's resistance to and discomfort with the drug is generally short-lived. After an occasionally difficult initial period, many children take the drug in a very matter-of-fact way (in a manner similar to that in which a child with rheumatic fever will take penicillin or an epileptic child Dilantin). As mentioned, the effect on the parents' localization of responsibility can be minimized by handling it in a flexible and noncommittal way. An honest admission of some ignorance does not harm the therapist's image and will permit him to later work with the family if this seems indicated. Theoretically, another potential danger involves taking a child who is appropriately rebellious to a bad environment and corseting him with a chemical straitjacket into docility. I have not, however, seen a clear-cut instance of this. Nearly always a child's improvement produces relief in his parents and an improvement in his home environment.

In contrast to these risks of treatment, what about the risks of nontreatment? It is quite uncommon for psychiatrists to consider this question seriously except in the case of suicidal patients. In the case of MBD children the risks of nondrug treatment are two: (1) the possibility of long-term effects of early psychological deviancy on the child; (2) the possibility of long-term effects of nontreatment on the family. There are both empirical and theoretical reasons for concern about the long-term effects of deviancy in the child. The follow-up studies cited in the chapter on prognosis, for example, contribute some clinical evidence but also require *a priori* projection: they seem to indicate that MBD children, when not treated, are at a greater risk for future psychiatric disability than are non-MBD children, but these studies refer to a fairly sick group of MBD children. We do not know either the relationship of prognosis to the severity of illness, or the effectiveness of drug intervention in preventing future psychiatric disability. Nevertheless, there are theoretical reasons for believing that intervention might be of preventive value. It is a widely held belief—although not a carefully documented one—that early psychological experience is of crucial importance for later personality formation. If this is so, interventions which promote "healthier" early psychological experience should obviously result in "healthier" personality in later life. Empirically one finds that a successfully treated child's self-esteem and self-confidence are apt to improve greatly as his impulse control improves, his grades improve, his peer relations improve, and he is better able to function in a way consonant with the demands of his peers, parents, and internal standards (superego and ego ideal). It is hard to see these changes as not promoting psychological health. Likewise, it is quite easy to see the vicious circle engendered by the untreated MBD child's behavior. By the time the untreated child has physiologically outgrown his behavior—if this ever occurs—we should expect him to have relatively permanent psychological scars. He will justifiably regard himself as a poor student, a bad son (or daughter), and an unlovable and unpopular person of little worth; he will have accurately incorporated the views of others. If general self-esteem is like perception of body image we would expect the effects of early low self-esteem to be permanent. Svelte adults, formerly fat adolescents, continue to regard themselves as unattractive in later life (Stunkard and Burt, 1967).

Let us now turn to the possible ill effects of nontreatment on the family of a child who has or may have a good response to drugs. Although one may assure the parents that the child's problems are not reactive to theirs, most parents find this virtually impossible to accept unless the situation is remedied by successful treatment of the child. Without such treatment one might predict that the parents would be chronically angry and guilty toward and about their difficult child. Reassurance that they were not to blame would probably be useless. As mentioned, many parents have difficulty adjusting to their child's improvement on drugs and only gradually come to accept the apparently absurd view that a child's behavioral difficulties might be secondary to his body chemistry, and remediable by the treatment of that chemistry; responsibility is given up with difficulty.

Since the decision not to medicate is usually a decision to substitute another form of treatment, namely psychotherapy, one must also weigh the relative merits and demerits of such treatment. In addition to the possible advantages and disadvantages of psychotherapy that have been discussed previously, there is another psychonoxious effect that should be mentioned. Since psychotherapy is quite clearly ineffective in the vast majority of MBD children, it frequently serves to worsen the rapport between the parent and the therapist. This frequently results in withdrawal of the child from treatment or poorer parental cooperation in the future.

Given the above array of imponderables, the most logical decision might seem to be to employ the safest and easiest form of therapy at first and reserve drug treatment for those patients who failed to respond. A logical case might be made for operating in a sequential fashion, placing all children on a placebo to begin with and then treating the nonresponders with medication. The difficulty of deteriorating parental rapport could be minimized by informing the parents that, as is indeed the case, several medications are effective and the doctor may have to try several before he finds the one that is best for the child. To many physicians such an approach would seem ethically untenable and they might choose to initiate treatment with psychotherapy. With such a plan one might eliminate from the rolls those "pseudo-MBD" children for whom drug treatment would present no advantages and only a disadvantage—that is, possible toxicities. Such an approach would be ethical only with better than expectable follow-up techniques. Most parents and/or doctors are apt to terminate treatment with some signs of improvement whereas the question at hand is whether a child has received optimal treatment and maximum improvement. The question of whether improvement without medication has been optimal is a problem except in those rare instances in which a child has "complete" recovery without medication. Otherwise one cannot know if still greater benefit might have been achieved with medication. The question is epistemologically akin to the status of the icebox light when the door is shut: the question cannot be answered without a trial of medication.

I am obviously opting for a trial of stimulant (amphetamine or methylphenidate) therapy in all children in whom the diagnosis of MBD is suspected. To those who have seen the results of such treatment in MBD children, many of whom had failed to improve or had worsened with traditional therapies, the present limited use of drug therapy is as upsetting as it is unbelievable. The failure to employ stimulant drugs in MBD children is not a sign of their doubtful therapeutic efficacy but is rather a clear-cut indication of the biases and prejudices of American child psychiatry over the past thirty years. Comparably effective drugs could never remain hidden or unused for so long in internal medicine. Only the views that most children's problems are psychological in origin and that the administration of drugs to children represents poisoning of the brains and minds of the innocent could prevent widespread use of such effective agents. With increasing documentation of the efficacy of the stimulant drugs, the burden of responsibility in not using them now falls on the child psychotherapist. It would not be hard to argue that in many instances psychotherapy of children with this syndrome virtually constitutes malpractice—a harmful withholding of useful treatment from a child. Undoubtedly cultural momentum will permit the child psychotherapist to earn an unstigmatized living from treating such children, but what the community will bear or approve of and what benefits the patient are two vastly different matters. Barring the future disclosure of chronic toxic consequences of stimulant drug therapy for such children, one must argue that it is the treatment of choice, and that withholding it represents an injury to the patient and his family.

Cost Considerations: A Final Note for the Pragmatist

In public health programs with insufficient resources (i.e., all public health programs), therapeutic efficacy is usually only one of the determinants in the choice of treatment modality. Another determinant is, obviously, the cost per person treated. One must calculate the cost per "unit" of achievement. With a costlier therapeutic modality, and hence, under existing circumstances, with a smaller number of patients who can be treated, one needs stronger evidence to justify its use. A particular expensive therapeutic approach may be extremely effective for an occasional patient who has failed to respond to more simple types of intervention. Even then it may be unjustified. With limited resources—and psychiatric resources are severely limited—the expense necessary for an elaborate treatment for a few patients might permit the simpler and effective treatment of many more patients. Adequate evaluation and treatment of the average MBD child requires approximately 4 to 6 hours for the first year and less thereafter. Long-term psychotherapy (which is the only sort that *might* be useful since short-term psychotherapy does not work) requires at least 40 hours per year for a few years—during which period the child might outgrow the symptoms anyway, and in either case might also be saddled with the cumulative effects of persisting deviancy.

The social conclusion should be obvious. In the absence of any convincing evidence for the efficacy of expensive nonorganic therapies, such as psychotherapy, the burden of justification falls on their proponents. Even if such therapies were the best treatment for *any* child, they might still be completely useless in terms of a community program, given our society's present allocation of funds for psychiatric treatment. If at some future time it is demonstrated that a new and expensive form of psychological treatment is more effective than current organic therapies, the question will be changed to how much our society is willing to pay for the best. That question is far off: at present we are not supplying enough of the adequate.

THE MANAGEMENT OF MBD CHILDREN: A CONCLUDING REMARK

I have come down rather heavily on the usefulness of psychotherapy with MBD children; I hope that I have not been unfair. The affect which must permeate the arguments has been generated by experience with these children. Unfortunately, raw experience cannot be transmitted; only its verbal summary can. I have worked with many families who have been either unhelped or hindered by psychological treatment alone.[28] I have had the real satisfaction, by the use of medication, of helping many MBD children and their families. Psychological treatment is a popular and accepted mode of treatment while drug treatment is not, but for those of us who are pragmatists the question is not what is popular but *what works*. There is considerable risk that future generations of psychiatrists will look back upon our modish psychological techniques of treatment with (hopefully, tolerant) amusement. We are so proud of our emergence from the bonds of superstition and belief in word magic, so smug about our elimination of demonology from the treatment of mental illness, that we must be particularly cautious lest we have placed our faith in new superstitions, formulas, and rituals. To progress beyond the primitive we must allow mere experience to contravene our faith in our ideas.

[28] See case histories, especially 2, "Eugene"; 3, "Thomas"; and 12, "Hal."

PART TWO

The Theoretical Basis of the MBD Syndrome

CHAPTER 6

A Psychological Theory

In attempting to understand the phenomenology of the MBD syndrome, it may be useful to consider the behavioral signs and symptoms as the results of both "primary" and "secondary" dysfunctioning. The term "primary" here refers to those behavioral abnormalities which are (1) the *more* direct and simple manifestations of the putative underlying cerebral or psychological abnormalities; (2) present in all instances of the syndrome; (3) incapable of further reduction at the same level of explanation;[1] (4) the postulates—that is, symptoms—from which all others may be derived (analogous to axioms in plane geometry, and like them, minimal in number). The term "secondary" here refers to symptoms which are reactions to, or attempts to compensate for, the primary symptoms.

These definitions of "primary" and "secondary" are most vague. The reasons are several. First, since MBD is a syndrome, there may be several different underlying defects, each with its own primary deficits. Second, even if all the different etiologies operate through a common pathway, we do not know enough of the operation of the mind to determine with *certainty* which of the observed abnormalities are casually antecedent and

---

[1] By analogy, consider the attempt to "understand" the functioning of the heart. At one level of abstraction its function as a pump may be explained in terms of its anatomy—its geometrical configuration and mechanical arrangements: one considers variables such as volume, volume change, the fluid properties of blood, etc. One may choose to consider variations in cardiac output, which is a "secondary" descriptive variable, in terms of such "primary" variables. In attempting to understand the heart's pumping action, one may also turn to an underlying level of abstraction and consider factors influencing the contractility of cardiac muscle. This level of abstraction constitutes a qualitative "jump," involving a discussion of the muscle's physiology and biochemistry, topics which may be regarded as more basic. In the consideration of MBD, the presenting signs may be considered "secondary" and thus as analogous to cardiac output; the "primary signs" that I am postulating—such as decreased experiencing of pleasure and pain—may be considered as on the same level of abstraction as the underlying anatomical characteristics of the heart; and the putative "basic" neurophysiological substructure may be considered analogous to the biochemistry and physiology of the heart.

which consequent. Nonetheless, it may be possible to make some educated guesses. The distinction between primary and secondary symptoms may be theoretically useful in directing our attention to those phenomena which are capable of psychological explanation and those which are not. The distinction may be practically useful in determining our therapy: we might expect to be unsuccessful in attempting to change reaction(s) to the primary effect(s); we would be unwise in attempting to treat the restitutive symptoms.

The following list may not be accurate and/or complete, but it may be helpful in illustrating this distinction. Among the primary symptoms I posit are the following: (1) decreased experience of both pleasure and pain (anhedonia, or more accurately "hypohedonia," and psychological hypalgesia); (2) a generally high and poorly modulated level of activation; (3) extroversion. I do not know if the above characteristics are the only primary defects and/or whether they themselves are derived from one or more still more "intrinsic" psychological defects.[2]

However, these three defects do seem to appear in most MBD children and can explain a large number of the other symptoms—that is, the other symptoms may be regarded as the consequence of the three postulated primary symptoms. Let me proceed by first discussing these primary reactions and then providing illustrations of the manner in which they generate the secondary reactions. The description of the secondary reactions will in turn lead to a description of the compensatory and restitutive mechanisms, and to a summarizing statement on the psychological theory. Finally, the psychological theory concerning the MBD child can lead to analogous theories concerning other psychiatric disorders; I shall conclude the chapter with speculations in this direction.

PRIMARY REACTIONS

Decreased Experience of Pleasure and Pain

Bentham described pleasure and pain as the sovereign masters of human existence. If MBD children do have a diminished experience of pleasure and pain, we should expect to see certain direct and indirect

---

[2] Obviously, "primary" and "secondary" are the end points of a continuum. Anhedonia might be due—as I shall speculate later—to underactivity of the positive reinforcing system, which underactivity might then be considered "primary." However, the underactivity of the positive reinforcing system might be due to defective amine metabolism, which might itself then be considered "primary." The term "primary" may be used at any given level of explanation, psychological, physiological, or biochemical, as referring to phenomena which can be explained only by appeal to a "lower" level of explanation. The discussion of "primary" symptoms in this chapter will be restricted to the psychological level of abstraction.

effects on their feelings and behavior. If we assume that the "need," the "hunger," for pleasure is as great in MBD children as it is in normal children but that the ability to experience pleasure is less, we would expect such children to be less satisfied by past, present, and anticipated pleasure. We would expect them to claim that things are not enjoyable and to be (1) difficult to please, (2) hard to satisfy, (3) insatiable for "good things"—love, attention, etc., (4) pleasure- and sensation-seeking— "daredevils," (5) looking for "kicks."[3] If we assume that these children experience less psychological pain, we would likewise expect them to be relatively less upset by present "negative" experience—censure, rebuff, punishment; and to show diminished anticipatory "negative" emotion— fear, anxiety.

If pleasure and pain are subjective experiences associated with (or manifestations of) underlying integrating forces, one would expect anhedonia and psychological hypalgesia to have additional behavioral consequences. Specifically, it is reasonable to assume that since pleasure is a subjective concomitant of positive reward (or reinforcement), the ability to experience pleasure parallels (and to at least some degree is a measure of) the sensitivity to positive reinforcement; and the diminished ability to experience pleasure should be associated with the diminished sensitivity to positive reinforcement. Similarly, it is reasonable to assume that since psychological pain is a concomitant of negative reinforcement, a diminished ability to experience such pain should be associated with a diminished sensitivity to negative reinforcement.

The consequence of the above line of reasoning is that MBD children should be less responsive to reward and punishment, to positive and negative reinforcement, to operant and avoidance conditioning.[4] These children should be less susceptible to social influence: they should be less easy both to push and to pull.[5]

[3] The fact that anhedonic individuals actively seek pleasure is probably a manifestation of a reasonably high energy level. Nonenergetic anhedonics would appear discouraged and depressed: they would not be attempting to compensate for that which they lacked. MBD children—who are both "hypohedonic" and energetic—seem to make active efforts to fill a void that they feel.

[4] Direct (laboratory) evidence supporting this assertion is not available and is very much needed.

[5] I have postulated that MBD children show a decreased susceptibility to learning by reward and punishment and that this decreased learning ability is secondary to a diminished ability to experience both pleasure and pain. Rado has hypothesized that schizophrenics are anhedonic. From clinical histories, it would seem that children destined later to become schizophrenic are anhedonic but not psychologically analgesic. They are unmoved by pleasure but controlled by anxiety. They are somewhat like the devout followers of fundamentalist faiths who Hume described as "being terrified, but not bribed into a continuance of their existence" (p. 740).

138 A Psychological Theory

Although one would therefore expect MBD children to be difficult to control by reward and punishment, one need not expect them to be impossible to control. Presumably, factors which strengthen the effect of positive reward should work as they do in normal children but to a lesser degree: according to Hullian learning theory, habit strength is, among other things, dependent upon the size of the reward. Since MBD children presumably experience a given reward as "less rewarding," one would expect that for them to maintain a high level of performance one would need more consistency of reward, larger rewards, more training trials. An anecdotal confirmation of this prediction is in the frequent report of teachers that an MBD child does poorly in general but "works very well with one-to-one attention" and much praise. More formal documentation is found in the literature dealing with reinforcement in the treatment of "hyperactive children." Likewise, factors that strengthen the effects of negative reinforcement should be helpful in controlling these children's behavior. Predictability and rapid administration of punishment should increase the effectiveness of negative reinforcement.[6]

Since parents seem less apt to use, or at least to be less aware of their use of, positive reward, they are more apt to *report* a child's unresponsiveness to punishment rather than his resistance to a reward. They are likewise more apt to report the more salient disturbing *indirect* consequences of the child's impaired ability to learn by negative reinforcement: recklessness, failure to be deterred by the painful consequences of acts ("failure to learn by experience"), diminished inhibition, decreased fear of social rebuff, decreased social anxiety, and less social poise. Careful historical inquiry will, I believe, usually elicit the less conspicuous—but theoretically equally important—diminished pleasure sensitivity and diminished responsiveness to positive reward.

In summary, the MBD child may be characterized and contrasted with the neurotic child as follows: the MBD child responds to social pressures as insensitively as if he were granite while fixing them like wax, while the neurotic child takes these impressions like wax and fixes them like granite.

Other authors have proposed theories linking the development of psychopathology to "conditionability" but have not linked "conditionability" to the activity and sensitivity of the reward and punishment system. Mednick (1962) has proposed that the basis of schizophrenia is an increased tendency to avoidance conditioning secondary to an increased experiencing of anxiety. Eysenck (1957) has proposed the existence of two polar personality types, the hysterical or extroverted and the dysthymic or introverted. The hysterical are postulated to manifest many of the behavioral characteristics of the MBD child: they condition with difficulty, are impulsive, and extroverted.

[6] See Zeilberger et al.'s (1968), report on the favorable consequences of the absolutely predictable use of an isolation room in controlling a very hyperactive child.

Generally High and Poorly Modulated Level of Activation

The characteristic described here is a somewhat vague and perhaps "neurometaphysical" concept. What I want to denote—by analogy—is a thermostat which is set too high and which also overshoots excessively in both directions.

The phrase "generally high activation" is a more abstract restatement of what is readily observable at the behavioral level. It is designed to permit inclusion of MBD children of normal activity and the small but important group of hypoactive MBD children. The phrase "poorly modulated" refers to an attribute which is less conspicuous but which is generally present. Both are postulated to be aspects of inadequate inhibition.

Generally High Level

The high level of activation, of course, is denoted by the term "hyperactive" and by such adjectives as "restless," "irritable," and so on. As noted in the chapter on symptoms, gross physical overactivity is difficult to document, but does often seem to be present.

Distractibility and inattentiveness seem to be related to the high level of activation. The reason for believing that these cognitive problems may be products of excessive activation comes from the observation of and subjective experience of adult patients. Anxious, hypomanic, and manic adults—all of whom may be perceived as overactivated—all manifest attentional changes similar to those seen in MBD children: the inability to fixate attention for long periods, an inability to "register" (forgetfulness), and increased distractibility. Like MBD children, anxious adults shift from one task to another; manic individuals shift from one subject or thought to another without completion. Early schizophrenia is believed to be a state accompanied or perhaps produced by increased activation. The change in subjective experiences of very early schizophrenics—which are seen in association with, and seem to parallel, their increased "excitability"—have been described by Chapman (1966). As such patients become more excited, they become increasingly unable to fix and focus attention, shut out the irrelevant, and discriminate the figure from the ground. The appearance of such MBD-like cognitive problems in direct relation to increased activation strongly *suggests* that in MBD children the attentional problems may also be the result of increased activation.

Poorly Modulated Activation

One aspect of poor modulation of activity level in MBD children is conspicuous and universally described—their overreactivity to stress. This overreactivity is described in such phrases as "low frustration tolerance," "temper tantrums," "rage outbursts," etc. The spontaneous variability that is another aspect of poor modulation is less often commented upon but when looked for is often found to be present: "His mood changes from one moment to the next. He's mercurial."

The last aspect of poor modulation of activity level that I wish to comment on is another that is infrequently reported spontaneously but which may be elicited with some frequency: the tendency of some MBD children to sleep either restlessly or particularly profoundly. This tendency is of additional interest because of the increased incidence of enuresis among MBD children. Studies of sleep patterns in enuretics (many of whom are presumably MBD children) have shown that they may have "disorders of arousal" (Broughton, 1968). Enuretics are difficult to arouse from nondreaming sleep and yet show an apparently excessive level of activation (as manifested by tachycardia) throughout sleep. The enuresis itself occurs not in dreaming sleep (REM sleep, Stage I sleep) but during arousal from nondreaming sleep. (This suggests that *specific* psychological factors[7] do not play a role in its etiology except insofar as they affect the general level of activation.) At any rate, the results of the physiological studies of sleep in enuretics correspond to parental reports regarding the sleep patterns of some MBD children.

That the excessive activity is a release phenomenon, a manifestation of a hypoactive inhibitory system, is suggested by two pieces of evidence: the appearance of the syndrome following destructive lesions of the central nervous system (e.g., encephalitis), and the response of the syndrome to stimulant drugs. The increased variability of response may also be seen as a function of the hypoactivity of a negative feedback system, diminished activity preventing modulation of response.

Extroversion

MBD children are frequently described as "outgoing," "forthright," and "socially aggressive." They are not described as "timid," "shy," or "afraid of strangers." It is unusual to elicit a history of separation anxiety. They do not seem to be concerned and occupied with their inner lives, although this is difficult to assess accurately.

Compared with the other two postulated "primary" characteristics, extroversion seems to be a "higher" level process—to represent more complex and "integrated" behavior. Nonetheless, extroversion does seem to have some biological basis. In dogs, Scott and Fuller (1965) have found

---

[7] That is, specific psychological factors apparently do not play a role in all forms of nocturnal enuresis. Early morning bed-wetting, loosely called "nocturnal," does seem related to psychological factors (Ritvo et al., 1969).

that different inbred species manifest more and less social timidity toward humans from an early age. The crucial longitudinal studies in humans are not yet available, but such evidence as is available does suggest that quality of social response is a variable in which individual differences may be noted at an early age and which tends to remain fairly constant over time. After an extensive review of the child development literature, Bell[8] concluded that during early and preschool years, level of activity and intensity of positive social response tend to covary in the same direction (i.e., children with a high activity level tend to be more socially assertive and vice versa).

In the field of psychopathology, even authors with disparate theoretical perspectives—such as Jung and Eysenck—have found it useful to postulate extroversion-introversion as a fundamental dimension of personality.

Another factor suggesting that a "basic" biological component contributes to extroversion is the MBD child's behavioral response to medication. Some MBD children when treated with small doses of d-amphetamine become shy, timid, socially withdrawn, less aggressive,[9] thoughtful, and occasionally preoccupied with fantasies. In a few instances children have become somewhat autistic (in the Bleulerian sense). That is, a drug that reduces activity level tends to reduce extroversion as well, suggesting that the two dimensions possibly share a common biological pathway. (With regard to the provocative fact that some MBD children become seemingly schizoid on d-amphetamine, more will be said later.)

The foregoing is an enumeration of the simpler manifestations of the putative primary dysfunctions. I would like now to consider a few of the secondary reactions.

SECONDARY REACTIONS: INTRAPERSONAL AND INTERPERSONAL

Intrapersonal Reactions: Cognitive and Personality Characteristics

Cognitive Characteristics

Under cognitive characteristics, two attributes will be considered: forced responsiveness and poor academic performance.

[8] Richard Q. Bell, personal communication. For example, Schaefer and Bayley's analysis (1963) of the Berkeley Growth Study finds a positive relationship between activity at one year and inattentiveness and distractibility at age 12. A high activity level between one and 3 years is associated with positive and negative extroversion in adolescence: social and friendly behavior, and hostile, irritable, and bold behavior, respectively.

[9] This is true for genetically aggressive rodents. Rats who will kill mice refrain from muricide when treated with amphetamine (Kulkarni, 1968).

An obvious and pervasive characteristic of the MBD child which may be a product of his inability to fix attention, is his forced responsiveness to both internal and external stimuli, which is manifested by both distractibility and perseveration. With the MBD child, as with an infant, striking external stimuli will interrupt a mental set. When he is told to perform a task he may start willingly enough and then forget to complete it; he abandons tasks in the middle. An irrelevant stimulus, a bright toy, an interesting noise, fixes his attention and "distracts" him from his task, holding his attention until another stimulus seizes it. These arresting stimuli may also come from within. The child's mental set, his internal "plan ahead," may also be interrupted by "ideas," "wishes," or drives which well up suddenly, disrupting the smooth performance and completion of extended tasks or behavior patterns. Parents frequently comment that the child has "wonderful attentiveness and is indistractible when *he wants* to do something." It is this persistence, or quasi stick-to-itiveness, which constitutes the perseverative behavior seen in many MBD children. This apparently incongruous persistence would seem to follow from the child's forced responsiveness to internal stimuli: when an internal stimulus occupies the center of the stage nothing else can reach the child. It appears that this seeming attentiveness is the other side of the coin of distractibility: that both are manifestations of a generally short duration of attention and excessive attraction to stimuli. Thus both distractibility and perseveration are products of an inability to attenuate the attractive power of internal and external stimuli, and are related to the postulated primary deficit concerning activity.

With regard to academic performance, it is possible that the poor learning ability many of these children show is another primary manifestation of the MBD syndrome. However, even if there are no primary contributions to learning inability, it is not surprising that these children learn poorly. A long attention span, a high frustration tolerance, and an eagerness to please are attributes which facilitate learning. One would anticipate that a child deficient in such attributes would not learn as readily as a child endowed with them.

These factors do not account for poor academic performance in all instances. In many children there exist, either primarily, or in addition to these problems, "special learning difficulties"—such as perceptual-cognitive characteristics of younger children, as manifested in difficulties of right-left discrimination, letter reversals, and mirror writing, and in test measures such as the Bender-Gestalt. The model presented here does *not* account for these difficulties.

Personality Characteristics

As has been implied in the descriptions of MBD functioning, certain personality characteristics have a marked association with MBD children.

1. Impulsivity. The epithet "impulsive," frequently applied to MBD children, can be seen as a compound of the primary deficits, possibly related to inhibitory defects arising from decreased reinforceability and activity malfunction. The cause of the children's lack of "inhibition" is problematic. Logically this lack of push could be due to either excessive "drive" or insufficient "control." "Control" is a metaphor that has no clear operational referents and is hard to measure independently (i.e., other than by signs of its absence). The disinhibition of these children does not *seem* to be satisfactorily explainable only by the postulated defective reinforcement mechanism. They do *seem* to have excessive "drive": they may have "poor braking" but it also seems as if their "motor is running too fast."

Subjective reports might be of some value in clarifying our thinking, but few children are good reporters. Kahn and Cohen (1934) do report on the subjective alterations in postencephalitic adults[10] who were characterized as having a "compulsion" to activity. These adults described themselves as "driven," but unlike the children many seemed able to "channel" their drivenness into areas other than motor activity—that is, some of these adults *did* possess apparently adequate controls with which they were able to mask their apparently independently increased level of drive.

These hints about the mechanism of impulsivity are quite vague. The hyperactive child's response to drug treatment may shed a few more glimmers of light on the problem. In psychoanalytic theory the term "controls" is generally used to refer to learned techniques for dealing with impulses. If we adopt this crude definition, how are we to interpret the increased "inhibition" which many children manifest with drug treatment? Probably as mediated not by cognitive modifications but by noncognitive ones, that is, not by an improved technique of drive channeling, but by diminished drive strength. It is this increased drive strength which I have subsumed under the vague abstract category of "generally high level of activation." Together with a defective reinforcement mechanism associated with "decreased pleasure and pain," the "high level of activation" may account for the "impulsivity" which is such a prominent characteristic of the syndrome.

2. Diminished identification. A striking and disturbing aspect of the

---

[10] It should be remembered that in children the disease sometimes produced a behavioral syndrome indistinguishable from idiopathic MBD.

MBD child's development is his failure, compared with other children, to assume the attitudes and values of his parents and subculture. It is evident that he is not unaware of or totally unaffected by them; the difference is in degree and is not qualitative. Like the felon with full knowledge of the law, the child is aware of the attitudes and values of others but does not absorb them nor act in accordance with them.

The assumption of the attitudes and values of significant others plays a crucial role in the socialization of the child. This process—variously designated as identification, internalization, or introjection—may occur under the influence of a variety of motives. Schafer (1968) lists at least 18 major motives—for example, the wish to preserve objects or to give them up, the wish to bolster or lower self-esteem, the wish to increase or relieve guilt, the wish to enhance or give up the subjective self. If anything is common to all of these motives it seems to be the intensity of the relationship between the child and the adult. Variables that affect the intensity of this bond should likewise affect the process of identification and hence the readiness with which attitudes and values are assumed.

It has been hypothesized that the intensity with which the MBD child experiences pleasure and pain is diminished. It will shortly be argued that this diminution accounts in part for the child's increased "independence" and a probably weakened affective tie between him and his parents. On the basis of Schafer's comments one would expect that such a weakened affective tie would be followed by diminished identification, with diminished superego and ego-ideal formation. That is, of course, what is seen in the MBD child.

The reaction of the MBD child to medication provides a clear insight into the dissociation between cognition and conation in the formation of superego and the ego-ideal. Following the administration of stimulant medication one observes the very rapid (and reversible) development of a superego: in an animalistic metaphor, the mule becomes a parrot. Medication obviously could not provide cognitive information but could only have supplied the willingness and/or eagerness to behave in accordance with already learned standards. These children have apparently been aware of the sanctioned norms of child behavior but have failed to behave in accordance with them. The information had been available; the control of behavior on the basis of that information had not. Prior to medication there had been a clear-cut dissociation between awareness of standards (both prescriptions and proscriptions) and whatever factors compel behavior to adhere to them. A satisfactory explanation of the action of medication is difficult to reach. To assert that it increases "inhibition" is no explanation but only an abstract restatement of an already known fact. To attribute the effects of medication to increased anxiety also seems unsatisfactory since these children sometimes seem anxious to begin with. (One could assert that they were "not anxious enough" but this would be begging the question.)

Whether a successful response to medication fosters (either on the short-term or long-term basis) an identification with positive values is less than certain. It seems as if it does: children appear increasingly to value and behave in accordance with parental "shoulds" as well as parental "shouldn'ts;" achievement and success may become highly prized values.

3. Negativism and stubbornness. Negativism and stubbornness are the product of several forces. First, for reasons already given, the child is unresponsive to social demands and hence is judged "willful." Second, negativism and stubbornness are devices for increasing a child's sense of autonomy and this sense may be impaired in a child who is excessively susceptible to external and internal stimuli and who is swayed by forces outside his control; stubbornness may be looked upon as a reaction formation to an inadequate sense of self-control. Lastly, negativism and stubbornness are standard passive mechanisms for fighting back (see the reference to passive-aggressive style in the discussion of interpersonal relations).

4. Immaturity. The epithet "immature," which is applied to these children, refers to their social ineptitude, their lack of internalization of social regulations and expectations, their deficient academic and (often) athletic skills. As mentioned, these features should not be viewed as regressive for they do not represent the child's returning to an earlier (and lower) level of functioning. They represent failure to have progressed, and if they disappear with time they justifiably earn the designation of "maturational lag."

5. Narcissism. All children are narcissistic. Language does not contain such similes as "generous as a child" or "altruistic as an infant." Nonetheless the MBD child may stand out as more "selfish" or "self-centered" than his fellows. His parents frequently report that "he's always wrapped up in himself," "he never thinks of others," "you can't get through to him." These attributes become more salient as he becomes older since the average adult at least feigns a modicum of altruism. The self-centeredness of the MBD child does not appear to be self-love—he is apt to have low self-esteem—nor is it a preoccupation with inner fantasies. It is the position of one who does not care much about other people or what they think.

The MBD child's narcissism and egocentricity can be explained in terms of his diminished dependency drives (needs), diminished proclivity to identify and take the position of the other, and diminished sensitivity to censure. One develops a consideration for the needs and rights of others— which is generally considered altruism or at least non-egocentricity—in part because of a desire to please or avoid the criticism of others, others being regarded as important. This position is strengthened by the repeated act of putting oneself consciously or unconsciously in the other's place. But what if one is insensitive? The armadillo would not hesitate to lead others through the briar patch and would be surprised at their accusations of his insensitivity.

In summary, the MBD child's egocentricity may be viewed as partly a product of his accentuated childlike characteristics and partly a product of his lack of dependency and his insensitivity to social reinforcement.

6. *Cross-sexual identification.* Certain features of the MBD syndrome— which are seen in a very few instances—may tend to foster the develop- ment of cross-sexual identification. In girls the reasons are obvious. Ex- cessive physical activity, a lack of docility, adventurousness, and irascibility are all characteristics which are more masculine than feminine. If the female who possesses these attributes likes baseball, football, and being a member of the "gang," she is likely to be perceived by adults, peers, and herself as a tomboy; she is more like and does fit in better with boys. If, for some reason she limits herself to traditionally more acceptable "fem- inine" pursuits, such as roller skating, jumping rope, or squabbling with her friends, she is more apt to escape being seen by others as masculine.

The possession of the above characteristics, the salient and usual char- acteristics of the syndrome, obviously would not foster a feminine identity in a boy. In my experience, effeminacy has been confined to the small *hypo*- active subgroup—boys who have particularly poor motor coordination, with resultant athletic ineptitude,[11] and have developed excessive instru- mental dependence. Poor motor performance may lead not only to rejection by a boy's peer group but also to a defensive assertion that such activities are unimportant; this disclaimer leads to decreased participation, worse performance, and still less acceptance; it is apt to be followed by a com- pensatory overvaluation of "neuter" or feminine activities. Excessive in- strumental dependence—having someone do "too many" things for him— is fostered by general inadequacy, but requires in addition the services of an oversolicitous mother. So aided, a boy is apt to develop less self-suffi- ciency than is considered sex-appropriate and to be categorized as a sissy and a "mamma's boy."[12]

7. *Guilt and anxiety.* MBD children do transgress more than is "nor- mal." If they have incorporated any societal standards they should and do

---

[11] See Anderson (1956), who reported that several of the male homosexual patients gave a history of being inept and clumsy, which caused them to be left out and clas- sified as "sissies" by both girls and boys.

[12] For exemplary case histories, see Levy's *Maternal Overprotection* (1943).

feel guilty—they are repeatedly acting in ways that they know are wrong.[13] They fit Mowrer's (1948) definition of a "pseudoneurotic" subgroup of neurotics. Mowrer perceives some neurotics not as oversocialized, hypermature persons who are inhibited in performing normal acts, but as partially socialized individuals who have been socialized enough to feel guilty for misdemeanors performed, but not socialized enough to fully control themselves. Their sense of guilt and fraudulence is, therefore, appropriate.

The anxiety that these children feel is likewise appropriate. They are the poor controllers of an unruly state. Aware that their controls are inadequate, they can accurately foresee that they are likely to act in ways that have resulted and will continue to result in rejection, rebuff, loss of love, and shame or guilt.

Whether the reactive (signal) explanation of anxiety is sufficient may be questioned. Bender (1949) feels that children with organic brain disease have profuse and diffuse nonspecific anxiety because of their "disorganization, the difficulty in relating themselves to reality, and the frustration in achieving normal maturation" (pp. 406–407). However, Bender is describing a group of organically damaged children *including schizophrenic children*. In my experience—which is considerably less extensive—such disabling anxiety is not seen in "pure" MBD children but only in those MBD children who have schizophrenic features as well.

8. *Social impulsivity—"acting up" and "acting out."* The common problem of asocial and antisocial behavior in MBD children can be understood largely in terms of the features already discussed. Poor impulse control, the impaired ability to identify, and a relatively decreased concern over the immediate consequences of transgression are all factors that predispose a child to behave in unacceptable ways, but these variables are probably not sufficient in themselves. To these factors may be added the low self-esteem and the feelings of rejection that these children have. Even these factors may not be sufficient but they do place a child at greater risk. One gets the clinical impression, however, that only a small fraction of MBD children do become seriously delinquent and that most such delinquents come from particularly noxious psychological environments.[14]

The motives for a given piece of "acting up," for example, stealing or promiscuity, are obviously extremely varied. The motivation for stealing

[13] "For the good I would I do not; but the evil which I would not, that I do." Romans 7:19.

[14] This view is favored by other psychiatrists, for example, Bender (1968). Noting that only a small fraction of MBD children—and children with other organic defects—become delinquents and that likewise only a small group of children from "delinquent-ogenic" environments become delinquent, she proposes that in general both sets of factors must be operative if serious delinquent behavior is to result.

may be a simple desire to have, a desire to have things with which to buy affection, an attempt to achieve status among peers, a search for a new method of obtaining excitement or avoiding boredom, retaliation, or an attempt to obtain attention or punishment. What is important is that most children do not steal compulsively and that many MBD children do. The dynamic factors promoting stealing are qualitatively the same in normal and MBD children. The differences are in intensity: the MBD child feels less loved, feels less status, feels more bored. To repeat, the factors involved in the "drive" toward acting out are not confined to the MBD child, but he is apt to have them to a greater degree and—far more important—he is not susceptible to the controlling influences which ordinarily serve to inhibit such behavior.

9. *Feeling of being unloved.* The feeling of being unloved is also veridical. MBD children are unpopular with their peers; they are rejected by their parents. Though charming in some respects they are often impossible in others. The frequent mild paranoia of these children is a predictable response of an immature (or regressed) individual to rebuff: "I am not at fault—he is."

10. *Low self-esteem.* The low self-esteem that is often seen in MBD children is not surprising. Children with the MBD syndrome perform poorly in areas in which successful performance is necessary for high self-esteem in childhood: in school, in peer relations, and—for boys—in athletics. In addition, because these children are difficult to socialize they do not behave in accordance with the parental prescriptions and proscriptions. The children may deny their concern over their performance but in more open moments they report that they are stupid and bad. Such self-perceptions are not neurotic, for the children *are* poor athletes, they *are* poor students, they *are* bad "sports," and they are the recipients of such comments as the following: "Why don't you ever pay attention? You could learn if you wanted to." "Why are you always a bad boy? Why don't you ever do what we want you to?" "If you want to play with your own rules don't play with us." In other words, the children's self-perceptions are accurate incorporations of the comments of adults and peers.

11. *Depression.* As indicated, the depressive symptoms seen in many MBD children are sometimes interpreted as "masked" depression, as manifestations or equivalents of or defenses against depression. As has been discussed in the chapter on etiology, the syndrome may occur as a reaction to circumstances that might be regarded as "depressing," but not commonly. Certainly many of the behavioral signs and symptoms of these children are depressive. Anhedonia and its more direct manifestations— boredom, ennui, pleasure-seeking—are important components of depression. Some of the secondary reactions already discussed are also symptoms

of depression: low self-esteem, feelings of being unloved, and guilt. The child may also have preoccupations or concerns about the illness or loss of loved ones. Whether these depressive features are symptoms of the *reaction to* the syndrome or intrinsic features of the syndrome is a question of more than hair-splitting importance—primarily because of its relevance to etiology.

There are good reasons for seeing these attributes, with the exception of anhedonia, as reactive. Anhedonia, it is agreed, is an intrinsic part of the syndrome. Sadness—a frequent if not an essential depressive characteristic—is generally not present. It is not present at the onset of a child's signs and symptoms and it seems to be absent rather than defended against. The other "depressive" symptoms—the low self-esteem, the sense of being unloved, the guilt—may be seen, of course, as accurate reflections of the opinions others hold of him. He can "justifiably" feel depressed: he is a failure, he is unloved, he is worthless. His fear of the loss of loved ones can be variously interpreted. One interpretation, consistent with the explanation of the syndrome as a depressive manifestation, would be as a concrete representation of a loss that has *already occurred* in fantasy: it would be argued that the depression which is manifested as MBD has been caused by the loss of love and is symbolized by death of the loved one. The alternative explanation, proposed here, is that because of his behavior the child both experiences and fears a loss of love, and this feared loss is concretely represented as a fear of death of the loved one.

Strengthening the view that the child's depression is a reaction to, rather than the cause of the behavioral difficulties, is the MBD child's response to effective medication. Following the initiation of therapy, there is often an interesting course of response. First—and rather promptly—the child's behavior improves. Following this behavioral improvement the child initially tends to become *increasingly* guilty, ashamed, and depressed over his past misdemeanors. After a period of time these self-recriminations disappear. The sequence—and the time lag—suggest a psychological working through, not a pharmacological response:[15] the reformed miscreant

---

[15] At this juncture, further theorizing suffers from the lack of an established theory of depression. The amphetamine-produced depression of the MBD child can be explained by still other mechanics. If, for example, one employs the model of depression as a manifestation of nonexpressed anger, the response to medication might be interpreted as follows: amphetamine inhibits the expression but not the intensity of the aggressive drive. Accordingly the aggressive feelings—still present—would be directed "in" not "out"; depression would be the outcome. Or—and this is a statement, not an explanation—amphetamine may, for pharmacological reasons, produce a biphasic response, first acting as a depressant and then as an antidepressant; when that "core symptom" is removed, the other manifestations of the syndrome disappear as well.

looks back with remorse upon his former crimes; after a period of "going straight" he is better able to live with himself.

12. Ego dystonicity. Many MBD children regard their misbehavior as due to forces in themselves which they cannot fully control. They do not generally acknowledge such feelings at first, and the examiner may overlook them. Not only do most of us—children included—tend to deny that there are seemingly forces in us that we cannot control, but also no one likes to acknowledge that these result in socially undesirable behaviors. Most children, particularly when brought for "behavioral" rather than subjective problems, deny the existence of any problems, and this is to be expected. As the child's confidence is won, and as he begins to expose his feelings, he often expresses his awareness of an unhappiness about his lack of self-control—frequently expressed as: "I don't know why I do it."

Interpersonal Relations

Interpersonal relations will be considered in terms of alterations of the child's behavior and alterations in the parents' behavior.

Alterations in Child's Behavior

One frequent complaint of parents is the child's excessive "independence." In part this term alludes to the child's insulation from the parents' control mechanisms and in part it refers to the child's diminished affectual dependence. If the tie to the parent is partly dependent upon the receipt of gratification from the parent,[16] one would expect these children to have weaker ties than "normal" children: one might assume that because of the partial anhedonia, a given amount of parental affection would be perceived by MBD children as smaller and generate a weaker tie than the same amount received by a "normal" child. If there is a minimal fixed amount of love (subjectively) which a child strives to obtain, one would expect an MBD child to demand more since he receives a "smaller amount" than he "needs." This *post hoc* prediction jibes with the facts. Such children (like deprived and orphanage children) seem to vacillate between indifference and excessive demandingness.

Another frequent mode of interaction between MBD children and significant others (parents, teachers, etc.) is the passive-aggressive style. The child's nonsocializability "pulls" exasperated demands from his parents. These parents are often perceived—by psychiatrists, psychologists, and social workers—as being extremely strict and punitive, and are often ad-

---

[16] This view is based on the learning theory and classical psychoanalytic hypothesis that the object is loved because it is the gratifier of instinctive needs. This hypothesis —and with it my interpretation—is questionable.

judged as being thus responsible for the child's behavior; it must be pointed out that such disciplinary measures might be adopted in reaction to the child's behavior.

The repertoire of techniques with which the weak may deal with the strong oppressor is limited, and passive resistance in the child is to be expected. Such behavior, unfortunately, is apt to generate a vicious cycle, and to become deeply entrenched.

Alterations in the Parents' Behavior

The MBD child is often a conspicuous and chronically difficult member of his family. Although parental patterns will differ, certain patterns that the child's behavior elicits are (*post hoc*) predictable and occur with considerable frequency.

As an infant, the MBD child is apt to be "colicky," insatiable, irritable, and unpredictable. His mother cannot relieve his tension and meet his needs. Depending on her confidence in her maternal abilities she is apt to feel more or less inadequate and deficient in the maternal role. This in turn may be expected to produce—and does produce—intensified nurturant efforts and/or increasing (and generally unconscious) rejection.

As the child becomes older, parental difficulties intensify. The child continues to be insatiable and demanding (because ungratified) and is as unrewarding as he feels unrewarded. Both reward and punishment are ineffective in discipline, and the parent is apt to feel angry, confused, frustrated, and baffled. Failure to find effective techniques frequently tends to make the parent experiment and vacillate. Excessive punitiveness tends to exacerbate the child's problem and tends to produce guilt in the parent, who then atones by being *more* lenient. This alternating pattern tends to aggravate the problem in a child who functions best in a *structured,* predictable environment (Bond, 1935). To compound the difficulties, the child's behavior often causes disagreement and dispute between the parents, each of whom accurately accuses the other of disciplining the child "poorly," that is, ineffectively. The resultant split favors the development of further familial psychopathology: the promotion of an alliance between the child and one parent with the extrusion of the other parent, the competition of the extruded parent and the child for the favor of the spouse, and so on— again in the manner of a vicious circle.

The possible complications include an area I have not even touched upon—the complex effects of interaction with siblings: the excessive attention the MBD child receives, the tacit—and not so tacit—unfavorable comparison with his sibs, his envy of them, and their resentment of him, to mention but a few.

The family imbroglios which MBD children both precipitate and react to are often, and most unfortunately, explained simplistically in terms of parental ineptitude—or worse. Most behavioral scientists are aware that correlation does not mean causation, at least in controlled experiments. But in human affairs the tendency to perceive interactions as unidirectional cause-and-effect relationships seems to be overwhelmingly strong. This view, that the child is a Lockean *tabula rasa,* who is entirely molded by his experiences and who does nothing to generate the experiences, is reflected both in behaviorism and in the American reading of psychoanalysis, which has tended to suppress very fundamental theses of Freud's: (1) children have congenital drives—whose strength varies constitutionally; (2) the child is an active agent who must be—against his protests—turned into a socialized being; (3) the child's behavior—for example, during the Oepidal phase—has typically predictable effects on his family. Whatever the historical antecedents of the unidirectional model of psychological causation, its utilization seems "natural," as does the tendency to see *all action as psychologically motivated.*

It is most important to consider that (1) abnormalities seen in the parents may be a manifestation of a genetic illness in them and may or may not be a psychogenic contributor to the illness in the child, and (2) psychological deviance in the parent may be a *response to* deviance in the child.[17] Angry children breed resentful parents; confusing children breed confused parents; ungratifying children breed disappointed parents.[18]

The theoretical attribution of responsibility has great practical consequence. If the parent is seen as the major contributor to a child's problems, it is the parent who receives the major brunt of the therapeutic assault (in both senses of the word). The ultimate clinical insult is apt to be iatrogenic when the parents, with subtlety or otherwise, are confidently informed by a mental health worker that they are *the cause* of their child's problems. Such "information" will reinforce the parents' guilt, intensify their defensiveness, and increase their sense of inadequacy; it can prove most psychonoxious, both compounding the problem and driving the parents away from

[17] Failure to include these possibilities has contributed to much of the murk in studies attempting to evaluate the roles of nature and nurture in schizophrenia. For a further elaboration see Wender et al. (1968).

[18] A naturalistic test of this hypothesis has been made by Margolis and Wortis (1956), who studied the parents of children with cerebral palsy. The parents were found to be overprotective, controlled by the child, afraid to thwart him, unduly restrictive of his activities, and occupied with feelings of guilt, inadequacy, and ambivalence. A re-inspection and re-interpretation of data purporting to show the effect of the child on the parent may be found in Bell (1968). Concerning the effects of the postencephalitic child on his parents, Bond (1932) observed that such children's behavior was "exactly calculated to bring out the most 'intense emotional reaction in the families' unfortunate enough to be exposed to the children" (p. 311).

more useful intervention. The last portion of the spiral occurs with sufficient frequency to be considered a common part of the presenting picture.

Before concluding, I wish to make it entirely clear that I do not feel that all the problems seen in the parents of MBD children are either simply reactive or the result of a vicious circle. Clinically, it appears that *many* (not all) of the parents of MBD children were seriously inadequate, immature, or impulsive individuals long before they had to contend with their children. It is my bias—supported by Safer's study (1969) of MBD children and their sibs who had been reared separately—that these psychiatric difficulties in the parents are the manifestations of a biological abnormality which is genetically transmitted to their offspring, in whom the disorder appears as the MBD syndrome. The subgroup of parents who are inadequate, impulsive, and infantile is a group most readily affected by difficult children and least equipped to provide the necessary well-structured family environment which these children require. In these families it seems that the parental behavior—which is correlated with both their own and their offsprings' genotype—interacts with the children's problems in a maximally disadvantageous manner.

COMPENSATORY AND RESTITUTIVE MECHANISMS

A number of common behavior patterns of the MBD child—which are not characteristic of him alone—may be viewed as restitutive and defensive. These behaviors, attempts at psychological homeostasis, become problems when they become excessive in degree of rigidity. A partial list would include the following: provocative behavior, attention-seeking behavior, "camouflaging behavior" (after Thomas et al., 1968), withdrawal, and various neurotic defenses.

Provocative and attention-seeking behaviors tend to overlap somewhat since what provokes inevitably gains attention. (The reverse, however, is not true.) In addition to being a mechanism of attention-seeking, provocation is to varying degrees a method of disguised attack. The MBD child is not only likely to engage in increased assault (e.g., bullying or domineering behavior) but is also more prone to react. In addition to making use of obvious expressions of anger and frustration, such as tantrums and direct assaults, he is apt to develop more muted techniques of venting such emotions. In older children provocation often takes the form of the "passive-aggressive" behavior discussed above.

Attention-seeking without vengeance is almost ubiquitous among MBD children. They are frequently described by teachers as being "class clowns" and by their parents as "doing anything for attention." Both sets of behaviors can reasonably be seen as the product of low self-esteem, a failure to receive interpersonal gratification through the normal channels of successful adaptation, and the normal need to receive approval and recognition. What is abnormal is not the technique chosen but the extent to which it is utilized. Its excessive employment is understandable when we realize that it is one of the few techniques by which the child may obtain any form of gratification from others.

"Camouflaging," or concealing behavior, is self-explanatory in both character and motivation. The MBD child is a frequent wrongdoer and like other wrongdoers is apt to excuse, lie, and conceal.

Withdrawal is not a common compensatory device of MBD children. As has been hypothesized, their primary proclivity is approach, not avoidance. Sometimes, particularly among older children whose behavior has been particularly obnoxious to others, a continued history of rebuff leads to defensive withdrawal. Such children are more likely to be misanthropic than withdrawn into themselves—it is not that they seek their own company but that they avoid the company of others. As I have mentioned, this mechanism may be more common among MBD girls than MBD boys; it would seem that the mechanism of withdrawal would be more readily available to less extroverted types and this would favor its employment by girls.

Neurotic defenses are not the prerogative of the functionally afflicted alone. As mentioned, anxiety and guilt ("realistic" in origin) are frequent concomitants of the MBD syndrome. Defenses against consciousness of deviance may manifest themselves as symptoms. The denial, rationalization, or projection of responsibility is very common. A large fraction of the full panoply of defense mechanisms can be employed by the MBD child; the dynamics of some seem similar to those found in the organically impaired adult. For example, the compulsiveness described by Goldstein (1942) in brain-damaged patients is quite clearly seen in some MBD children (it is also frequently seen in schizophrenic children). In my experience such compulsiveness has appeared only in well-organized families with a compulsive life style; but in these families the MBD child has been described as being the most compulsive member. It would seem that his compulsiveness is of the nature of a reaction formation to the inwardly perceived lack of structure and control, and it seems to fulfill the same function here that it does in schizophrenic and brain-damaged adults—that of providing structure and certainty and thus reducing anxiety.

A SUMMARY NOTE ON PSYCHOLOGICAL CAUSATION OF MBD

It is important to emphasize the intricate tangle that is produced by the interaction of temperament and experience. It is logically important and extremely difficult to distinguish between impaired functioning due to current neurophysiological difficulties and that which is the result of cumulative experience in earlier psychological development. The MBD child or adolescent is often seen by a prospective therapist when he already has had considerable psychological experience, which has itself been produced and influenced by complex interrelationships among subjective experience, objective environment, and physiology. For example, conspicuous and nonendearing qualities of many MBD infants would tend to impair the mother-child relationship from the beginning. Irritability, insatiability, and unpredictability do not reinforce the mother in her child-rearing efforts, but rather tend to weaken her ties to the infant. Whether or not the child outgrows these characteristics, their presence has affected his mother in ways that will continue to affect him. In any such case it is possible that even if all the apparently neurophysiological abnormalities of infancy disappeared at an early age, many of the behavioral difficulties seen currently could be the indirect product of the earlier neurophysiological abnormalities rather than their current manifestation. The child's old attitudes—the psychological product of the earlier physiological deviation—and the reaction patterns they produced in the parent might both persist on the basis of "psychological momentum."

The complex tangle may not be unravelable but sometimes may be cuttable. When drug treatment is effective it gives one some insight into the psychological as opposed to the physiological fixation of habits. If medication is employed and patterns persist one is at a logical loss: persistence might be due either to the drug's inability to change the putative physiological abnormality or it *might be due* to a "psychological overgrowth" which remains unaffected while the underlying physiology is affected. When signs and symptoms do disappear—as they often do—it can be inferred that they were maintained solely by a current physiological abnormality. Finally, when symptoms are initially abated and continue to remit over time, one may infer that the behavioral abnormality has a current physiological basis (which responds immediately to treatment) and also a learned component which may be gradually unlearned when its physiological props are removed. This pattern is frequently seen clinically and may account for the effectiveness of short-term drug treatment.[19]

[19] Drug treatment may institute a "virtuous cycle" (Wender, 1968). Although such benefit may be attributed to a placebo effect (e.g., McDermott, 1965), it is equally tenable that drug treatment interrupts a fixed pattern that is partially dependent on physiology and allows the appearance and development of more adaptive behavior patterns.

THE THEORETICAL RELATIONSHIP OF MBD TO OTHER PSYCHIATRIC DISORDERS

The following discussion is both frankly speculative and tangential to the main body of argument already presented. The issue to be discussed is whether the model posited for the MBD syndrome has any bearing on other psychiatric disorders.

Two interwoven theses will be advanced: (1) that the dimensions posited to account for the MBD syndrome provide useful dimensions for classifying other psychiatric syndromes; (2) that the response of MBD children to medication sheds some light on the possible biochemical basis of neurosis. Special questions that arise with reference to schizophrenia will also be explored. The tangential excursion will conclude by relating the theories advanced here to other theories of psychopathology.

In accounting for the manifestations of the MBD syndrome it was found useful to posit three major dimensions of quantitative variation: (1) the ability to experience pleasure and pain (and the susceptibility to conditioning); (2) activation level (and the ability to inhibit cognitively); (3) extroversion-introversion. The first of these dimensions will be explored here. With the MBD child, the impaired ability to experience pleasure and pain and the impaired conditionability move in parallel: they are both decreased to begin with and often they are both simultaneously increased by stimulant drugs. There are some clinical data, as will be discussed later—that suggest that the two systems might vary independently, that is, that people might have various combinations of high or low attributes on the two dimensions. There might be individuals with an increased susceptibility to conditioning (reinforcement) and either an increased or a decreased ability to experience pleasure and pain, or there *might* be individuals with a decreased susceptibility to conditioning and either an increased or a decreased ability to experience pleasure and pain. Let us examine the varying possibilities, as shown in Table 6. First, it is obvious that all the represented cells are not filled. Some cells are left empty since the author could think of no psychiatric syndromes possessing certain attributes. (What psychiatric *syndrome* is characterized primarily by an increased ability to experience both pleasure and pain? (What personality type is characterized by a decreased ability to experience both pleasure and pain and an increased susceptibility to reinforcement?[20])

[20] Although some cells do not characterize specific psychiatric syndromes, they may characterize certain personality types. Decreased ability to experience pleasure, an increased ability to experience pain, and a decreased sensitivity to reinforcement might describe the campus rebel. Or an increased ability to experience pleasure, a decreased ability to experience pain, and an increased sensitivity to reinforcement might describe the inspirational personality type.

Table 6. Theoretical Combinations of Susceptibility to Conditioning and Ability to Experience Pleasure and Pain[a]

| | | Ability to Experience Pleasure or Pain Increased (↑) or Decreased (↓) | | | |
		Pleasure ↑ Pain ↑	Pleasure ↑ Pain ↓	Pleasure same or ↓ Pain ↑	Pleasure ↓ Pain ↓
Susceptibility to conditioning (reinforcement)	Increased	. . .	. . .	Cell 2	. . .
	Decreased	. . .	Cell 1	. . .	Cell 3

[a] Diagnostic types *might* be related to the cells as follows: Cell 1, hypomanic; Cell 2, schizoid, obsessive, depressive, some "mixed neurotic"; Cell 3, MBD child and MBD child grown up.

What of the occupied cells? What groups of individuals constitute the three categories?

Cell 3 is occupied by the MBD child and the MBD child grown up: the impulsive character neurosis; the emotionally unstable and immature personality; the sociopath.

Cell 1, characterized by a diminished ability to experience pain, a decreased susceptibility to reinforcement, and an increased ability to experience pleasure, *might* constitute the attributes of the hypomanic. "Might" is an important qualification since it is questionable whether hypomanics do experience pleasure more intensely or whether *they seek it more furiously because they experience it less* (which is summarized in the familiar dynamic formulation that "mania is a defense against depression"). If manics do not experience pleasure more intensely they might be included in category 2.

The "Contra-MBD Syndrome"

The naturally occurring combination of attributes that is summarized in Cell 2 seems to characterize several diverse pathologies, which can be subjected to the following explanatory analysis. If, as will be discussed in the section on biochemistry, the MBD syndrome can perhaps be attributed to the hypoactivity of certain functional systems, one is inclined to ask what the consequence of hyperactivity of these systems would be. It is reasonable to suppose that if hypoactivity of these hypothetical neurophysiological systems leads to diminished psychological pain perception, decreased sensitivity to reinforcement, distractibility, and extroversion, then excessive activity of the *postulated* system(s) might lead to an increased perception of pain (and possibly pleasure), increased susceptibility to reinforcement, nondistractibility, and introversion. The combination of these qualities is characteristic of several *seemingly* disparate psychiatric entities: depressive, obsessive, schizoid, and some forms of "mixed neurotic" characters. These varying types of patients all appear to be characterized by easy conditionability. The concept of someone who "learns too quickly" and cannot forget overlaps many authors' formulations of the concept of neurosis. The neurotic is variously described as a person who fixates, as a person who cannot unlearn and so continues to behave in a manner once adaptive but no longer realistic, as a person who cannot "extinguish" behavior that is no longer appropriate. All of these characterological types have several features in common. The schizoid (particularly the child) "learns too well"—he is an "easy" (i.e., compliant, readily trainable) child—he readily learns to develop (conditioned) anxieties and phobias. He is, as Rado has described him, "anhedonic": he does not readily experience pleasure or, perhaps, too readily experiences pain. The obsessive is considered a different species, but he may be a member of the same genus: Sullivan observed that the obsessive was a first cousin to the schizophrenic. The obsessive's diminished ability to experience pleasure is not usually directly noted: it is indirectly noted in the stereotyped dynamic assertion that these patients, like manics, often seem to be "defending against depression," which means descriptively (not inferentially) that depressive features are often present, and that depressive behavior is oozing out along the edges. The susceptibility of the obsessive to reinforcement is recognizable in his being oversocialized: he is—impulses aside—a "goody-goody" grown up, a rigid, law-abiding individual "obsessed" with shoulds and should nots. Lastly, there is the depressive character. Most of the comments addressed to the obsessive apply to the depressive character as well. The descriptive psychiatric link between the obsessive and the depressive consists not only in "masked depression" of the obsessive, but in the often stated and plausible assertion that the premorbid character structure of the endogenous depressive is obsessive in character.

Cell 2, which is occupied by what may be ponderously designated as the "contra-MBD syndrome" (CMBD), carries considerable, apparently dissimilar, pathological baggage. Two points are in order. First, the polar opposite of the MBD patient should have an *increased* ability to experience pleasure, but CMBD individuals apparently are not so blessed. While they do experience increased pain, it is not obvious that they experience increased pleasure. One could argue—circularly—that they do but that it is concealed by the increased pain susceptibility. This might be true but it is *ad hoc,* circular, and not very readily testable. Second, most patients are diagnostically impure. Definitions of diagnostic categories may be clear and distinct enough but few patients appear to read textbooks of descriptive psychiatry. It is more common to find individuals with mixed neuroses than those with "pure" neuroses. One finds individuals with obsessive, depressive, and schizoid characteristics, but generally not in pure form. Thus, in grouping apparently dissimilar states together, we may not in fact be "lumping" dissimilar individuals together; the names apply to pure instances while the usual patient is a hybrid. Individuals in the same category may vary because of disparate accidentals (i.e., not essential) features. Members of the same category need logically only have some essential defining characteristics in common. Cows, goats, and yaks are all ruminants. The theory advanced does not attempt to account for everything: it points out similarities among these groups; there are differences which it cannot and does not attempt to explain.

In the hypothesis that the "CMBD" syndrome might be seen as an overactivity of the neurochemical systems in question whose underactivity conceivably produces MBD, a theoretical difficulty worth repeating is that the two are not exact opposites. The CMBD is more susceptible to conditioning and more sensitive to pain but he is *apparently* no more sensitive to pleasure. The meaning of this fact is not clear: stimulant drugs (methylphenidate) increase the susceptibility to conditioning in adults (Schneider and Costiloe, 1957) while generally producing a sense of euphoria (and possibly increased pleasure responsiveness).

Schizophrenia and MBD

In the chapter on prognosis, studies were reviewed which suggested that the MBD syndrome might at times be an antecedent of schizophrenia. If one speculates that schizoidness is a CMBD characteristic, how can it be that in some instances MBD children become schizophrenics?

There are two important considerations in answering the question. The first is factual; not only do MBD children seem to be at greater risk for schizophrenia, but it is problematic if shy, withdrawn children—often called "schizoid"—are at greater risk for the illness.[21] The second point involves an attempt to see the similarities—if any—between the two syndromes, for certainly schizoidness does appear to be quite "un-MBD-like." Schizoid patients are stereotyped as introverted rather than extroverted, and quiet rather than active, and are here described as sensitive to conditioning rather than refractory to it. However, part of the schizophrenic syndrome—

---

[21] Robins (1966) found that shy, withdrawn children were not at appreciably greater risk for later mental illness than were controls.

borderline states—is quite MBD-like. Many borderline, ambulatory, "pseudoneurotic" schizophrenics[22] do have MBD characteristics. They may be perseveratively object-seeking, extroverted (although perhaps pseudo-social), behaviorally active (sometimes frenetically so), and unable to check their own behavior or thoughts (i.e., insensitive to inhibition whether from self or others). The cognitive disabilities of these patients also overlap those of the MBD child: undirected, desultory thinking which lacks goal orientation and persistence.

Some MBD characteristics that obviously do not overlap borderline schizophrenic characteristics are the more gross psychotic abnormalities (the Bleulerian "secondary" attributes such as delusions and hallucinations). These attributes are not explained by the above arguments. It should be emphasized that these secondary symptoms are neither essential to the diagnosis of schizophrenia nor peculiar to that diagnosis.

MBD and Mowrer's Theory of Neurosis

It has been implied that neurosis (the CMBD syndrome) and the MBD syndrome constitute polar opposites: the overconditionable, oversocialized and the underconditionable, undersocialized. As mentioned, Mowrer (1948) has theorized that many "neurotics" are not excessively socialized and inhibited but instead are periodically undersocialized and disinhibited, that is, that some neurotics have patchy or occasional MBD behavior. Their anxiety and guilt, he argues, stem not from repressed drives but from awareness of *expressed* drives. This sort of neurotic is anxious from a fear of disclosure of acts rather than wishes. He is anxious about being found out and guilty about what he has done. He is the opposite of the "criminal from a sense of guilt"—he is, so to speak, guilt-ridden from a sense of criminality. Such persons are unsocialized enough to periodically transgress and socialized enough to be concerned about their transgression. Their inhibitory clutch slips periodically, they act up, and subsequently feel fearful and regretful. Mowrer's suggested technique of treatment is not disinhibition and derepression, but (1) the act of confession to relieve pain from past transgressions, and (2) the strengthening of controls to prevent further transgressions.

The prevalence of Mowrer's "impulsive pseudoneurotic" in the potpourri

---

[22] Although the question of whether borderline schizophrenics should be included in the syndrome of schizophrenia is sometimes considered debatable, recent evidence indicates that they should be. Borderline schizophrenics share genetic factors with core schizophrenics: the relatives of core (process) schizophrenics have an increased prevalence of borderline schizophrenia even when reared apart. For a summary, see Wender (1969a).

of neurosis and character disorders is unknown. However, it seems clear that the MBD syndrome does contribute to this diagnostic category. Should Mowrer's description apply to a significant portion of neurotic character problems, the MBD syndrome would be of increasing explanatory relevance.

Conclusion: Intersection with Other Theories of Psychopathology

In current psychoanalytic theorizing, a considerable fraction of serious psychopathology is conceptualized under two dimensions: (1) dependency-depression-orality; (2) ego strength. It is of interest that starting from a completely different vantage point, descriptive child psychiatry and comparative psychology, the chain of reasoning presented here has led to postulation of very similar dimensions of function and dysfunction. The postulated underactivity of the pleasure-pain system and the reinforcement system generates difficulties which may be categorized as: (1) disordered interpersonal relations characterized behaviorally by excessive object-seeking and diminished object attachment, and subjectively by a sense of insatiability; and (2) a weakness of "ego strength" whose specific attributes are deficient inhibitability and an inability to postpone gratification, to withstand frustration, or to stay impulses. The second postulated malfunction, that of the activation-inhibition system, leads to further defects in "ego strength"—the inability to think in an abstract, planful, detached manner (i.e., in a fashion characterized as possessing "secondary process" attributes).

One purpose of this addendum has been to show that the overlapping of the MBD syndrome and various other psychiatric syndromes is not only a fact, but a fact that makes some sense. A sketchy delineation of the manner in which the postulated defects might interact to form other psychiatric syndromes has been presented; the details can be supplied in a variety of ways. Whether a correct picture will be drawn is a different matter; the diligent filling in of details may result in the construction of a creature that never was, a psychiatric chimera.

A second intention has been to sketch out the negative state, the CMBD syndrome, an entity which appears to overlap the area of neurosis. If this "entity" is the phenomenological inverse of the MBD syndrome, it *might* be the biochemical inverse as well, so that a biochemical model of the one would shed light on the biochemical nature of the other as well.

CHAPTER 7

A Physiological Theory: Some Suggestions for a Neurological and Biochemical Model of the MBD Syndrome

The fact that amphetamine (and other stimulants and antidepressants—methylphenidate, imipramine, amitriptyline) has a quieting effect on MBD children is of some interest, but a characteristic of considerably greater interest—and one that is generally unrecognized—is its effect on complex psychological functioning. Many reversible poisons (ether, alcohol) are capable of quieting—often while impairing consciousness and "higher mental functioning" (impulse control, secondary process thinking, etc.). A few agents are capable of helping an individual to return from an impaired to a previous, more or less normal, level of functioning. In the latter category would be included the actions of phenothiazines on acute schizophrenic reactions, minor tranquilizers on behavior impaired by anxiety, the tricyclic and MAO inhibitor antidepressants on some psychotic depressions. To the best of my knowledge one aspect of the drug action of certain stimulant drugs (amphetamine, methylphenidate) on MBD children is unique: they produce immediate psychological growth; while the drug is active children may demonstrate age-appropriate psychological functioning which they have never attained previously. The unfortunate usage of the term "anti-regressive" to describe the action of the drug obscures the unusual effect. Such children are not regressed—they have never progressed as they should; these children are, so to speak, psychologically retarded and the unique effect of these stimulants is to produce temporary psychological maturation.

The class of drugs that are effective in treatment and the nature of the behavioral changes produced *suggest,* respectively, a biochemical abnormality in several of the subgroups of these children and a possible neurophysiological localization of the biochemical lesion. Specifically my hypotheses are as follows: (1) MBD children have an abnormality in the

163

metabolism of monoamines: serotonin (5-HT), norepinephrine (NE), or dopamine (DA) (see Figure 5). (2) This biochemical abnormality affects behavior by the impairment produced in (a) the reward mechanism of the brain and (b) the activating system of the brain.

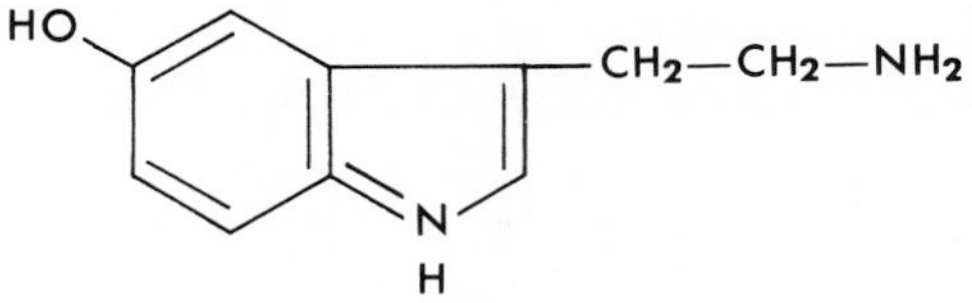

5—Hydroxytryptamine (Serotonin, 5-HT)

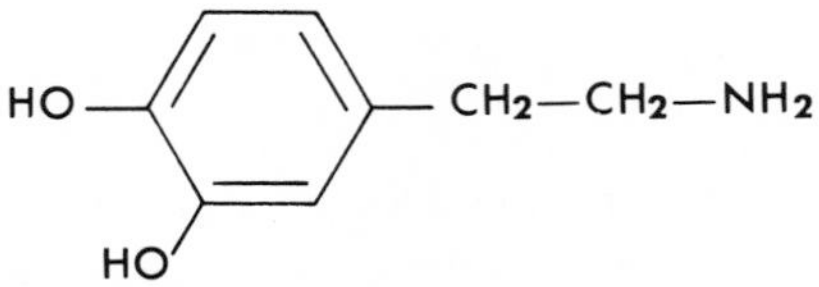

Dopamine (DA)

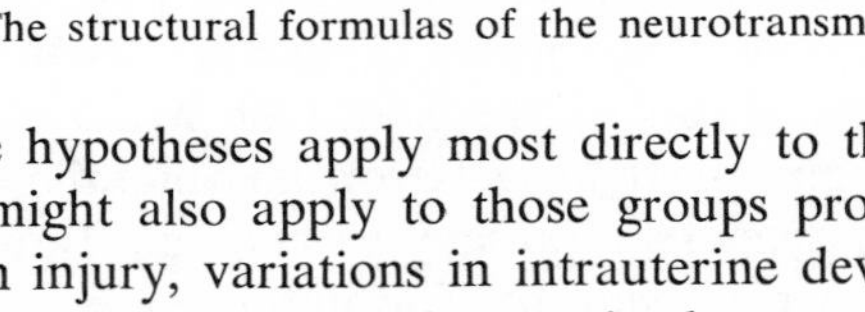

Norepinephrine (NE)

Figure 5.   The structural formulas of the neurotransmitters.

Although the above hypotheses apply most directly to the putative genetic subgroup, they might also apply to those groups produced by fetal maldevelopment, brain injury, variations in intrauterine development, and psychological privation. Hypoxic brain damage in the premature newborn *may* impair reward areas;[1] postencephalitic brain injury can semi-selectively affect the reticular[2] activating system; Mongolism, a disorder produced by

---

[1] Towbrin (1969) has shown that such damage in the premature newborn is associated with brain damage located primarily in the deep strata—particularly the periventricular areas—and not the cortex. Since the structures subserving the reward system are (as will be discussed later) in these areas, it is possible that they are particularly subject to injury from such damage.

[2] For example, the extreme somnolence seen in von Economo's encephalitis was associated with brain-stem damage.

chromosomal abnormalities, is associated with metabolic abnormalities. Logically the fetal maldevelopment subgroup of MBD might likewise be associated with enzymatic abnormalities. Similarly, as was noted in the chapter on etiology, intrauterine variation, and psychological privation may be associated with alterations in brain chemistry.

The suggestive data supporting the hypotheses come from animal experimentation whose relevance depends on the legitimacy of extrapolation from animal to man. Such extrapolation—both in the biological and the behavioral spheres—is of questionable validity, but since the data are being adduced *only to suggest, not to prove,* the question of "legitimacy" may be waived. The biological data are assumed to be isomorphic, the same mechanisms applying in animal and man, and animal behavioral analogues of the MBD syndrome are used.

I have suggested that two primary abnormalities of behavior in MBD children are (1) their diminished experience of pleasure and pain—which is paralleled by a diminished susceptibility to positive and negative reinforcement, and (2) an excessive and poorly modulated level of activity. This chapter will present evidence for a possible biological basis for these behavioral abnormalities. The chapter will also examine evidence pertaining to inherited differences in such behavior, and will consider possible reasons for the paradoxical response to certain drugs.

REINFORCEMENT DATA

I have presented clinical evidence that MBD children behave in ways consistent with a diminished sensivity to negative and positive "external" rewards. Not only do these children fail to respond to "external" rewards, but they also appear to fail to respond to or to have an "internal" system of reward. These are not children who strive to comply with socially sanctioned values or standards; they do not appear to strive to control, change, or perfect themselves. Such failure to learn adequately and to behave acceptably might theoretically be either cognitive or "motivational." They might either fail to understand others' expectations, or understand them but be unwilling to comply with them. A third possibility is that they might understand the expectations but be unable to comply with them. The prompt response to stimulants in the absence of an opportunity for additional learning indicates that the defect is *not* cognitive. Children will suddenly strive to behave in accordance with rules they have heard but have never previously acted upon—a phenomenon parallel to "latent learning" in animal experiments. Apparently the child has already "heard" and learned the relevant relationships between acts and consequences, but has previously not evidenced his awareness by his behavior; under medication such awareness of these relationships does influence his behavior.

I have phrased the impairments of MBD children in terms of reinforcement theory because such phraseology permits immediate—if unjustified—translation to an animal model. The learning theory to be employed is the so-called "two-factor" theory of learning which posits separate characteristics for operant (instrumental, Skinnerian) conditioning and Pavlovian (classical) conditioning. A two-factor theory of learning asserts that in the operant mode of learning, behavior followed by the presentation of a positive reinforcer ("reward," e.g., food) should be more apt to occur in the future while that followed by a negative reinforcer ("punishment," e.g., electric shock) should be less apt to occur. Similarly, behavior followed by the removal of a negative reinforcer (e.g., escape from or avoidance of shock) should be positively reinforced and more apt to occur while that followed by the removal of a positive reinforcer should be less apt to occur. The behavior whose frequency is affected by these reinforcers is referred to as "operant behavior." In the classical conditioning paradigm, a stimulus (conditioned stimulus, CS) when paired with an unconditioned stimulus (US) acquires the "power" of eliciting the same response (unconditioned response, UR) that the unconditioned stimulus had. The CS then can produce a "conditioned response," a CR. For example, a light (CS) repeatedly paired with an electric shock (US) will acquire the "power" of producing the same response (UR) that the US did. If the electric shock produced increased heart rate, sweating or "anxiety," the light will tend to have the same effect. The light would then be the CS, and increased heart rate, sweating, and "anxiety" would be the CR.

Using the two-factor theory, the postulated psychological "lesion"—diminished sensitivity to reinforcement—might occur in either type of conditioning or in both. In the operant mode, impairment of such learning could be due to an impairment of the reinforcement mechanism. Subjectively we might expect the individual to perceive pleasure and pain to a diminished degree, although he might perceive normally and still have a defect in the reinforcement mechanism operationally, normally effective reinforcers being ineffective.[3] The second locus of possible impairment might be in classical conditioning. Under most circumstances, in humans operant behavior is generated and maintained not by "primary" (unlearned) reinforcers but by "secondary" (learned) reinforcers. Examples of primary reinforcers are food, water, and sexual contact, while some

---

[3] It should be noted that a postulated operational defect in the reinforcement mechanism is different from temporary circumstances in which stimuli that are usually reinforcing may not be: for example, food will not reinforce an animal that has eaten to satiety.

examples of secondary reinforcers are praise, approval, or money, which some social learning theorists would assert are reinforcing because of a learned association with primary reinforcers. Presumably the efficacy with which such associations are learned varies, and a child with an impaired ability to form such associative connections would have diminished social conditionability. Obviously, therefore, failure to learn in an operant situation with secondary reinforcement might be produced not only by a failure in the operant process itself, but also by an impairment in the classical conditioning process that has prevented the secondary reinforcer (e.g., praise) from acquiring a reinforcing effect.

To be adequately explanatory, experimental data would eventually have to specify impairment in either or both of these two behavioral mechanisms.

In the initial search for supportive evidence, I have considered an animal as having some important behavioral characteristics of the MBD child if: (1) the animal conditioned with difficulty; (2) this behavioral deficit was reduced when the animal received amphetamines. The data cited do not, in many instances, permit a discrimination between the two possible sites of impairment discussed above. The reader should bear this in mind while evaluating the data.

The evidence to be presented describes the neuroanatomical and biochemical substrate of reinforcement, the behavioral effects of brain lesions, and the behavioral effects of biochemical alterations of neurohumors.[4]

The Neuroanatomical and Biochemical Substrate of Reinforcement

Beginning with the discovery by Olds and Milner (1954) that a rat's behavior could be reinforced by electrical stimulation of the brain, there has been an accumulation of evidence concerning the anatomical locus and neurohormonal characteristics of the positive reinforcement system of the brain. Olds (1962) states that in the rat, cat, and monkey the strongest locus of positive reinforcement seems to be the medial forebrain bundle (MFB), a phylogenetically old multisynaptic pathway that in the primitive mammal runs most of the length of the brain. In the rat the positive reinforcement system is formed by the MFB, the supramammillary area, and an area in the posterior diencephalon beneath the medial meniscus. (The anatomical localization of the MFB is depicted in Figures 6 and 7). Stein

---

[4] In all of the animal studies to be cited, age is not varied as an independent variable. Since the MBD syndrome appears to be age-dependent—that is, it often disappears or subsides with puberty—and response to amphetamines is likewise age-dependent, a lack of control for age may be critical: it is *possible* that very different results might be obtained in younger versus older animals.

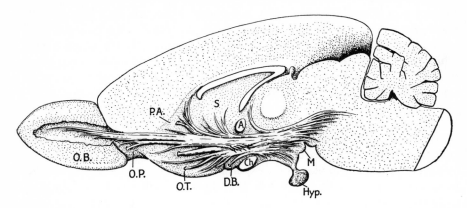

Figure 6. Medial forebrain bundle portrayed in a generalized and primitive mammalian brain. Landmarks include: A.—Anterior Commissure; Ch.—Optic Chiasm; Hyp.—Hypophysis; M.—Mammillary Body; S.—Septum (from LeGros, Clark et al., 1938).

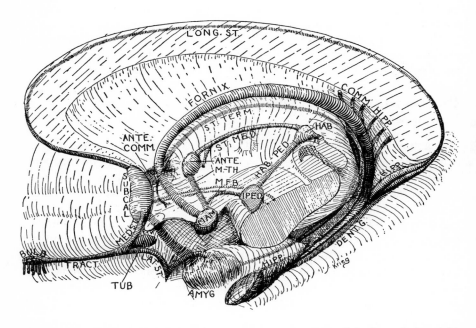

Figure 7. Human rhinencephalon, as seen in a ventromedial view of the right cerebrum and illustrating the medial forebrain bundle. Note the considerable reduction in size in the human, as compared with the primitive mammalian brain. Structures include: Ante. Comm.—Anterior Commissure; Hipp.—Hippocampus; Mam.—Mammillary Body; MFB.—Median Forebrain Bundle (from Krieg, 1953).

(1966) has discussed the possible relationship between this system and the "limbic midbrain area"[5] described by Nauta (1960). In man, stimulation of the positive reinforcement system has produced a variety of positive feelings: "Electrodes believed to be in the hypothalamus and tegmentum have produced extreme euphoria, electrodes in septal areas have inhibited pain and produced feelings of 'well being'" (Olds, 1962, p. 557).

The anatomical localization of the negative reinforcement system is more diffuse. In the rat the negative reinforcement system surrounds the reticular activating system in the midbrain and the periventricular region more rostrally. Physiological localization is also less exact than in the positive reinforcement system. Areas of negative reinforcement may be found mixed with areas of postive reinforcement. In some instances electrical stimulation of the *same* area produces mixed positive and negative reinforcement; such "ambivalent reactions" occur in several locations, including the MFB itself. In other regions, discrete areas of positive and negative reinforcement are very closely juxtaposed.

The psychological interrelations of the positive and negative reinforcement system are likewise not entirely straightforward. The positive and negative reinforcement systems have the effect (by definition) of increasing and decreasing, respectively, the probability of antecedent behavior; surprisingly, electrical stimulation of the positive reinforcement system facilitates negatively reinforced escape (Olds, 1962) and avoidance (Stein, 1965) behavior. This effect—*that stimulation of the positive reward system potentiates behavior learned through punishment*—is of considerable importance in legitimizing generalization from clinical experimentation to the MBD syndrome in children.

In the past few years the neurohumoral basis of the system has begun to be understood, and evidence has accumulated that the system is monoaminergic. Using a fluorescent technique for visualizing monoamine neurons, Hillarp et al. (1966) were able to trace the pathways of such neurons in the central nervous system. Employing this technique, they described a group of neurons containing DA, NE, and 5-HT, whose cell bodies are located in Nauta's limbic midbrain[6] area and whose fibers ascend through the medial forebrain bundle and terminate in the lateral hypothalamus and cortex. Further evidence, employing a different technique, suggests that the function of the positive reinforcement system is intimately related to the monoamines. It has been demonstrated that the anatomical intactness of the MFB is related to the monoamine content of the telencephalon.

[5] This has close connections with but is distinct from the midbrain reticular formation.

[6] As noted, Stein (1966) has suggested that this overlies Olds' positive reinforcement system.

Harvey et al. (1965), Heller and Moore (1965), and Sheard et al. (1967) have shown that lesions of the lateral hypothalamus which section the MFB are associated with a homolateral decrease in 5-HT and NE in the whole brain and telencephalon. These latter studies may be interpreted to mean either that (1) the neurons containing monoamines and *running to the cortex* have had their axons sectioned, with resulting degeneration and loss of monoamines in the cortex, or (2) the fall in cortical amines is, at least in part, due to a transsynaptic effect[7] (Heller and Moore, 1965). The transsynaptic hypothesis does not necessarily imply that the sectioned and the affected neurons employ the same mechanism of neurohumoral transmission; it is only a plausible interpretation.

The tentative conclusions that may be drawn from the combination of the neuroanatomical, neurochemical, and psychological data are as follows: (1) the medial forebrain bundle (MFB) forms an essential part of the positive reinforcement system; (2) the positive reinforcement system is monoaminergic (its neurohormones are DA and/or NE and/or 5-HT); (3) the activity of the positive reinforcement system is possibly related to the effects of negative reinforcement.

Effects of Selective Brain Lesions on Conditioned Emotional Behavior and "Emotional Reactivity"

The production of physiologically meaningful brain lesions can produce marked impairment of conditioned behavior reactivity.

Focal lesions of the brain can interfere with classical conditioning. Brady and Nauta (1953), for example, investigated the effects of septal forebrain lesions in the rat. One of the dependent variables investigated was the "conditioned emotional response" (CER). The CER is defined as the change in behavior which is presumably due to the production of an emotional state. The usual technique for the generation of a CER is to present a neutral conditioned stimulus in association with a traumatic unconditioned stimulus (US) such as electric shock. Through classical conditioning the neutral conditioned stimulus acquires the power of eliciting the same behavior as does the electric shock. In this experiment the CER was the amount of "freezing" produced by the conditioned stimulus, a clicking noise which had been associated with electric shock. Following the introduction of septal lesion the authors found a diminution in the strength of the CER. In anthropomorphic terms, the rats had become "less fearful;"

---

[7] That is, an effect in one group of distinct neurons (here destruction) has an effect (here reducing the concentration of a neurohumor) in another distinct group of neurons (presumably contiguous or related).

the anticipation of pain did not produce "anxiety." In the operated animals, the magnitude of the changes in behavior appeared to be "roughly commensurate with the extent of injury to the fornix column" (p. 345), rather than to the septal area, suggesting that lesions in the structure mediating maximum positive reinforcement produce diminished anticipatory "fear."

Focal brain lesions can also impair avoidance conditioning. Krieckhaus (1965) describes the effects of mammillothalamic tract (MTT) lesions in the retention of the conditioned avoidance response (CAR). The lateral mammillary nucleus and the supramammillary area constitute part of the system yielding maximal positive reinforcement effects (Olds, 1962). In the CAR paradigm an animal is given a warning signal, a conditioned stimulus, which is followed at a fixed time interval by an electric shock delivered through the grid floor of the animal's cage. Following the onset of the conditioned stimulus, the animal has access to another portion of the cage in which he will not be shocked; movement to the safe portion following the conditioned stimulus and prior to the delivery of the electric shock constitutes a successful avoidance response. Those animals who successfully avoided at least 85% of the shock trials were subjected to operative lesions of the MTT. Postoperatively the animals with bilateral lesions successfully avoided the shock on only 10% of the trials. Following the administration of d-amphetamine the animals returned to their previous level of success, 83%. When the drug was discontinued, performance deteriorated to its postoperative, predrug level. As has been noted before, certain experiments, of which this is an example, do not localize the behavioral site of the lesion: in this experiment, either classical or operant conditioning or both might be impaired.

Sheard et al. (1967) investigated the effects of medial and lateral hypothalamic lesions on *escape* behavior (conditioning) in the rat; the dependent variable was latency to escape. In this design, the animal had to rotate a wheel to terminate a periodically presented electric shock whose avoidance was impossible. These authors found that lesions which interrupted the medial forebrain bundle greatly prolonged the escape latency (by a factor of 9 to 12). Biochemical analysis revealed a decline in telencephalic concentration of 5-HT (-40%) and NE (-15%). Further, the correlation between escape latency and the concentrations of the two substances was high ($r = -0.77$ and -0.61, respectively). Unfortunately, d-amphetamine was not administered postoperatively to see if it would reverse the behavioral defect produced by the lesion. In Krieckhaus' experiment, the drug did reverse the effects of the lesions, but the lesions were probably produced in another portion of the positive reinforcement system; it would be of interest to see if such a reversal of effects is independent of the specific site of the lesion within the reinforcement system.

Lesions can also affect "behavorial reactivity" which is also called "emotional reactivity" in the literature.[8] In the experiment already cited, Brady and Nauta examined the effect of septal lesions on "behavioral reactivity," here defined as "hostile" defensive behavior, such as resistance to capture and handling and aggressive reactions to prodding with implements. Postoperatively the animals showed increased reactivity.[9] Although the operated animals displayed an impairment in learned reaction to a conditioned stimulus, they displayed hyperreactivity to unconditioned stimuli. "The sudden presentation of almost any auditory stimulus produced an explosive startle reaction . . . . Attempts to capture or handle the animal were responded to by fierce attacks [on the experimenter] . . . . When placed in a group cage, five or six such septal animals would fight continuously and vigorously for extended periods of time with loud and frequent vocalizations . . ." (p. 343).

As is apparent, the operation had produced some characteristics of MBD children: diminished conditionability and hyperreactivity. It should be emphasized again that the same lesion—in an area related to the positive reinforcement system—produced two behavioral changes: *increased* "behavioral reactivity" and *decreased* conditioned emotional responsiveness. Since these behavioral traits are commonly clustered in the MBD syndrome, the data suggest that the fornix and/or systems functionally related to it are anatomically impaired or physiologically underactive in children with the syndrome.[10]

Effects of Biochemical Alterations of the Neurohumors on Conditioned Behavior and "Emotional Reactivity"

As part of the increasing body of knowledge of neurochemistry, a large number of compounds which affect the handling of monoamines by neurons have been discovered and developed. Compounds are now available that will (1) impair the synthesis of monoamines, (2) decrease their breakdown, (3) affect their storage, and (4) influence their "re-uptake." A current model of the noradrenergic neuron (Schildkraut and Kety, 1967)

---

[8] "Emotional reactivity" is used here in a sense quite different from that used in the description of the behavior of Maudsley rats (which will be discussed later).

[9] Rats generally show such altered reactivity only for periods of a few weeks. The limited duration is confusing: one cannot know if the lesion was initiating (and stimulating) or ablative (and inhibiting).

[10] Of relevance is the fact that the MFB has "massive" descending contribution to the ascending and descending reticular systems of the midbrain (Zanchetti, 1967) and may act to modulate the activity of these systems. Caution is indicated in interpreting this fact since the function of these connections has not yet been explicated.

proposes the following mechanism of NE transport and metabolism: NE is synthesized within the neuron and stored within intracellular granules which occur at the presynaptic nerve endings of the neuron. NE may be released into the intersynaptic cleft from these endings either by nerve impulses or sympathomimetic agents. The released NE stimulates the receptor neurons and is inactivated either (1) by metabolic breakdown within the intersynaptic cleft (via the enzyme catechol-O-methyltransferase), or (2) by re-uptake into the presynaptic cell. NE which has been re-uptaken may be either returned to the storage granules or degraded by the enzyme monoamine oxidase (MAO), which likewise degrades NE released *within* the neuron.

Schildkraut and Kety propose that the action of certain depressive and antidepressive drugs can be explained by their actions on NE metabolism as follows: the behaviorally depressive drug reserpine releases NE (and 5-HT) from its storage granules within the cell, permitting catabolism by MAO and a depletion of the cell's store of NE; the antidepressive MAO inhibitors block the catabolism of, and increase the cell's stores of NE; the antidepressant imipramine prevents the re-uptake of NE by the presynaptic neuron which has released it, thus increasing the concentration of NE in the intersynaptic cleft, which presumably facilitates discharge by the postsynaptic neuron; amphetamine releases NE, inhibits its re-uptake, and, lastly, acts as a sympathomimetic itself. The effects of these agents on the metabolism and release of DA and 5-HT are less well understood but seem to be quite similar: the MAO inhibitors prevent their intracellular catabolism; imipramine prevents their re-uptake; amphetamine impedes the re-uptake of both and stimulates the release of DA. (At this time its effect on 5-HT release is not known.)

I will now examine some experiments dealing with the biochemical manipulations of 5-HT and NE and the effects of such manipulations on animal behavior.

Effects of Manipulation of Monoamines on Avoidance Conditioning

It is possible to inhibit the synthesis of brain 5-HT and NE by the administration of certain blocking compounds. Para-chlorophenylalanine (PACA) interferes with the rate-limiting enzyme in the synthesis of serotonin (Koe and Weissman, 1968), and α-methyltyrosine (α-MT) interferes with the rate-limiting enzyme in the synthesis of NE (Iversen, 1967).

Moore (1966) studied the effects of α-MT on guinea pigs in a conditioned avoidance situation and found that α-MT disrupted avoidance behavior in approximate relation to the depletion of brain NE and DA. Although the behavior impairment more closely paralleled the levels of

NE and DA than the levels of α-MT, it was impossible to be certain that the behavioral impairment was not due to MT toxicity, itself. Another experiment (Moore and Rech, 1967) answered this difficulty by giving α-MT to rats with and without a MAO inhibitor. Since the MAO inhibitor prevented intracellular breakdown of DA and NE, the combination of MAO inhibitor plus α-MT produced higher brain NE levels than α-MT alone without affecting the brain levels of α-MT. The behavioral deficit—failure to maintain conditioned avoidance behavior—was absent when DA and NE levels were normal despite the presence of α-MT; thus it was demonstrated that the diminution in conditioned avoidance is associated with a reduction of brain DA and NE levels, rather than being produced by a toxic effect of the α-MT.

Direct evidence relating activity of the catecholamine systems and the conditioned avoidance response (CAR) is reported by Fuxe and Hanson (1967). These authors studied the histochemical and behavioral consequences of the administration of a blocker of NE synthesis. They found that the conditioned avoidance response in rats was appreciably reduced and that such impaired avoidance was accompanied by histochemical evidence of depleted NE (and to a lesser extent DA) stores in the brain. In those animals in whom avoidance was not impaired there was no histochemical evidence of depletion of NE stores. Stress alone did not result in such depletion: electric shock administered to rats treated with the blocking agents did not result in a depletion of NE stores. The authors reasoned that during CAR performance there is a widespread activation of NE neurons and to a lesser extent of DA neurons and that such activation utilizes the stores of DA and NE which, in the presence of the blocking agent, cannot be resynthesized.

The drug correction of avoidance conditioning impaired by blockers is reported by Hanson (1967). This author administered both a compound (3, α-dimethyltyrosine) which blocks DA and NE synthesis *and* reserpine (which *releases* and thus depletes *both* 5-HT and NE) and found the expected decrement in conditioned avoidance. This decrement was diminished by amphetamine.[11] The implication is that amphetamine will reverse—to some extent—the conditioned avoidance impairment associated with DA and NE depletion. It should be noted that in the above experiments DA and NE have not been manipulated individually—although this can be done. Accordingly, we cannot associate the behavioral effects with either compound alone.

---

[11] And reversed by the combination of DOPA (a DA and NE precursor) *plus* amphetamine. The large number of drugs employed tends to cloud the interpretation: that amphetamine requires small amounts of DA and/or NE (provided by the DOPA) for its action.

The effects of the manipulation of 5-HT levels on behavior are more complex and difficult to evaluate. Aprison (1965) administered 5-hydroxy-tryptophan, the immediate precursor of 5-HT, and studied its effects on operant conditioning (employing a food reward) and avoidance conditioning. He found that brain levels of 5-HT increased and that this was not accompanied by an effect on avoidance conditioning. Operant conditioning by reward *was* affected, which will be discussed in the next section.

Depleting brain levels of 5-HT through the use of the blocking agent PACA, Tenen (1967) studied the relation of such depletion to the conditioned avoidance response, the "emotional reactivity," and the activity level of rats. He found an *increased* sensitivity to electric shock; when he controlled for this variable,[12] he found that lowered brain 5-HT was *not* correlated with changes in avoidance behavior. Thus neither decreasing nor increasing brain 5-HT seems to affect the conditioned avoidance response.

In summary, it seems that (1) diminished levels of NE are associated with impaired conditioned avoidance behavior, and (2) neither an increase nor a decrease in 5-HT is associated with changed conditioned avoidance behavior.

Effects of Manipulation of Monoamines on Positively Reinforced Behavior

As noted, experiments have been conducted studying the effect of manipulation of brain monoamines on positively rewarded operant behavior. When Aprison (1965) increased brain levels of 5-HT by the administration of its precursor, he found that such increased brain levels were accompanied by a disruption of food-rewarded operant behavior. Some ambiguity is introduced in such an experiment since there is no control for the effect of 5-HT on food intake itself; it is conceivable that the increased 5-HT could diminish food-maintained operant behavior by decreasing "appetite." It is obvious, for example, that one could not study the effect of amphetamine on positively reinforced behavior if the reinforcers employed were either food or water since amphetamine decreases both "hunger" and "thirst." The effects on drive and "behavior strength" would be confounded.

A method of circumventing this difficulty has been described by Stein (1964) and Poschel and Ninteman (1966, 1968). This technique utilizes

---

[12] The author found that for low levels of shock, animals treated with PACA had both a lower threshold to electric shock and a more rapid acquisition of conditioned avoidance. When the intensity of the shock was raised above the threshold of both groups, the rate of acquisition of the conditioned avoidance response was the same for the PACA-treated and untreated animals.

the effect of manipulation of monoamine levels and/or drugs on operant behavior maintained by electrical stimulation of the brain. Stein (1966) studied the effect of a number of drugs on the frequency of operant response in rats. He decreased the rate of the animals' responses to a very low level by either reducing the intensity of the current to very low levels or decreasing the frequency of positive electrical reward. He then studied the effects of a number of agents whose presumed mechanism of action is via their effects on NE metabolism. Stein found that amphetamine and MAO inhibitors facilitated response maintained by self-stimulation and that compounds that released amines rapidly from stores in the brain likewise facilitated such response. Using these data, Stein argued that the self-stimulation mechanism is norepinephrinergic.

Poschel and Ninteman (1966) investigated the effect of lowering brain catecholamines on operant behavior maintained by electrical self-stimulation. They administered the NE synthesis blocker α-MT to rats and found that the rate of response dropped from approximately 5000 bar presses per hour in controls to virtually none in the drug-treated animals. Such failure to respond was not accompanied by any obvious sedation. They then administered methamphetamine and found that it restored rates of response to approximately pre-α-MT levels.

The most direct evidence implicating NE as the neurotransmitter of the positive reinforcement system comes from two recent experiments. In the first (Stein and Wise, 1969), a "classical" demonstration of NE release was displayed using a perfusion technique. Rats whose brain NE had been radioactively labeled were implanted with electrodes in the positive reinforcement system. While the animals bar-pressed to receive electrical stimulation, their hypothalami were perfused and the perfusates' radioactivity measured. Increased radio-NE metabolites were found in the perfusate only when electrical stimuli were positively rewarding, indicating that NE release is a concomitant of electrical stimulation of the positive reward system and suggesting that NE is the mediator of that system. Further evidence implicating NE as the critical neurotransmitter of the reward system comes from experiments of Wise and Stein (1969). In these experiments rats were first implanted with electrodes in the positive reinforcement system. After it had been established that the animals would work to receive electrical stimulation, they were injected with substances (e.g., disulfiram) that interfered with the synthesis of NE from its immediate precursor, DA. It was found that this inhibition of NE synthesis resulted in diminished rate of response, that is, low levels of NE with normal levels of DA and 5-HT were accompanied by low levels of response. Intraventricular administration of neurotransmitters allows their uptake by functionally active portions of the brain. Wise found that administration of NE restored animals to previous levels of electrically rewarded behavior and that administration of DA or 5-HT did not. The finding that a depletion of NE results in a diminished activity of the positive reward system and that a restitution of NE—but not of excess exogenous DA or 5-HT—results in a return of activity in the system strongly implicates NE as the neurotransmitter of the positive reward system.

Poschel and Ninteman (1968) also investigated the effects of 5-HT levels on electrical self-stimulation of the brain in rats. In these studies the animals were first administered MAO inhibitors and then the 5-HT precursor, 5-hydroxytryptophan (5-HTP). The rationale for the administration of MAO inhibitors was that such agents have been found to potentiate the effects of 5-HTP on *behavioral* depression in animals and of affective depression in humans. In rats, the administration of MAO inhibitors is followed by an approximately 24-hour increase in the rate of spontaneous self-stimulation of the brain. Following the return to pretreatment levels, Poschel and Ninteman administered 5-HTP and found a greatly increased rate of operant response in the animals. This increased rate of responding occurred with a fixed latency; the authors argued that the delayed onset might be explained by the time required for 5-HTP to be converted to 5-HT. These findings contradict the findings of Aprison, cited previously. Poschel and Ninteman present some speculations to account for their contradictory results: (1) that the difference in experimental outcome is related to dose levels and that previous experiments employed much higher (and possibly toxic) doses of 5-HTP; (2) that the action of the exogenously administered 5-HTP may not produce physiologically meaningful responses—that exogenous 5-HTP may cause a release of endogenous NE, so that what apparently is a serotoninergic effect is actually a norepinephrinergic effect.

Thus there is considerable evidence that monoamines are involved in the functioning of the positive reward system. The available data most strongly suggest that the neurohumoral transmitter is NE but the possibility that DA and/or 5-HT are involved as well cannot be ruled out at present.

Effects of Manipulation of Monoamines on the "Conditioned Emotional Response" and "Emotional" Behavior

The maintenance of the conditioned avoidance response is dependent on both classical conditioning (learning that "the light is followed by shock") and operant conditioning (ostensibly jumping avoids anxiety, a negative reinforcer, and the diminution in that negative reinforcer strengthens jumping). An experiment that would test the effects of manipulation of monoamines on the conditioned emotional response itself would provide evidence as to whether classical conditioning can be selectively impaired.

Manipulation of 5-HT levels does affect this response. In an experiment already discussed, Tenen (1967) investigated the effects of diminished 5-HT on the conditioned *emotional* response. In this experiment the operational measures of the CER were (1) the disruption in drinking produced by a conditioned stimulus which had been paired with an electric shock, and (2) the amount of defecation under such stress. The data showed that depletion of 5-HT is associated with a diminished CER and a more rapid extinction ("unlearning") of the CER.

Of relevance to the MBD syndrome in children is the effect of certain monoamine-influencing drugs on hostile behavior in animals. Kulkarni (1968) has reported on the effect of a variety of drugs on "mouse-killing" in the "killer" rat. Such rats are defined as those animals who will invariably kill a mouse placed in their cage within 15 minutes. Kulkarni found that amphetamine, imipramine, and 5-HTP produced a "muricidal" (mouse-killing) block. Since 5-HTP is converted to 5-HT, it is presumably the latter compound which is "antimuricidal." Stimulation of the amygdala typically results in rage behavior and amygdalectomy produces "placidity or calmness . . . [which is] specific" (Ruch and Fulton, 1960, p. 492). Amygdaloid lesions (King and Meyer, 1958) will produce such calmness even when hyperemotionality has been produced by septal lesions (already discussed). Since 5-HT has been shown to inhibit the activity of amygdaloid neurons when applied microelectrophoretically, Kulkarni speculated that the administration of 5-HTP and amphetamine might inhibit their "muricidal rat" by inhibiting the activity of the amygdaloid. Since amphetamine is often effective in diminishing aggression in MBD children and since I have been advancing the hypothesis that such children have diminished levels of catecholamines and/or 5-HT, these findings are of obvious interest.

ACTIVITY LEVEL: THE EFFECTS OF BRAIN INJURY AND THE RELATIONS OF MONOAMINE LEVELS

Before discussing animal models of hyperactivity and their possible parallels with hyperactivity in children, I must repeat that (1) some authors question whether all MBD children are, in fact, actually "hyperactive"; (2) some studies have revealed that children judged to be "clinically hyperactive" do not display more gross activity per day than do normal children; and (3) what is judged as "hyperactivity" may not be due to excess total activity but rather to a failure to inhibit motor activity when appropriate. Accordingly, a manipulation which produces an animal in ceaseless motion may not be an entirely appropriate model for an MBD child. Since, however, the data relating to children are not certain and since there is no model of response to social inhibition in hyperactive animals, it may be appropriate to tentatively note this potential objection and then waive it.

Naturalistic evidence exists which indicates brain injury not only in the production of the MBD syndrome but also in the generation of the specific symptom (or, more properly, "sign") of hyperactivity. Hohman (1922) and Strecker and Ebaugh (1924) reported hyperactivity which occurred in children following encephalitic and traumatic injury to the brain. Ruch and Fulton (1960) state that in monkeys motoric hyperactivity occurs after ablation of the entire orbitofrontal lobule or its subareas or the ventromedial nucleus of the hypothalamus.

Maire and Patton (1956) demonstrated that lesions in the septal-preoptic regions (again related to the fornix) resulted in increasing running behavior. Apparently, lesions at the head of the caudate nucleus can likewise increase motoric hyperactivity. Ruch and Fulton quote the work of Smith and DeVito, who were able to observe fine terminals of degeneration in the head of the caudate nucleus of the monkey following prefrontal lobule ablation, which obviously suggests an anatomic relationship between the two areas.

Davis (1958) investigated the effect of a number of drugs on spontaneous and induced motor hyperactivity in rhesus monkeys. In this study, one animal was hyperactive before and without operative intervention, and the other animals were made hyperactive by unilateral and bilateral lesions of the caudate nucleus.[13] Among the drugs administered to these animals were methylphenidate and amphetamine. Both agents dramatically reduced motor hyperactivity; the animals became slightly tolerant to both drugs, but as with children, the tolerance "never became very marked."

Routtenberg (1968) has reported data linking lesions of the reward system and increased activity level. Rats with lesions in one area of self-stimulation (the ventral tegmentum) were found postoperatively to be "continually active in an open field situation" (p. 57) and failed to habituate. If such a lesion produced diminished sensitivity to reinforcement, one localized lesion would have been shown to both effect reinforcement and increase activity.

The fact that hyperactivity is produced by lesions of the caudate nu-

[13] Towbrin's (1969) findings are again of interest. Hypoxic brain damage in prematures affects the basal ganglia.

cleus is provocative and suggestive biochemically. The caudate nucleus and the corpus striatum have the highest concentrations of dopamine of any areas of the central nervous system.[14] The caudate nucleus concentration of other neurohumors is of the same order of magnitude as those of other areas of the central nervous system. This datum suggests that dopamine is the probable neurohumor in this nucleus. A naturalistic datum which *suggests* that the spontaneous hyperactivity in children may possibly be due to injury of a catecholamine-functioning nucleus is presented by the pathology resulting from von Economo's encephalitis. This illness sometimes produced a Parkinsonian syndrome in adults. Idiopathic Parkinsonism is associated with marked depletion of DA (Hornzkiewicz, 1966) and responds to treatment with DOPA (a DA and NE precursor). As the virus in question appeared to have certain preferential sites of attack, one might reason analogically that catecholamine (possibly DA) nuclei had been affected when children became hyperactive following von Economo's encephalitis.[15]

A further datum suggesting that functional underactivity of the caudate nucleus may be responsible for the hyperactivity in MBD children is provided by a finding of Coyle and Snyder (1969), who report that *l*-amphetamine and *d*-amphetamine are equally effective in preventing the re-uptake of DA and NE in the striatum but that the *l*-isomer is one-tenth as active as the *d*-isomer in preventing re-uptake of NE in the cortex. Benzedrine (*dl*-amphetamine) has been found to be more effective than *d*-amphetamine alone in the treatment of some hyperactive children (Bradley, 1950). If this is so, benzedrine's differential activity must be attributed to its content of *l*-amphetamine. Taken with Coyle and Snyder's finding, the implication is that benzedrine's increased therapeutic efficacy is not mediated through its action on the cortex, but possibly through its effects on subcortical areas, including the caudate nucleus, and possibly—since the caudate is so rich in DA—via a dopaminergic system.[16]

A final datum suggesting that dysfunction of the caudate nucleus may be involved in the pathogenesis of the MBD syndrome comes from a study of Neill and Grossman (1970). These authors implanted cannulas in the dorsal and ventral portions of rats' caudate nuclei and injected

[14] Namely, 3 to 8 µg/g in the caudate nucleus versus 0.13 µg/g in the hippocampus, 0.26–0.75 µg/g in the hypothalamus, 0–0.1 µg/g in the cerebral cortex (Fuxe, 1965).

[15] Another reasonable supposition, suggested by Seymour Kety (personal communication), is that the virus had a predilection for catecholamine-containing neurons and where these were mainly DA-containing the result was Parkinsonism and where they were NE-containing and in children the result was MBD.

[16] Although, equally logically, *l*-amphetamine might exert its quieting effect via caudate NE.

scopolamine to produce cholinergic blockade. They found that injections of scopolamine in the dorsal portion of the caudate nucleus both decreased the animals' conditioned avoidance response and increased the animals' activity level in novel situations. Thus a single biochemical lesion apparently produced the two postulated deficits of MBD children: decreased conditionability and increased activity. The lesion was, however, cholinergic. It remains to be seen if local adrenergic or dopaminergic blockade would produce similar effects or if local injection of DA or NE would counteract the effects of cholinergic blockade.

The above data are obviously inconclusive, but they do document that anatomical lesions—whose location in some instances is related to that of the positive reinforcement system—can produce motoric hyperactivity. No data have been presented to show that decreased amounts of 5-HT, DA, or NE produce increased motor activity. In fact, a general reduction in activity of the monoamine systems, as is produced by the administration of reserpine—is accompanied by sedation and/or depression. However, from the data presented it seems that focal depletion of catecholamines, either in the positive reinforcing system or in the caudate nucleus, might be accompanied by motor hyperactivity. Again, the evidence is only suggestive: no firm conclusions may be drawn.

GENETIC DIFFERENCES IN CONDITIONABILITY AND THEIR RELATIONS TO MONOAMINES

I have been proposing the thesis that the MBD syndrome may be based on alteration of monoamine metabolism, and that such a biochemical etiology may particularly apply to children in the genetic MBD subgroup. Therefore it will be relevant to present the available evidence which links inherited differences in conditionability and monoamine metabolism.

In outline, evidence exists to support the following points.

1. Within groups of animals there are individual ones who avoidance condition with difficulty.

2. Many of these "poor" avoidance conditioners respond to amphetamine with increased rates of avoidance conditioning.

3. "Good" and "poor" avoiders can be inbred, producing purebred strains which avoid with ease or difficulty.

4. As is the case within nonpurebred strains, inbred strains of "poor avoiders" respond to amphetamine.

5. Monoamine levels in the brain correlate with these differences in conditionability.

The supporting data will now be presented and their relevance for the MBD syndrome discussed.

Rech (1966) found that approximately one-third of a large group of rats were unable to learn to avoid on more than half of their trials in a conditioned avoidance situation. He found that administration of amphetamine to such rats raised their levels of avoidance to levels approximating those of the spontaneous "good" performers (i.e., those rats that avoided shock more than 50% of the time following the routine training trials). Closer inspection of his data revealed to Rech that "poor performers" fell into two categories. The first group were animals who had performed as well as the "good performers" during the early sessions but later regressed to the level of "poor performers." The second group of animals were never able to perform as well as the "good performers." Interestingly, only the second group of performers responded favorably to treatment with amphetamines. Performance of the first group did not. Rech speculates that the poor performance of the first group may not be related to an inactive "adrenergic" system but may involve another, possibly cholinergic, mechanism.

Bignami (1965a) selectively bred Wistar albino rats for high and low rates of avoidance conditioning. The percentage of conditioned avoidance responses in the line selected for a high rate of avoidance conditioning gradually increased until the fifth generation, when the male rates were approximately 70% greater than those in the initial parental generation, and the female rates were approximately 35% greater; similarly, the downward selection resulted in males whose avoidance rates were 45% lower than those of the initial parental generation and females whose rates were 60% lower. Another finding of mild interest was that initially the female rats of the parental generation avoided considerably better than did the males. This is of interest in that the MBD syndrome in humans seems to be sex-linked, males having the syndrome far more frequently than females.

Broadhurst and Bignami (1965) have compared Bignami's rats with the "Maudsley" Reactive (MR) and Non-Reactive strains (MNR). The MR and MNR rats are inbred strains selected over many generations for high and low rates of "emotional elimination in the open-field test" (i.e., defecation in a presumably stressful situation). Bignami's high-avoidance strain was correlated with the Maudsley Non-Reactive strain with regard to superiority in escape-avoidance conditioning, and both were more active than the low-avoidance and MR strains, respectively, but Bignami's high- and low-avoidance strains did not differ in "emotionality." In both groups of animals, high avoidance was correlated with a high exploratory activity level. High exploratory movement is presumably correlated with "fearlessness." With that interpretation, the correlation between fear and conditioning is opposite to that seen in MBD children. From these data one can infer that the Bignami and Maudsley strains are "phenocopies," with similar behavior being mediated by different genotypes. In any event, it is obvious that the genotypes governing speed of acquisition of avoidance response need not correlate simply with those influencing "emotionality."

An additional finding of interest is reported by Bignami (1965b), who investigated the effects of amphetamine on the Roman low-avoidance strain and found that the drug produced an improvement in the level of performance and a reduction in the amount of time taken for daily learning of the conditioned avoidance task.

The above evidence, taken together, documents the following points.

1. Individual differences in susceptibility to avoidance conditioning occur and these differences are often reversible by the administration of amphetamine.

2. Such differences can occur on a genetic—and therefore presumably biochemical—basis.[17] It seems likely, therefore, that such variations might occur in humans as well and that such variations in humans might be mediated by a similar biochemical difference.

Correlation between 5-HT levels and behavior in the Maudsley Reactive and Non-Reactive rats is reported by Sudak and Maas (1964a). The authors found that the MR males had a higher level of 5-HT in the limbic areas than did the MNR males. There was no difference in limbic 5-HT between the Reactive and Non-Reactive females. The authors also found a negative correlation between limbic 5-HT and ambulation scores: the greater the limbic 5-HT, the less the ambulation score. The meaning of these findings in regard to MBD children is not immediately clear: a higher 5-HT level was correlated with slower conditioning, a MBD characteristic; while a lower 5-HT level was correlated with lower "fearfulness" which is likewise a MBD characteristic.[18] Sudak and Maas (1964b) have also reported on the 5-HT and NE content of the brain stem (diencephalon, mesencephalon, pons) and hippocampus of "emotional" and "nonemotional" strains of mice. The "emotional" (reactive) mice were found to have higher hippocampal 5-HT, lower hippocampal NE, and higher brain-stem NE. The serotonin finding is similar to that in the Maudsley

---

[17] In order to test this hypothesis experiments are now being conducted at the National Institute of Mental Health to determine the levels, uptake, and turnover of DA, NE, and 5-HT in the Roman high- and low-avoidance strains.

[18] A resolution of the dilemma may be found in Tenen's (1967) data which have already been cited. Tenen found that at low levels of shock (approximately the levels employed by Broadhurst and Bignami) animals with less 5-HT—such as the MNR strain—conditioned better; the suggestion is that if higher shock levels had been employed by Broadhurst and Bignami they would have found no differences between the MR and MNR strains in conditionability.

Reactive and Non-Reactive rats. If nonemotionality in the mouse can be equated with fearlessness in the MBD child, the fact that the "nonemotional" mice have lower brain-stem NE levels corresponds to the hypothesis concerning MBD children; however, the higher hippocampal NE levels found in such mice does not correspond to the hypothesis concerning MBD children.

Karczmar and Scudder (1967) have investigated the behavioral characteristics, brain monoamine levels, and response to amphetamine of several different genera and strains of mice. They report several findings that are of suggestive interest concerning MBD children: brain levels of monoamines vary by a threefold factor between the various genera studied; there are correlations between brain monoamine levels and exploratory behavior—flexible, exploratory behavior was accompanied by a low level of brain monoamines; amphetamine had differential effects on the same behavioral variable depending upon the genus studied—for example, in some strains a given activity was increased while in others it was decreased.

THE PARADOXICAL EFFECT OF THE AMPHETAMINES

One important issue which has not been touched upon in this theoretical model is that of the "paradoxical response" of MBD children to the amphetamines. As will be recalled, this phrase is generally used to refer to the quieting and depressing effect the agent has on such children, as opposed to the activating and euphoriant effect it has upon adults. Another peculiarity of children's response to this drug is not generally mentioned: *apparently,* unlike adults, children very rarely develop a tolerance to the effect of amphetamines. In attempting to account for the paradoxical effects, it would be useful to know if they are confined to MBD children or if they are characteristic of children in general. Unfortunately, such data are not available. The few relevant data will be presented, and will be followed by hypotheses concerning the paradoxical response.

Relevant Data

Changes in Monoamines During Maturation

Agrawal et al. (1966) have studied changes in monoamine levels during the maturation of the brains of rats. They reported that brain levels of 5-HT and NE increased progressively with age, adult levels being reached 5 to 6 weeks after birth. DA "continued to increase until adult life" (p. 511). (For purposes of unjustified cross-species extrapolation, I will add that weaning in the rat takes place at about 3 weeks, sexual maturation at 2 to 3 months.) These data seem to relate to the diminution of some MBD signs (e.g., hyperactivity) with maturation. If the syndrome is partly caused by deficient monoamines, their increase with age should cause its amelioration.

MAO Levels and Androgens

Klaiber et al. (1967) cite Zeller, who observed that "castration elevated brain MAO activity in male rats while testosterone administration to castrated rats lowered the brain MAO activity" (p. 321). This datum suggests a mechanism by which monoamines should increase following sexual maturation. Since the intracellular level of monoamines is controlled largely by MAO activity, monoamine levels should increase with increased androgen levels. Sexual maturation should increase monoamine levels (by decreasing MAO levels) not only in the male but in the female as well, since adrenal 17-keto-steroids with androgenic activity are produced in both sexes at puberty.

Effect of Sex Hormones on Reinforcement Mediated by Electrical Stimulation of the Brain

In the above paragraph a datum was presented which explained how androgens *might* be expected to affect the reinforcement systems. *Direct* evidence for such action is available: Olds (1958) has reported on the effects of androgens on operant behavior reinforced by electrical stimulation of the brain in the rat. In a study that is of particular relevance to my previous speculations linking defects in the caudate nucleus and an increased activity level, Olds found that with electrodes placed in the dorsomedial caudate nucleus, an all-or-none relationship between rate of response and testosterone level was obtained. Castration produced total failure to respond to even very high levels of electrical stimulation, while administration of testosterone restored the nucleus' previous level of sensitivity to electrical stimulation.

The above data may help to explain why there is some improvement in the MBD syndrome at the time of puberty. Increased androgenic activity at this time would increase the levels and/or functional activity of the monoamines, which in turn would potentiate the activity of the positive and negative reinforcement systems.

Hypotheses Accounting for the Paradoxical Response

What has not been explained is why drugs that affect the handling of monoamines have different effects before and after puberty. There are a number of possible *ad hoc* solutions.

The Quieting Effect of Amphetamine

There are regional differences in the levels of monoamine activity in different areas in the brain and these levels change with maturation (it will be remembered that DA continued to increase until adult life in the rat). In the previous discussions in this chapter, the data cited referred to whole brain levels of the compounds in question. It is possible that there are differential rates of maturation of various neurohumoral systems within the brain. For example, it has been hypothesized that the hyperactivity seen in some MBD children might be a result of functional underactivity of a DA system within the caudate nucleus. In the adult, amphetamine apparently stimulates neurons acting within the reticular activating system. If it were the case that the hyperactive MBD child had only small amounts of DA within his caudate nucleus and none of the (unspecified) neurohumor(s) which mediated the activity of the reticular activating system, administration of amphetamine would stimulate his caudate nucleus but not his reticular activating system, and decrease rather than increase his hyperactivity. If, as the child matured, the levels of the mediator within the reticular activating system increased at a greater rate than DA within the caudate nucleus, administration of amphetamine would activate the excitatory RAS system more than it would the inhibitory DA system.

Some support for the above speculations is provided by children's differing patterns of response to amphetamine. Some children are sedated as well as quieted and a very small number may even go to sleep. Far more common responses, however, are decreased motor activity, increased attentiveness, increased susceptibility to social demands, and *increased wakefulness*. In fact, this insomnia is occasionally a distressing side effect of amphetamine administration in children. The fact that amphetamine generally increases wakefulness while decreasing motor activity and inattentiveness in children would suggest that its effect on the reticular activating system is not qualitatively different from that seen in adults, but that its action does differ in children in that it selectively stimulates the inhibiory system to an even greater degree.

In general, the stimulant drugs seem to have a biphasic effect in MBD children: in lower doses they are calming and in higher doses they are activating. In normal children their effect seems to be constantly activating: as the dose is increased the child becomes increasingly irritable. An *ad hoc* —but plausible—hypothesis is as follows: assume that both the inhibiting and excitatory arousal systems are monoaminergic so that both respond to amphetamine. In Figure 8, excitatory level is a function of the comparative levels of the inhibitory and excitatory system: if the excitatory system is at a greater level of activation, the child is excited; if the inhibitory system is more active, he is sedated; if both are equal, he is "normally" aroused. If we assume that the inhibitory system is less active at a low level of mono-amine activity, that it increases its activity more rapidly with increasing levels of monoamines, and that it peaks sooner, the following situation is generated.

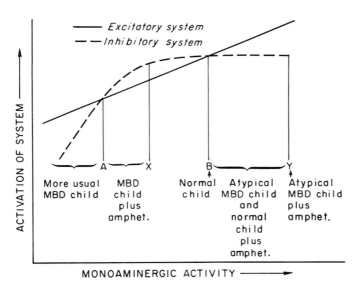

The higher line at any point indicates dominant behavior

Figure 8.   Level of arousal and monoaminergic activity.

Low and high levels of monoamines produce hyperarousal, while inter-mediate levels produce normo-arousal or, possibly, sedation. The MBD child starts to either the left of point A or the right of point B. In the former instance, amphetamines "push the child" to a point such as "X" and sedate him; in the latter instance (atypical but occurring), they push him to a point such as "Y," producing further activation.[19] The normally aroused

---

[19] It would be of interest to see if hyperactive MBD children who become more excited with the administration of *d*-amphetamine consistently become quieter with the administration of *l*-amphetamine or lithium, tentatively indicated in the sec-tion on drug management. If such children are overactive because they are too far to the right of point "B," *d*-amphetamine would stimulate the excitatory systems more than the inhibitory system and produce greater activation. Preliminary evidence sug-gests that *l*-amphetamine might produce a different effect. If the drug stimulated the inhibitory (?DOPA) system without stimulating the excitatory system (i.e., by shift-ing the line depicting inhibitory activity upward), it might quiet these children. How-ever, if in such children the inhibitory system was already maximally active (or

child begins at point B, so that further increases in monoamine activity produce increased arousal.

There is suggestive evidence for the existence of a catecholamine inhibitory system—since destructive lesions may increase arousal, as in postencephalitic children—but its exact location and neurohumoral basis is uncertain. It is known that stimulation of certain portions of the reinforcement system of the brain activates an animal while stimulation of other portions of the system sedates the animal (Routtenberg, 1968). If *both* portions of the system were shown to be monoaminergic, there would be evidence for the plausibility of the proposed model.

There is evidence supporting the existence of a behaviorally depressing monoaminergic system (Mandell and Spooner, 1968); the evidence suggests that the system is noradrenergic—*not* dopaminergic, however. The authors cite a number of studies in which NE was administered either intraventricularly or intravenously into young animals with an immature blood-brain barrier. In all instances there was either no effect or behavioral depression. This data, taken together with that of Stein and Wise (1969), would suggest that both the activity dampening and reinforcement systems are noradrenergic and that the beneficial effect of amphetamine is mediated only by its effects on NE.

The Failure of Amphetamine to Produce Euphoria in the Young Child

It is generally asserted that amphetamine does not have an euphoriant effect in children. However, it often does produce an affective change. Interestingly—and inexplicably—the administration of amphetamine occasionally produce a transient (generally less than a week) period of sadness with many qualities of adult depression: guilt, low self-esteem, self-recriminations. Further, although the drug does not produce euphoria, in some postpubescent MBD children it may produce a calming effect and

---

absent), stimulation of that system would be impossible and *l*-amphetamine would not be effective. In that case lithium might be useful by reducing the activation of the excitatory system. Since lithium acts to facilitate the re-uptake of monomines by the presynaptic neuron, decreasing postsynaptic stimulation, then if both the inhibitory and excitatory systems are monoaminergic, lithium should decrease the activity of both systems. If the more active system is the more sensitive to chemical dampening (as should obviously be the case if the inhibitory system is totally inactive), the excitatory system should be dampened more and behavioral quieting should result; if the inhibitory system is completely inactive, then lithium could only act to decrease the activity of the excitatory system and behavioral quieting should likewise result. The above is grossly speculative. Obviously the effectiveness of both agents needs to be tested.

a positively toned mood. Amphetamine thus does influence affectivity although it does so in neither a marked nor a prolonged fashion.

Since it may alleviate the MBD syndrome while producing (1) no change in affect, (2) a positive change in affect, or (3) a negative change in affect, amphetamine's paradoxical affective action would seem to be independent of its beneficial effect. It should also be noted that the "monoamine hypothesis" does not explain why amphetamine produces euphoria in normal subjects while other antidepressant agents (imipramine, MAO inhibitors), in general, do not.[20]

Perhaps relevant to the question of amphetamine's failure to produce euphoria in young children is the apparent absence of prolonged, intense, nonreactive, affective states in such children. *Nonreactive* euphoria is not seen in young children. Similarly, although many children do become sad, many child psychiatrists would question whether serious depression—in the adult sense—occurs in young children. Manic-depressive illness occurs rarely, if at all, in the young child (Kanner, 1962). Why this is so is problematic. It suggests that the systems necessary for producing euphoric states do not exist or cannot be activated in an immature brain. In view of the appearance of such states following puberty and the discussed effects of androgens on the positive reinforcing system, one might speculate that the ability to experience intense affective states is androgen-dependent.

The dilemma can, however, be avoided (perhaps unfairly) by positing a partial functioning of the neurohumoral mechanism in the reinforcement system but an absence of such functioning in the positive affective system. Accordingly, potentiation of the former system would take place with the administration of amphetamine while potentiation of the latter would be impossible. This is the most special of *ad hoc* hypotheses and *may* be lent a small measure of credence by the following clinical observation. A certain percent of MBD children fail to respond to amphetamine and it seems to be common clinical opinion that lack of response is particularly marked in the preschool-age group. Since the percent responding to amphetamine treatment increases apparently with age, one must assume that some nonresponders have become responders. If this is so, one might postulate that their positive reward and activity inhibiting systems have matured enough to become stimulatable. The foregoing is, I realize, a fragile chain composed of weak hypothetical links.

---

[20] Since there is some evidence that these other agents affecting NE metabolism can successfully be used to treat the MBD child, it is possible that amphetamine's euphoriant effect in adults and its depressive effect in children may be not only paradoxical but also irrelevant. This assertion would be strengthened if it could be documented that the other antidepressants were as effective in the treatment of MBD children as is amphetamine.

Failure to Develop Tolerance to Amphetamine

It is commonly believed that a tolerance is developed in adults to the behavioral effects of the amphetamines, and this relative absence of tolerance[21] in children appears to be another paradoxical response. The continued usefulness of the drug in children—the absence of tolerance—may not be a phenomenon peculiar to them. Kosman and Unna (1968) have observed that although in adults tolerance develops to the anorexic and euphoric effects, it does not develop to the awakening action of the drug. Amphetamine is of continued usefulness in the treatment of narcolepsy, and addicts who are tolerant to the euphoric effects of the drug continue to manifest insomnia. Likewise, MBD children rarely develop a tolerance to the effect of amphetamine on either reinforcement or awakening.

Kosman and Unna note that in animals chronic administration of amphetamine continues to produce hyperactivity and *continues to potentiate avoidance behavior.* The latter datum is entirely consonant with the clinical findings with children. Tolerance, therefore, would appear to be normal for the affective component of the drug and not for the conditioning effect. Children's failure to develop conditioning tolerance would therefore not be paradoxical. Whether adults fail to develop tolerance to the potentiating effects on conditioning is not known,[22] although the evidence reviewed would suggest that that would be the case. If adults do develop such tolerance another explanation would have to be invoked.

A DISCLAIMER

These data, taken together, may provide support for the plausibility of the hypothesis that the MBD syndrome may be based on a defect in monoamine metabolism, and that the biochemical defect is most likely to occur in the MBD subgroups with genetic etiology.

I wish to emphasize that the data presented are, at most, suggestive.

---

[21] Many children do develop a *mild* tolerance to d-amphetamine, and the daily dose must be increased from 10 mg to perhaps 20–30 mg over a period of a few weeks. By comparison, adults taking the drug for its euphoric effects may increase their daily intake from 10–50 mg to 1000 mg per day. Another indication of at least some development of tolerance occurs in the children who have a depressive reaction upon initial administration of amphetamine. The reaction disappears quickly with continued administration; this is analogous to the disappearance of the euphoric effect in adults who have developed amphetamine tolerance.

[22] Methylphenidate facilitates acquisition of classical conditioning in man (with nonchronic administration, Schneider and Costiloe, 1957). Since the action of that drug and amphetamine are very similar, it may be supposed that amphetamine would likewise potentiate such conditioning.

The inferences drawn from the experiments on stimulation and lesions must be interpreted with considerable caution. As Routtenberg (1968) observes, "It is typically thought that stimulation at a point X influences those areas to which X sends its output, and a lesion of X removes that influence. Unfortunately, it appears that the situation may become, at times, quite the reverse" (p. 73). Citing the work of others, he adds, "Stimulation may disrupt brain function and act more like a lesion . . . and lesions may act more like stimulation by augmenting the excitability or lowering the threshold of denervated structures" (p. 73).

The inferences drawn from biochemical manipulations must likewise be considered with caution. Most of the experiments cited deal with brain *levels* of monoamines. Unfortunately, the variables which correlate with the activity of given neurohumoral system may not be the levels of a neurohumor but its rates of turnover or release, or the sensitivity of the postsynaptic neurons to this neurohumor. By analogy, one cannot predict the speed of an automobile from the amount of gasoline in its tank; its speed usually correlates better with the rate of flow of gasoline to the cylinders, provided that all the cylinders are "sensitive," that is, firing consistently in response to gasoline received. Nor can the effect of the administration of precursors or blocking agents be assumed to be unambiguous. It is generally assumed that the administration of a large quantity of a precursor simply increases the amounts of other substances along the normal metabolic pathway. Likewise, "blockers" are generally assumed to only prevent the production of a normally present substance. The effects of such manipulations may be more complex. Precursors may interfere with the metabolism of other compounds, while blocking agents may facilitate alternate metabolic pathways and induce the production of abnormal metabolites (Mandell and Spooner, 1968). Finally, as has been alluded to, the concentrations of critical neurohumors may vary independently in different regions of the brain. Excessive activity or deficient reinforceability might be a manifestation of a localized deficiency in certain substances which are present in normal (or even, logically, excessive) amounts elsewhere. Thus, evaluations of total brain metabolism of these substances might well lead to misleading conclusions.

The clarity of this rather impressionistic picture—as is the case non-metaphorically—disappears upon closer inspection. The data must be interpreted cautiously; the inferences are most tentative. *Caveat lector*!

CHAPTER 8

Theory: Conclusion

One of the theoretical intents of this essay is to illustrate how variations in the activity of rather simple neurophysiological systems might be manifested by qualitative differences in complex psychological functioning. This is more than an idle exercise. Recent studies in the genetics of schizophrenia conducted by Heston, Kety, Rosenthal, and myself have suggested a genetic relatedness between a variety of phenomenologically distinct disorders: schizophrenia, sociopathy, certain characterological disorders, and inadequate personality. Biologically it is possible to account for such data by at least two models. First, one can postulate polygenetic modes of transmission, with several genes regulating the production of several enzymes, and with various segregations of these genes resulting in varying patterns of enzyme dysfunction and varying clinical pictures. In the second model, one can theorize that several genes control the production of one or a very few enzymes, with the varying genotypes differing only in the amount of these few enzymes they produce. In the second instance, it might seem difficult to see how quantitative differences in one or a few neuroenzymes might result in qualitatively different psychiatric syndromes. It has been the purpose of this theoretical excursion to illustrate how such simple variations in the levels and/or activity of one or a few neurohumors might result in changes in complex psychological functions. Differences in the intensity of deviation of these functions might well result in the appearance of qualitatively different patterns—which patterns constitute psychiatric diagnostic entities. To be specific and redundant, defective monoamine metabolism might be expected to result in poor avoidance conditioning, attentional and cognitive problems, variability of behavior, and poor socialization. As summarized in the section on prognosis, differential degrees of such dysfunction would result in distinct psychiatric syndromes: accentuated failure to learn by avoidance conditioning might result in sociopathic personality types; accentuation of cognitive abnormalities in schizophrenia-like syndromes; accentuation of volatility and impulsivity in immature, inadequate, and infantile character types.

Epilogue

At the end of a journey, particularly if it has been somewhat involved, it is sometimes useful to review one's wanderings.

The points (or facts or biases) which I hope the reader will take away with him from the first part of this essay include the following: (1) that the MBD syndrome is extremely common, being probably the most common single diagnostic entity seen in child guidance clinics; (2) that the symptoms (to be more exact, the signs) of the syndrome are exceedingly varied, and that the basic symptoms of the disorder may be masked by neurotic or sociopathic problems, or by the presence of a "special learning disorder"; the investigator must actively *search* for the core signs in these more ambiguous cases—and in many instances such diligence, as is fitting, will be rewarded; (3) that adjunctive techniques of diagnosis are of considerably less value than a careful history in which the historian knows what he is seeking; the psychologist and neurologist may provide confirmatory evidence but cannot make the diagnosis; (4) that the diagnosis will sometimes be made by administering a trial of medication; (5) that the treatment of choice in virtually all instances consists first of medication, second of counseling, and last of "psychotherapy;" (6) that the psychiatrist or pediatrician who follows this therapeutic course can anticipate a very high probability of success; (7) that with regard to its relevance for adult psychiatry, the syndrome, at least in its more severe instances, may be a forerunner of certain forms of psychopathology of later life, including impulsive character disorders, immature characters, sociopathy, and, perhaps, schizophrenia; and (8) that the defect which is postulated to lie at the base of the MBD syndrome of children may conceivably form the base for these psychiatric disorders in later life.

In the second portion of this essay, which dealt with the psychological and neurophysiological bases of the syndrome, my major assertion was that the syndrome was not only a disorder of activation, but was also a *disorder of reinforcement.* I asserted that many of the manifestations of the syndrome could be explained by a decreased sensitivity to positive and negative reinforcement, and that this decreased sensitivity could be explained on the basis of either brain damage or innate biochemical abnormalities. The thesis, I feel, is simple and satisfies the demands of parsimony, of Occam's razor. The simple *may* be beautiful but it may not always be *true,* particularly when attempting to explain a complicated state of affairs. Although the theory does suggest certain critical tests (Wender, 1969b, in press) it is perhaps too all-encompassing; it perhaps explains too much. Popper (1963) has asserted that a concept that explains too much may explain nothing because concepts that explain too much are generally not testable. I am aware of these deficits. I have advanced this theory with the intention and caution reflected in Whitehead's dictate: "Seek simplicity and distrust it."

APPENDIX 1

Case Histories

A number of cases, illustrating varying manifestations of the MBD syndrome, are presented below. Only a few instances of the "classical" subtype are provided; they are extremely repetitious in pattern and, with practice, exceedingly easy to recognize. More examples are given of the atypical forms: the psychopathic, the neurotic, the learning disorder subtypes.

It is difficult to communicate a "feel" for the syndrome by a simple recitation of its salient characteristics. It is easier to communicate by ostensive definition, by providing concrete gestalts and allowing the reader to add to more formal descriptions by abstracting the concept himself. The MBD syndrome, like the concept of "dog" is difficult to define rigorously but easy to teach by example.

One final point. *The case selection has been nonrandom.* In most of the cases there is a singularly dramatic response to medication. I do not wish to convey that such dramatic responses happen with boring regularity, but only that they do happen frequently. Failure to respond to treatment also occurs frequently, but I do not believe such instances are in danger of being unrecognized. What is useful is the reporting of cases which are similar in all discernible respects to illustrative nonresponding cases but do dramatically respond to treatment.

The cases provided are, I feel, sufficient to illustrate the concept and suggest its scope. The examples should also be sufficient to illustrate MBD's possible varying disguises.

1. Michael

Diagnostic subsyndrome: Classical hyperactive.
Age at contact: 8 years.
Duration of symptoms: Lifelong.
Duration of follow-up: 6 months.
Etiology: Unknown; congenital developmental (premature, congenital strabismus).
Response to treatment: Excellent.
Special features: Initial correct evaluation for 3 years without treatment; prompt and dramatic response to treatment.
Illustrating: Diagnosis and mistreatment; prompt and dramatic response to correct brief therapy.

Mike was referred to the clinic when he was 8 years old because of persistent behavioral and academic problems. He was a foster child, then in the third grade, who had been described for many years as having an "overabundance of energy." His teachers described him as of "above average intelligence," a poor student, and increasingly distractible and hyperactive. At home, although his foster mother perceived him as "really a good boy," discipline was a problem: he had "a poor ability to learn from experience," and could not control himself. When he was 6, his foster mother characterized his behavioral problems as follows: "At school his teacher tells me that he disrupts the class socially although he is very bright. Michael is still hyperactive. There is hardly a still moment in his day, but by 8:00 pm, if he is put to bed, he goes to sleep quickly. . . . He cries a lot, especially when told he cannot do something, when told he must come in from play, and also at mealtimes, because he does not want to eat. . . . He does not play well with the neighborhood children . . . he always wants to fight, wrestle, and poke people . . . he finds it difficult to play any game that isn't all activity. . . . He is always playing he is Superman, Zorro, etc." He had nightly enuresis and had never been trained. He was diagnosed as hyperactive at a pediatric clinic; his foster mother was told he would outgrow it, and he received no treatment.

His medical history was mildly suggestive of congenital difficulties: he was one month premature and weighed 5 lb, 1 oz at birth, and has a convergent strabismus which necessitated operative correction. His growth and development were normal and there were no neurological signs.

When he was 8 he was evaluated briefly by a pediatrician, who correctly diagnosed the problem and placed the boy on 5 mg of *d*-amphetamine (long-acting). A report from his teacher 3 months later read as follows: "Mike has improved considerably. . . . He feels he's taking the 'magic' pill and so he can do no wrong while under the influence of it. Consequently his whole self-image appears to have changed. He is now considered by *himself* and his *classmates* to be the *new* Mike, a 'good' Mike, the Mike who helps everyone. It's a joy to watch him these days with his changed self-concept. Some of his recent accomplishments were: (1) Chairman of the Social Study Committee (did a fantastic job); (2) reading comprehension score on Weekly Reader test jumped from 15 over 48 (January) to 33 over 48 (June); (3) stopped other children from bullying someone (January he was the bully)."

His foster mother reported a marked improvement in behavior at home and an approximately 50% decrease in his enuresis.

Amount of treatment time expended: Initial evaluation, 2 hours; follow-up visits, 2 hours.

2. Eugene

Diagnostic subsyndrome: Classical hyperactive, severe.
Age of contact: 10 years.
Duration of symptoms: Lifelong, severe 5 years.
Duration of follow-up: 2 years.

Etiology: ? Premature, early illness, ? genetic—maternal grandfather was an alcoholic; his mother had been variously described as being immature and as having no psychiatric difficulties.

Response to treatment: Very good.

Special features: Initial inadequate pharmacological treatment and nonindicated psychological therapy with a resultant delay of adequate treatment for 4 years. Immediate response to adequate drug treatment.

This child was referred to the child guidance clinic by his mother, who stated that her son had multiple problems including "no impulse control. [He's] aggressive with other children. . . . When he starts things he can't stop. . . . [He] lies about anything and everything, plays with matches, [is] attracted to dangerous things [e.g., the oven], does poorly at school, can't concentrate, must touch everything . . . and takes things apart."

Possibly relevant aspects of his medical history included the following: he was 1½ months premature; his birth weight was 4 lb, 9 oz; he was placed in an incubator for 4 days and was kept in the hospital for 6 weeks; he was hospitalized several times during the first 7 months of life because of "immature kidneys" and generalized edema.

The boy had received his first psychiatric evaluation when he was 6 and the family was then seen in psychotherapy for the succeeding 3 years. Eugene was seen in once-a-week therapy for a period of 2 years, during which time his mother was seen in a mothers' group and then for individual counseling. Intermittent family sessions were held throughout this period, during which he was reported to have received a trial of *d*-amphetamine, ostensibly with no success; the drug trial had apparently been quite brief. From the data available one cannot determine if the boy's initial failure to respond to medication and later good response were due to a maturational factor or to the fact that he initially received an inadequate trial (which seems quite likely).

The comments of the various mental health workers involved in the case over a period of 3 years are representative of the interpretations and explanations which are sometimes generated to account for MBD children. The social worker commented that "none of the men in mother's life have ever given her as much of what she thinks she needs and her husband would like to do this for her but feels inadequate. She indicated that we might possibly find that there is nothing wrong with Gene but that she hopes that we will not turn them down because they as parents need help. Mother is angry with a private kindergarten because they have not been able to give her the answers to her problems. She is a determined mother and she is determined that Gene should perform as well as the other children do." The psychologist, having observed that the boy was bright, verbal, and possessed of an unusually short attention span, went on to observe that the boy seemed to have a high degree of sensitivity and vulnerability, was preoccupied with right and wrong, and desired the approval of authority figures. She felt that his "early experiences have not prepared him adequately to meet the kind of demands he encounters, nor has he developed a tolerance threshold to allow him to cope effectively with everyday stress situations." After 8 months of psychotherapy he received a psychiatric evaluation because of "some anxiety about the potential for destructive behavior . . . and lack of impulse control generally." The psychiatrist observed that "at no time was there any difficulty in keeping his behavior under control and there was not an unusual amount of hyperactivity or distractibility in his play." Psychiatric therapy was continued as noted and another psychological evaluation was obtained almost 4 years later.

This psychologist administered the Rorschach, the Bender-Gestalt an intelligence test, and the Illinois Test of Psycholinguistic Abilities (ITPA). On the basis of the Rorschach findings this observer commented that the "Rorschach responses are the most revealing of his sense of inner disequilibrium with impulses and emotions overly fluid, and a seeking out that's almost of their own accord. Identifying with a battered creature, Gene seems to be saying that although he would like to be a butterfly, his structure has prevented such a role. Instead he must be a monster, so filled with energy that it is constantly poured out into his environment with blood, smoke and fire. Sensitive to the reactions of others, wanting approval, Gene nevertheless seems unable to successfully to defend against his explosiveness." The psychologist went on to add that the figure drawings and the sentence completion test "suggest that evasiveness, withdrawal, and denial have been major defenses used in handling the fear of his own impulsivity. A dependent, needful, orally devouring boy, Gene would seem to have found little substance in relationships within his immediate family. Rather, he sees worthiness as emanating only from the use of his head, on developing a conscience, doing what mother said in avoiding trouble." Commenting on the Bender-Gestalt and the ITPA, the psychologist observed that these revealed "developmental perceptual immaturity and exceedingly poor visual memory" while the ITPA also showed "serious difficulties in correctly reproducing a sequence of symbols previously seen and in expressing his ideas in spoken words." For the first time this examiner raised the opinion that "there should be some consideration of the neurological basis for this youngster's learning and behavioral difficulties. Although there is a "tragic quality [sic] to the family dynamics, Gene does seem to be also struggling with inner difficulties which seem to represent structural handicaps. Although neurological examination probably would prove negative there are sufficient soft signs from the psychological test materials to suggest that benefits might accrue from the trial of medication."

When seen at another child guidance at age 10, the boy was found to be friendly and to relate well, and the history was obtained as noted. He denied the existence of most difficulties and projected the blame for those he did acknowledge. Neurological examination revealed impaired fine-motor coordination together with a moderate degree of adiadochokinesis. His Bender-Gestalt drawings were extremely immature but otherwise unremarkable. He was begun on a trial of d-amphetamine, 10 mg/day. His mother called in two weeks to say that he was doing "excellently in school" and had been very pleasant at home. She called a week later and reported with suprise that "he has friends . . . he's in on time . . . he does what he is told . . . children come to the house for him . . . he's never been so good for so long in his whole life before." The school reported that "Gene's behavioral change has been a grand improvement. He does not seem as flighty as he appeared during our first semester. His frustration level has been reduced to a level that allows his normal productive days in the classroom. He does *now* sit and work contentedly for a greater length of time than he previously was able to do. No drowsiness is noticeable. His mood has come to be one of a receptive nature to all guidelines of an academic and disciplinary nature. He seems to be more valued as a friend than before. Children now seek his opinion and respect his worth as part of the class."

Amount of treatment time expended: First treatment program (3 years): approximately 200 hours individual and group psychotherapy and counseling. Second treatment program: interviews, 4 hours; telephone contacts, 2 hours.

3. Thomas

Diagnostic subsyndrome: Classical hyperactive, severe.

Age at contact: 7 years.

Duration of symptoms: 2 years.

Duration of follow-up: 2 years.

Etiology: ? Genetic—mother had two postpartum depressions.

Response to treatment: Very good.

Special features: Previous initial diagnosis incorrect, made on the basis of an individual interview with the child; confusion of active and reactive family dynamics, inadequate drug therapy.

This child was referred by his school public health nurse with the following complaints: "Disruptive classroom behavior, a discipline problem at home. Outbursts of misbehavior—seems to lack self control, especially when not under direct supervision of teacher (hits other children for no reasons, rolls on floor, jumps off of chairs). Even under teacher's direct supervision he talks out, makes facial grimaces. He gets out of his seat frequently. Even during his 'quiet' moments he seems tense; cracks his knuckles, plays with buttons on clothes, can't sit still. Has no close friends at school; seems to reject other children's attempts to make friends. Has above average ability but not working up to that level now." He had been tried on a variety of drugs: Atarax (200 mg/day) plus Benadryl (200 mg/day), Thorazine (150 mg/day) plus Benadryl (200 mg/day) reportedly without appreciable benefit. The school personnel had considered special educational and residential placement because of an increasingly difficult management problem in the classroom.

The boy had been evaluated at a traditional child guidance clinic for purposes of "crisis intervention." At that time the examining psychiatrist stated that the boy "could not be classified during this interview as a hyperactive child, however, there was constant movement—mild and out of his awareness—throughout the interview, primarily 'squirming in his seat'." Additional comments of the physician included that the session with the parents "revealed a very pathological triangle with a very disturbed mother as the core. One can speculate that the interaction observed by this interviewer was typical of this family's interactions. The mother had rejected Thomas and has labeled him as 'bad' and the 'cause of all my problems.' Therefore, if he is removed, i.e., punished or locked up, things will be all right. The father is brought in by mother's excessive demands since she is being overwhelmed and is dismayed at his being out of control (as his father is usually the instrument of Thomas' punishment). Thomas' reaction to mother's inability to maintain control appears to be his falling apart, impulsivity and hyperactive taking over, primarily at school. Hence, when mother is upset, his acting out behavior is unbearable both at home as well as at school. It is my opinion that Thomas is developing a chronic character disorder but that without family intervention as well as therapy for him, specifically geared for their difficulties, therapy alone for him will be quite unsuccessful."

The boy's behavior had been exacerbated with a family move and entrance into a new school, and the referring history implied that his difficulties had begun at this time. Reports from his previous school revealed, however, that the child had never been well adjusted: he had "spit, hit and had temper tantrums . . . his behavior fluctuated drastically . . . sometimes he was moody and at other times exceptionally mean." The developmental history revealed that the boy had always been very active, that he had been "always into things and on the go," that he had had "no interest span," attentiveness, stick-to-itiveness, and that he had always blown up easily and cried readily. He had marked sibling rivalry, his 11-year-old brother always having been a model student and son. An interview with the parents revealed them to be indeed human—even if rather rigid—and people who might be expected to react poorly to a child with the characteristics of their son. The mother had a history of psychiatric illness, having been twice hospitalized for "postnatal depression." The parents stated that in addition to the drugs reported, the boy had been tried on Ritalin (dose unknown) and that this had aggravated his problem. Examination revealed a large, good-looking boy with two congenital stigmata (small incurving fingers; large, very low-slung ears). His Bender-Gestalt test was exceedingly careful and accurate. His neurological examination revealed no difficulties, his speech was well organized, his affect appropriate, his ability to relate good. His expressed concerns about his increasingly poor school record. He was begun on d-amphetamine, 10 mg/day, and on this dose he was reported to be cranky, irritable, slowed down, and moody, and to have insomnia. However, there was some slight improvement and accordingly it was decided to increase this medication until the boy had benefit or toxic symptoms. His behavioral response increased with increasing dosage and he responded optimally with 35 mg/day in divided dosage. He was returned to school, where his behavior was excellent: he had no difficulty with his peers or his teachers. At home his "temper" stopped entirely, discipline problems disappeared, and he no longer fought with his brother.

An ironic and informative side effect of Thomas' successful treatment was the appearance of slight behavioral problems in the brother as Thomas improved. The phenomenon of one family member becoming more ill as another becomes better is well recognized and is generally attributed to some form of "homeostasis," that is, one member's sickness was "serving a need for the family." In this family what occurred was that the parents had previously not noticed the brother's comparatively minor difficulties until Thomas' conspicuous problems were ameliorated. When this happened, his older brother's foibles became more visible, he began to be disciplined for them, and reacted predictably. Minimal counseling with the parents (whose standards were high) was able to change their expectations and demands of the older brother.

Amount of treatment time expended: Initial evaluation, 2 hours; follow-up visits, 8 hours; telephone follow-up, one hour.

4. Gilbert

Diagnostic subsyndrome: Classical hyperactive.
Age of contact: 8 years.
Duration of symptoms prior to contact: At least 6 years.
Duration of follow-up: 2 years.
Etiology: Unclear. No evidence of neurological insult, genetic background, or psychological stress.
Response to treatment: Very poor.
Special features: This case exemplifies those "classically" MBD children who, for reasons that are not understood, fail to respond adequately to drug therapy.

This 8-year-old boy was brought to a child guidance clinic with a lifelong history of "classic" hyperactivity. His mother stated that he had been very active from the time of birth, had shown rapid motor development, walking at under a year, and had as a toddler manifested extreme destructive behavior which was not malicious: the boy was good-natured but was always a "bull in a china shop," breaking toys and lamps, and wearing out his clothes at a prodigious rate. As a toddler and preschooler he had been impossible to discipline. He inevitably—and good-naturedly—"forgot," although when carefully supervised he would willingly perform a task. He was extremely outgoing and until the fourth grade he had adjusted well with teachers and peers. Despite his noncompliance, his genuine good nature had prevented anyone from becoming seriously resentful of the boy. The parents had been able to tolerate his behavior and consulted the clinic only because Gilbert was beginning to have academic difficulty in school, and was beginning to manifest antisocial behavior, stealing small amounts of money from his mother's purse and small articles from stores.

The parents were counseled and the boy was begun on drug therapy. Large doses of amphetamines (40 mg/day) and methylphenidate (up to 80 mg/day) proved ineffective as did tricyclic antidepressants (imipramine up to 100 mg/day). The boy was begun on phenothiazines (chlorpromazine), and by gradually increasing the dose to the point of producing lethargy (400 mg/day) the more extreme manifestations of his behavior were ameliorated. He became less fidgety, was able to sit still longer in the classroom, and was able to perform his work somewhat better. His refractoriness to discipline and his antisocial behavior continued. Counseling the parents to set extremely firm limits modified his behavior somewhat but at time of follow-up he was still an extremely difficult child who was producing such turmoil in his home, community, and school that institutionalization was seriously being considered.

Amount of treatment time expended: Approximately 10–15 hours, including visits and telephone calls. Considerable time had to be expended in attempts to regulate the boy's medication and in counseling and supporting his understandably troubled parents.

5. Robert

Diagnostic subsyndrome: Sociopathic.
Age of contact: 7½ years.
Duration of symptoms prior to contact: 3 years.
Duration of follow-up: 3 years.
Etiology: Suggestive genetic. Father—learning difficulties and uncoordination.
Response to treatment: Excellent but with abnormal features (see below).
Special features: Dramatic treatment response to amphetamines accompanied by the development of drug-induced schizoid characteristics.

This child was referred to a child guidance clinic at the age of 7½; the chief complaints were that he had been stealing and firesetting for the previous 2 years. The initial consultation was on an "emergency" basis. The boy had twice set fire to the family's living-room furniture within the previous week and on both occasions the fire department had to be called. This represented the zenith of his misbehavior; but his mother stated that for 2 years he had been stealing virtually "constantly" from her pocketbook, that he had taken things from drug stores and grocery stores on a number of occasions, that he had been playing more or less compulsively with matches (although hitherto with comparative lack of success—he had only succeeded in firing a few small wastepaper baskets).

His mother, a bright, psychologically minded, lower-middle-class woman, provided an explanation for Bobby's difficulties, attributing them to money problems at home during the past 2 years with resultant tensions between the parents: "Bobby certainly picks it up." The mother also saw a clear relation between Bobby's problems and differences in discipline techniques between the boy's grandparents and parents. The former, first-generation Italian immigrants, were immensely proud of their oldest grandson, could see no wrong in him, and "indulged the boy much too much." His mother felt that somehow his misbehavior was aggravated by "strictness" (a mixture of both firmness and punitiveness) and that, for example, the boy's enuresis increased with stress. She felt herself "over a barrel" in that what seemed to be a logical solution only made the problem worse.

The boy's mother was somewhat annoyed at the psychiatrist
a developmental and medical history. She seemed to be indicating
an irrelevant medical formality which was precluding the vital discus
problems between herself, her husband, and the boy's grandparents
mother had had a somewhat difficult pregnancy with probable pretoxe.
labor had lasted 38 hours and at the time of delivery the baby suff
"sprained neck muscle" and subsequently had a wry neck. Early moto
velopment seemed to be normal: he began to walk at 14 months: "He was
starting and never stopped after that." As an infant he had hypo-gamma glc
ulinemia, with repeated infections. The mother acknowledged—as an irrelevan
attribute of a boy whose major problems were not trivial—that he had always
been extremely active and fidgety, and easily bored. Another attribute she regarded as incidental was his very poor coordination: he had only recently
learned to tie his shoes, and that with difficulty and considerable practice; despite relative fearlessness he had been unable to learn to ride a bicycle; he
could not throw or catch a ball.

At home during the past 2 years the mother had noticed increasingly severe
temper tantrums and rebelliousness. He was affectionately independent and instrumentally dependent: "He would like to be independent but he can't. I have
to do a great many things for him." Enuresis was persistent; he had never
been trained at night and at the time of consultation was wetting several times
per week. He related well with his two younger sibs and peers. He was outgoing, somewhat aggressive, and inclined to be bossy, and on some occasions
other children rejected him because of this bossiness.

He had had school difficulties since kindergarten. He had to repeat kindergarten because he was "too immature." In the first grade he was described as
having reading difficulties and was thereafter placed in a special reading class.
His first-grade teacher described him as "slow to mature" with a short attention
span and an inability to sit still—he was continually getting up and wandering
around the classroom; he "could do his work but he won't. . . . When things
don't go his way he just rushes out."

The boy's family history was of some interest. His father described himself
as a slow starter in school who had been unusually poorly coordinated as a
boy. Bobby's 4-year-old brother had speech and hearing problems, possible
dysphasia, and seemingly relatively normal intelligence. He was enrolled in a
nursery school for multiply handicapped children.

It was felt that the boy had rather clear-cut MBD syndromes which had been
masked by his "acting-out." He was begun on d-amphetamine and referred to
a university treatment program in physical reeducation for poorly coordinated
children. His response to treatment was of considerable interest.

He was begun on 10 mg of amphetamine per day and one week later his
mother reported that "he is behaving like an angel . . . he is a different child."
The following week she spontaneously offered the doctor a note detailing his
progress: "(1) he has been practicing his numbers and reading by himself;
(2) he has been coloring and improving very rapidly [prior to beginning medication he had quite poor fine-motor control]; (3) he has been helpful to his

parents and brothers with and without being asked; (4) he hasn't been hanging on his grandmother like he usually does; (5) there has been no stealing and no fires; (6) he has had almost no outbursts of temper. It is like a miracle from heaven. For the first time in 4 years he is enjoying life instead of fighting it." He continued to maintain his progress for 2 months when his mother reported, "at first he was doing very well on the pills . . . now it's starting up again." He had begun to bedwet and had started to steal and have temper outbursts. His medication was gradually increased to between 15 and 20 mg of d-amphetamine per day, with resultant total control of his behavioral problems. Increase in dosage was accompanied by an unexpected and disturbing side effect. When the medication was increased to 20 mg/day, Bobby had no problems with impulsivity, hyperactivity, or disobedience but lost his previous gregariousness and ease with peers. His mother—who became quite adept at controlling his medication—found that there was a very narrow dose range in which her son could be maintained, i.e., in which his behavior was controlled without excessive inhibition. When the dose was increased by a very small amount above this level (5 mg/day) Bobby became "preoccupied, dreamy . . . and wanted to spend all his time by himself." During the 3-year period of follow-up (at the end of which he was still on medication), his behavioral difficulties at school disappeared, his grades became adequate, and he became increasingly popular with his peers, who began to seek him out. Although still not outgoing, he became genuinely responsive and was gradually learning to be appropriately social: he was now fond of other children and apparently *learning* to be outgoing. In retrospect, his extroversion prior to beginning treatment seemed less substantial than his social adjustment 2 years later. He has not outgrown his need for medication. On those few occasions on which his mother has forgotten to give it to him he has exhibited considerable behavioral aggression with excessive negativism, activity, and volatility. It appears that social learning has taken place but that such learning has not been sufficient to compensate for his still-present physiological difficulties.

Amount of treatment time expended: During 3-year period: initial interview, 2 hours; follow-up interviews, 6 hours; telephone calls, 4 hours.

6. Sean

Diagnostic subsyndrome: Sociopathic
Age of contact: 16 years.
Duration of symptoms: Lifelong.
Duration of follow-up: 2 months.
Etiology: Unknown.
Response to treatment: Too brief to evaluate with certainty—apparently good.
Special features: Chronic "sociopathy," unresponsive to residential care, hospitalization, or multiple drug trials; quickly responsive to stimulant drug therapy.

This 16-year-old boy was referred by the Juvenille Court for psychiatric evaluation of his delinquent behavior. During the previous year the boy had been convicted of auto theft, placed in a residential children's evaluation center for one month, referred for intensive treatment, and then sent to a State hospital because no adequate treatment facilities were available. The report to the Court implied that Sean's troubles had started at age 13: "Since then he has been running away from the military school when he became angry . . . has stolen two cars . . . and in public school was not disruptive but would not work or cooperate. He stole whiskey from home but stated he did not drink it on the school bus or at stops [sic]."

The boy had been adopted at five months and was the oldest of three brothers, having one adopted brother and another who was the biological offspring of the parents. His father was a rigid, stern, retired Army doctor, his mother less forceful and psychologically more absent. Previous agencies characterized both parents as lacking in affection and warmth toward the child. Both of the boy's siblings were described as having been well adjusted, having done well in school, having gotten along well with their peers and the parents.

A brief history revealed that the boy's problems extended much further back in time: his mother reported that "he was hard to train" and that he went through periods of soiling and smearing feces until 3 years of age. He was a thumb-sucker and a nail-biter "from an early age," "argued and argued until he got his way," and "would never mind his parents." From early latency he had stolen money from his mother's purse, and his parents considered him a "chronic thief." Previous psychological evaluation had stated "he showed little remorse about stealing from his brothers, from stores, from his parents. . . . Most recently he has shown a fascination for knives and razor blades and 'in jest' his parents reported he 'playfully' held a knife to his younger brother's throat, daring him to move."

The child's full case folder included many dynamic observations by previous observers.

1. Pupil personnel worker, Board of Education. "It became apparent that both Dr. and Mrs. X tend to be rather rigid parents but, at the same time, can be inconsistent in making the children follow through on requests. The most obvious finding on the psychological examination was the boiling hostility and undisguised rage Sean experiences, which is primarily directed towards his father. . . . He said his father does not understand him, won't listen when he has anything to say, and all he (that is, the father) thinks about is work and study. . . . Mother is described in more positive terms and he claims, at least verbally, to like her. One senses through psychological testing that he does not experience a great deal of warmth from her either, however.

"He is indeed a troubled, angry, and impulsive young man who, though having essentially average intellect, has little interest in academic activities at this time. He is expressing his negativism and resentment of his father in increasingly more open rebellion. . . . There is no indication of any severe psychopathology at the present time, but this does not obviate Sean's very real need for psychotherapy in order to help him cope with ever increasing anger toward authority figures."

2. Evaluation from children's residential center. Sean was observed to be a "rather immature, strong-willed youngster who had great difficulty adjusting to the group . . . he was noted to have a very quick temper, and was very belligerent when he could not have his way. He appeared to resent authority and had to be supervised rather closely. . . . He sought adult attention and preferred this on a one-to-one basis. . . . He can become very angry, hostile and sullen if his every request does not get immediate response. . . . He used profanity quite frequently and could act out in an aggressive manner." The dynamic formulation read partly as follows: "The extreme anxiety under which this youngster functions is quite striking . . . [it] is primarily in interpersonal relationships and certainly can be attributed to the home situation, which he perceives as being barren, a source of conflict to him and one which causes him to be extremely disorganized and impulsive. . . . He is an extremely insecure youngster who feels very inadequate and unsatisfied with himself . . . he has been rejected, feels deeply hurt, and is determined to retaliate against the father's authority and everything he represents. He attempts to overcome his own insecurity by acting in a very aggressive way, seeking attention and recognition by associating himself with the antisocial elements. He is an extremely dependent child who desperately tries to conceal his fears and his dependency, which is overwhelming and anxiety-arousing."

At the time of the clinic evaluation his parents were administered a standard children's behavior questionnaire which inquired, among other things, about the child's activity level. On a 1- to 4-point scale they reported that as a latency child Sean was judged to be scale point 4 on "can't keep still, always into things, fails to finish things he starts, easily discouraged and gives up, gets overexcited." None of the mental health workers who had spoken to the parents previously had inquired concerning this attribute of the child's behavior. The boy himself described his behavior as ego dystonic. The boy had a suprising amount of insight: he saw himself as going to prison if he didn't "straighten out" and was at a loss to understand what was causing him to behave in a self-injurious manner. He was not fond of his parents (as previous reports indicated), and indeed his father had reacted to the boy's impulsivity with extreme punitiveness. The parents were exceedingly eager to have the boy placed in a residential school—out of their jurisdiction and out of their home—and it was only possible to give him a brief trial of medication before he left the home. During his previous admission to the State hospital, the therapist had exhausted a substantial fraction of the psychiatric drug armamentarium, including Thorazine, Dilantin, and Tofranil, with no appreciable effects. As a therapeutic trial the boy was placed on methylphenidate, 10 mg B.I.D., and the surprised mother reported 2 weeks later that for the first time in the past 10 years he had stolen nothing. Arrangements had been made, however, for his residential placement, and the parents believing this improvement was magical and doomed not to last, carried through with their plans. The short trial documents nothing, but the change in his behavior was obviously not due to a drug placebo effect: until the trial of Ritalin he had been receiving two active placebos, Thorazine and Dilantin, at the clinic. The abrupt change in behavior, which included increased calmness and decreased feelings of hopelessness, began immediately following the drug trial.

What would have happened had he continued on the medication or remained at home must remain problemmatical.

Amount of treatment time expended: Psychiatric interviews, 2 hours.

7. Royce

Diagnostic subsyndrome: Mixed sociopathic and neurotic; adolescent school underachievement.
Age of contact: 14½ years.
Duration of symptoms prior to contact: At least 5 years.
Duration of follow-up: one year.
Etiology: Unclear. Temperamental MBD child reacting to familial stress.
Response to treatment: Very good.
Special features: MBD syndrome in adolescence with manifest behavioral problems, both antisocial and intrafamilial; seemingly causative (actually reactive) dynamic overlay—Oedipal problems.

This 14½-year-old boy was referred to a child guidance clinic by the Juvenile Court. The Court had become involved when the boy had been discovered repeatedly stealing small sums of money from the mother of a friend; he has used the money to make small purchases, not in any particularly meaningful way (e.g., he did not use the money to "buy" friends). He had not begun his stealing in response to any readily discernible change in his family's fortunes, either pecuniary or libidinal. The Court had apparently considered a psychiatric referral because the mother had stated that Royce had manifested other psychological difficulties as well.

At the time of referral he was in the ninth grade where he was getting C's and E's. This was representative of his past performance; he had never failed but had obtained barely passing grades throughout his school history. At school he apparently ingratiated himself with his teachers and only his mathematics teacher (in whose course he was doing most poorly) commented on Royce's inattentiveness, difficulty in concentrating, and poor peer relations. His other teachers were impressed with the seemingly psychodynamically relevant aspects of his home life. One teacher indicated that Royce "has some concerns over his relationship with his stepdad. He has not talked enough about it for me to be certain of how much disagreement there is between him and his stepdad. I think something important may be going on."

The mother indicated that at home there was indeed "something going on with the stepdad." Royce's father had died 5 years previously in an automobile accident. This was reported to have been an exceedingly traumatic event for the boy, who learned of his father's death on television before the family had been informed. Royce had been his father's favorite, and his mother—perhaps with a touch of jealousy—felt that Royce had always been overindulged and insufficiently disciplined. Most of his father's failings were "rectified" when the boy's mother had remarried a year and a half following the father's death. The boy's stepfather was rigid, hot-tempered, and, the mother felt, "perhaps a little bit violent . . . so I'm afraid to interfere . . . particularly when he has been drinking." The stepfather had been increasingly upset by the boy's close ties with his mother, his poor school performance, and his "instigating" the younger children into various acts of misbehavior.

When interviewed the boy was a good-looking, friendly, warm, open, sad child who was rather vague about the reasons for his appearance at the Court or clinic. His affect was seemingly appropriate and no cognitive abnormalities, gross or subtle, were present. He described his stepfather's abuse and his step-father's jealousy of the close relationship between him and his mother. He stated that his relationship with his mother had been intensified by his feelings of being unloved by his foster parent. The boy was so warm and appealing and related so well (in contrast to the usual adolescent who has been caught with his hand in the cookie jar) that it made the interviewer think that he might be dealing with an early sociopathic personality.

Royce had four siblings, the oldest of whom was married and out of the home. An older brother was also getting along poorly with the stepfather; the younger children, both girls, were not. It had seemed very clear to all mental health parties concerned that many of the boy's problems were secondary to a two-generation family triangle, which had been aggravated—as is often the case—by the presence of a stepparent.

Relevant aspects of Royce's past history were as follows: as a baby and toddler he had been "very restless . . . he always had to have something to do . . . he was never able to sit still . . . he had tons of nervous energy . . . he couldn't sit still with reading . . . he never sat for a moment in front of the TV." The mother described a low frustration tolerance, an extremely short attention span, and marked clumsiness, which in earlier days had resulted in his habitually breaking things and in later life had made him a conspicuously poor athlete. In regard to his peer relationships his mother said that he was "never shy. . . . He's always been forward enough . . . but he loses friends. . . . He's never had any close friends. . . . He likes younger children he can boss around." At school his marks had been at best C's and in the upper grades he had usually come home without his books claiming that there had been no homework. On those occasions on which he brought work home he failed to do it. His mother stated that his major problem was "a failure to learn to read right . . . like his sister . . . he can't grasp and retain, they say."

The mother was unable to explain why Royce's biological father had pre-ferred the boy to his older brother but stated that he always had. She felt that as a result Royce had learned to "take advantage of people and use them . . . he plays on their sympathy." She felt that the boy had little ability to discipline himself, that he had failed to learn by discipline at home but had learned to to blame others for his own problems. The mother described increasing diffi-culty with her second husband, whom she blamed for aggravating the boy's problems. She felt that this husband was probably right but "too strong," and felt an increasingly strong need to take the part of her son.

It was the evaluator's impression that Royce was an MBD child "partially grown up," with some beginning sociopathic characteristics. It was felt that his problems had been exacerbated by the handling of both fathers. The boy was begun on *d*-amphetamine with caution (because of his age), and gradually increased to 30 mg/day. His mother stated that on the medication he became quieter, more tractable, easier to talk to (in which judgment his probation officer concurred), and that his grades had improved at school, most E's having been advanced to C's. She still felt that the boy was unusually demanding of attention and fearful of being "left out." Royce described feeling "pretty good" and stated that the medicine made his head "feel clearer" so that he could concentrate much better," and [I] feel a lot more relaxed." The school reported improved academic performance: increased attention, better concentration, decreased daydreaming, decreased stubbornness with the teacher, and improved peer relations (his isolation had diminished considerably).

Amount of treatment time expanded: During one-year period: initial interview, 2 hours; follow-up interviews, 4 hours; telephone calls, one hour.

8. Carl and Jim

Diagnostic subsyndrome: Special learning disorder.
Age at contact: 11 and 12 years.
Duration of symptoms: Carl–6 years; Jim–lifelong.
Duration of follow-up: 3 years.
Etiology: Genetic—mother had identical reading problems, as did the boys' two
    brothers (to a much lesser degree).
Response to treatment: Excellent.
Special features: Familial dyslexia with occurrences in all siblings. Identical
    reading problems with differing early histories: Jim, the older sib, was more typ-
    ically hyperactive while Carl had a history of being withdrawn and hypoactive.

The boys' mother brought her younger son, Carl (then 11), with the chief complaint of behavior and learning problems in school. She reported that all four of her boys (the others were 9, 12, and 14) had had reading difficulties characterized by reversals. The mother herself had had rather serious reading difficulties as a child, and even now, at age 41, had some slight persistent difficulties, which were not preventing her from getting her Ph.D.

The boy himself had an interesting history. His neuromuscular development was somewhat slow; he walked at a year and a half; he spoke in sentences at about 3 years. The parents had considered him to be quiet as a baby and perhaps somewhat fidgety as a toddler. Of his attention span, the mother reported, "If he's interested he's there until its completely done." The parents reported him to be unassertive socially. In preschool he was shy. Having entered nursery school at age 4 he refused to talk and he began to talk again only when he was 5. "He forms long-term associations with several boys . . . he doesn't fight . . . he just doesn't relate . . . but the other children in my family are even less sociable." (Both parents described themselves as having been shy during childhood and both presented a picture of well-adjusted, somewhat schizoid people.) The school complaints had been typical: short attention span; inability to complete work; clowning in class and annoying his peers. His I.Q. was normal and he was reported to be "very dexterous manually."

The mother was seen once, the boy seen once, and the situation was fully explained to the parents. He was begun on *d*-amphetamine and the dosage was regulated via phone contacts (half a dozen) during the following year and a half. His mother reported that the treatment had been "marvelous" with a total disappearance of the boy's school difficulties and an unasked-for improvement in his behavior at home. Although the mother had previously not complained of his behavior at home she realized that when he was off medication in the summer his behavior had reverted to the *status quo ante,* which had been less good than she had remembered. On the medication his temper had disappeared, he stopped fighting with his friends, and he became more popular. The boy referred to *d*-amphetamine as his "magic pills" (as did case history 1., "Michael") and never failed to remind his mother to give them to him on those rare occasions on which she forgot to do so.

Because of the dramatic improvement in her 11-year-old son the mother referred his 12-year-old brother, Jim, who had had somewhat similar difficulties. This child's history was atypically hyperactive; although he was insensitive, fought religiously, and was not a bit withdrawn, he was not hyperactive at home. The mother reported that—unlike most "hyperactive" children—"tiredness and sleepiness have always been a problem" and that the boy had always required an "unusual" amount of sleep. Teachers' complaints had included daydreaming and "sleepiness." Unlike most such children he had a considerable degree of insight. The boy reported that he had difficulty concentrating, that the other children realized he had a low boiling point and consequently picked on him, and that he felt himself to be a loser, friendless, and unliked. Dynamically, the mother felt that she had first censured this boy because of his more blatantly objectionable behavior and subsequently attempted to make amends, with resultant diminished limit-setting. The family situation would have provided very fertile grounds for the confusion of cause and effect if the family interrelationships had been exposed to a dynamic interpretation.

The older boy was also placed on *d*-amphetamine and his response, although initially not as striking, became as good over the next several months. On medication the boy's grades improved, he developed increased initiative (setting up a newspaper route), and he began to get along much better with his teachers and peers.

Amount of treatment time expended: Initial evaluation, 2 hours (total, both boys); follow-up interviews, 2 hours; follow-up telephone calls, 2 hours.

9. Edward

Diagnostic subsyndrome: "Neurotic" with adolescent school underachievement.
Age at contact: 15 years.
Duration of symptoms prior to contact: ? 10 years.
Duration of follow-up: 6 months.

Etiology: Suggestive genetic: mother—cyclothymic personality and endogenous depression.

Response to treatment: Good but parents terminated because of other family problems.

Special features: Multiple familial occurrence of syndrome, modification of symptom picture in adolescence, complex obscuring family dynamics, response to tricyclic antidepressants.

This 15-year-old boy was referred by his parents because of continuing difficulties which had been unsuccessfully treated at a psychoanalytically oriented child guidance clinic. The parents were concerned about their son's "continuing to do very badly in school. . . . That's been true since kindergarten . . . his attitude is negativistic or at best indifferent."

Edward was the middle child of three brilliant children, all of whom had done poorly academically despite superior intelligence. His older sister, a sophomore in college, had ranked second in her class on the National Merit Scholarship Test (in a highly competitive upper-middle-class suburb where the mean I.Q. of her peers was probably 120) and was now flunking in college. His 9-year-old sister had a full-scale I.Q. of 148 on the WISC and was getting low B's. This sister was described as "unable to finish her work in school and unable to relate well to her peers." She was "wild, positive, domineering." On scholastic aptitude tests Edward himself placed in the 99th percentile verbally and the 87th percentile nonverbally. He was obtaining C's and D's in all his subjects at the time of his consultation.

The family background was most interesting. The boy's father was an extremely bright, obsessive, self-made man, an only child who had been reared in the backwoods of New England and was currently employed as a high-level computer executive. His wife was an English-speaking ex-war bride who appears to have been chronically hypomanic in her youth but who had been chronically depressed for a period of several years. The parents' marital adjustment was poor. Whereas formerly they had spent much time together, they now avoided each other assiduously. The boy's father took every opportunity to take long business trips while the mother kept to herself at home. She had a large and close-knit family several thousand miles away and had made no effort to develop close friends in this country. The family was initially seen together and group meetings were sparkling. The mother emerged from her depression to produce and parry incisive repartee in which the boy joined with a skill not to be expected in a clever adult. Underlying the banter, both parents were depressed and confused about their children's collective academic failure. Both had expressed their dissatisfaction with Edward articulately and he responded in kind. In their previous therapeutic experience the family had been treated in a two-generation group. What that therapist perceived as transpiring is not known, but the parents felt that he had implied repeatedly that they had been excessively demanding and had thereby caused their children's problems. It was quite clear that Edward's performance (like his siblings') was not in accordance with parental expectations. The parents were angry at the implication of the previous therapist that they had caused their children's troubles; they believed, rather, that they had merely reacted to them. As is usually the case after the fact, it was impossible to decide what might be an accurate interpretation from the history of the parent-child transactions. Because the two younger children seemed to have many MBD characteristics it seemed that the parents may have been partially justified in their indignation, that is, there was a strong suspicion that the two younger children would have done badly academically given any set of parents.

Edward's developmental history was "classically" that of a hyperactive MBD child. He was "crying when born . . . and had problems from age 2." He was described as hyperactive from early childhood, always on the go, and unable to sit still. He had "habitually" destroyed toys and clothes, and had always been negativistic and "excessively" independent. He "antagonized other children who . . . wouldn't play with him." He was "almost kicked out of kindergarten" and had been maintaining a marginal adjustment to authority ever since. He had been "destructive" in grade school and had continually made inappropriate comments in class. As a latency-age child he clowned and talked loudly. As a brilliant adolescent he baited his teachers, thought circles around many of them, and vented his proficient sarcasm on the slower ones; not surprisingly he was very unpopular with them.

His parents reported in passing that he had been poorly coordinated all his life. Despite their efforts to teach him he was unable to tie his shoes until he was 10 years old. He was still a bad athlete in visual-motor sports but had compensated by participating in track and swimming; the boy had seized upon a useful compensatory device for MBD children.

He had never gotten into serious difficulty outside the home. Both parents were hypermoralistic churchgoers and Edward voiced the virtues of a good ascetic life in a manner now 50 years anachronistic.

The boy partially acknowledged that he was having difficulties but attributed them—as did his family—to his superiority. He realized that others disliked him for his brilliance, but he totally failed to see that he goaded them into hostility. His poor academic performance he attributed to a lack of interest, and as a demonstration of his own academic abilities he cited his performance outside of school.

The boy was felt to be a MBD child "grown up," who was suffering not only from a continuation of his previous difficulties but also from psychological characteristics ingrained on the basis of those difficulties; in addition he was embroiled in a complex family dispute. Because of his age he was begun on amitriptyline, 75 mg/day, and within 3 weeks gradually began to "slow down" in the classroom. He described himself as decreasingly boisterous and manifested pride in what he perceived as his increasing ability to control his own behavior. Concomitantly his grades improved from C's and D's to B's and C's. He and his parents received psychotherapy once a week and then once every 2 weeks for a period of 4 months. During this time he managed a *modus vivendi* with his parents. He acknowledged his father's domineeringness and his mother's intrusiveness, agreed that these were defects that were unlikely to change, and became appropriately tolerant without becoming submissive. At the end of 6 months his school behavior and grades had improved, as had his family relations. The mother had become increasingly depressed and the boy's father increasingly unwilling to admit the now rather obvious mental illness in his wife and a possible biochemical defect in his children. He decided independently that he did not want his son treated with agents whose long-term effects were not known. That scientific rationalization was agreed with, but it was mentioned to him that such possible dangers had to be weighed against the present effects of discontinuing medication. The boy's father decided to discontinue the amitriptyline and over the next four weeks the boy's boisterous school behavior returned, his grades declined, and the familial problems reappeared. The boy's father became increasingly upset and depressed, withdrew from treatment, and refused to seek further treatment for either Edward or his mother. Follow-up is not known.

Amount of treatment time expended: Family and individual psychotherapy, 16 hours.

10. Tim

Diagnostic Subsyndrome: Special learning disorder; sociopathic ("acting up").
Age at contact: 14 years.
Duration of symptoms prior to contact: School difficulties, 8 years; behavioral problems, ? 2–4 years.
Duration of follow-up: 2 years.
Etiology: Unknown.
Response to treatment: Excellent.
Special features: MBD syndrome in early adolescence with overlay of psychopathology concealing the deviant manifestations of the syndrome; prompt and dramatic response to treatment.

Tim, a 14-year-old boy, was referred by his parents, who complained that within a period of a month he had been involved in two episodes of stealing: in the first he had premeditatively stolen a friend's mother's car keys and with some friends had taken a "joy ride"; he was caught by the police and severely reprimanded by his parents. His next misdemeanor was stealing 30¢ worth of candy in a drugstore while carrying several dollars in his pocket.

His parents had finally initiated psychiatric contact because of these two conspicuous social violations but stated that these represented only exaggerated instances of an increasing number of similar problems during his early adolescence. He had always maintained a trivial, passive, forgetful disobedience; he violated his curfews, "forgot" to put his clothes away, "forgot" to take out the garbage. In school he continued to get the C's and D's which he had maintained throughout his academic career. Tim was a somewhat soft boy and there were some mild indications of feminine identification; he was pudgy but not grossly feminine in appearance, was not interested in girls or athletics, and was slightly interested in feminine activities. His mother felt that she had never been able to "reach him" but that recently this difficulty had extended to her husband as well. The only other problem was persistent but relatively infrequent enuresis.

The boy himself was friendly, unusually open, seemed to relate very well (in a childish, not a psychopathic manner), and conveyed a strong impression of being both awkward and "dopey." He had no understanding of what had been happening or why.

Tim was one of two adopted children, having a sister 2 years his senior. She had never presented either academic or behavioral problems. His developmental history was relevant. His parents stated that there had been much crying during his first year of life, that he had always been motorically active, had worn out clothes very rapidly, had broken toys unmaliciously but consistently, and was—at least until the age of 8 or 9—very fidgety, twitchy, and unable to sit still. He was and had been stubborn, outgoing, and good-naturedly noncompliant. His "stick-to-itiveness" and boiling point had always been low. At school he was popular with peers and teachers, the latter always feeling that he might be quite bright if he "only settled down." His adoptive parents were relatively undisturbed people who were warm and neither fiercely bright nor blessed with excessive amounts of psychological insight.

Tim was given a battery of psychological tests and the most striking findings were in the style and manner with which he attempted to solve problems. The psychologist noted repeated indications of impulsivity: Tim would jump to an incorrect answer without delaying and then gradually correct himself. In contrast to some assertions about the patterning of psychological test responses, Tim showed superior motor performance and somewhat deficient verbal performance on the test administered. There were no indications of neurological damage on the Bender-Gestalt test or the Graham-Kendall Memory for Designs Test. There were likewise no indications of psychosis. The psychologist felt the boy's verbal inabilities were so gross that it was doubtful that he could finish high school.

He was begun on d-amphetamine, 10 mg/day, and promptly had a dramatic alteration in his behavior. The boy described himself as being able to concentrate better, his grades improved (going from C's and D's to B's), and, most striking to the parents, he began to follow all instructions both at home and in school. He became very communicative and eagerly discussed academic and other matters with his parents. The week the d-amphetamine was begun his enuresis stopped totally. A follow-up for one year revealed a maintenance of the improvement already reported.

Amount of treatment time expended: Interviews, 4 hours; telephone follow-up, one hour.

11. Larry

Diagnostic subsyndrome: Moderately severe classical hyperactivity with some schizophrenic features.

Age at contact: 8½ years.

Duration of symptoms: 5 years.

Duration of follow-up: 3 years.

Etiology: ? Genetic—maternal grandparents ? borderline psychotic, maternal great-aunt psychotic, mother chronically hypomanic.

Response to treatment: Fair to amphetamines; good to combined drug and operant therapy management.

Special features: Clear-cut therapeutic benefit from drug treatment (phenothiazines) of mother and operant therapy for boy.

The parents contacted the clinic when Larry was 8½, asking for help because he was continuing to bed-wet (he had never been trained completely), was stealing at home and at school, lied unnecessarily to his parents, and was excessively evasive.

His mother, a woman who was hypomanic at least, tended to deny appreciable problems in the past. She attributed her son's difficulties to the family's move from England to the U.S., which had been occasioned by his Army father's transfer. Pregnancy and birth history were described as normal. There was no history of neurological damage. Neuromuscular development was also described as normal. As an infant and toddler he was said not to have been particularly active or moody, stubborn, or balky. He was, said the mother, "closer to me . . . but he likes his father best." Peer relations were described as excellent: "He has buckets of friends . . . they come to play with him all the time." The only difficulties were as follows: "He just doesn't want to understand. . . . You can't believe him for a million dollars . . . he looks you in the eye and then goes out and does the same bad thing all over again. . . . You can't trust him." The boy had been evaluated at the age of 6 at an Army Hospital for "minor stealing" and enuresis. A psychological evaluation at the time showed him to have a full-scale I.Q. of 123 (verbal I.Q. 110, performance I.Q. 132) and "very astute perceptual motor skills." He was described as having "rich, imaginative process . . . [which] were brought to bear in a rather hostile, hypercritical manner." The dynamics were interpreted as follows: "His resentment seemed especially directed towards his mother for failing to satisfy his demands for attention, and indirectly towards the siblings, seeing them as rivals for his mother's attention. Thus he tends to express very intense needs for affection and attention and seems to resort to negative (e.g., stealing), 'babyish' (e.g., enuresis) behavior as a way of expressing this need." His enuresis was ameliorated by a small dose (25 mg) of imipramine; no information is available about its effect on his behavior.

The mother's judgment that the boy was neither excessively active nor distractible was apparently based on herself as an implicit criterion. She talked in a stentorian staccato voice, slept 5 hours a night, and could not sit still in the office. Larry's teacher saw a different child: "He is a nervous child. . . . He is constantly getting out of his seat or finding 'anything' to play with. He finds it hard to follow the classroom rules. Larry enjoys 'fun' and likes to be the joker of the group. He is a talker and often bothersome to his classmates, therefore making it necessary to separate him from the group." The teacher perceived him as "very intelligent" and stated that he read with the top reading group, that he learned and picked up new concepts without difficulty, and that "he is always one of the first to finish his work, though the work itself is not very legible. For a child his age, he frequently uses vulgar language. He has been reprimanded for this but it seems to do no good. After he has done something wrong and is caught, he will not admit the truth." The teacher noted and was concerned about his increasing stealing in the classroom.

The family history was of some interest. The mother described her own parents as "unusual": the maternal grandmother was described as such an unkempt, chaotic, filthy housekeeper that the mother always felt squeamish when the grandchildren ate off their grandmother's plates; the grandfather was described as "cruel"—when the mother kept a kitten against his wishes, he made her watch while he chopped off the heads of the entire litter. "If you liked something he'd hurt you . . . he beat us much too much . . . he didn't let us have our teeth fixed or get glasses until the County officials made him." The grandmother's sister was described as having been chronically psychotic since the age of 30. The mother described herself as generally "cheerful" and very active. There had been only one period when she had been upset: in England, for no reason that was apparent to her, she became depressed and began to drink very heavily. In general, Larry's mother described the marriage as having been happy and satisfying. The father concurred. Larry had two sisters, 2 and 3 years his senior. These children were inclined to be somewhat "messy;" one year after her initial contact the mother mentioned in passing that she still kept her 11-year-old in a bib.

Larry's mother had extreme difficulty in coping with him (as well as with the other children) at home. She was volatile, explosive, and inconsistent. She was aware of her inadequacies but felt unable to control them.

On examination Larry was a quiet, somewhat guarded child, who claimed he felt unhappy about his stealing and wished he could stop. He did not seem particularly anxious and there was a slight feeling he was play-acting his concern. His speech was well organized. He denied sexual, aggressive, or depressive preoccupations and/or concerns. His neurological examination was normal.

He was begun on d-amphetamine and manifested a dose-related improvement in his school behavior. He developed some tolerance to the drug's effects and the dose was gradually increased to first 20 and then 30 mg. The school reported a "100% improvement." The school report read as follows: "The teacher, being completely unaware of psychiatric help and medication that Larry was now undergoing, noticed a great change in the child. He, who had been an extremely hyperactive child, sat quietly and calmly in his seat when expected to do so. It was the first time I could remember seeing him with nothing in his hands. Listening had always been extremely difficult for Larry. His day had been so good that the teacher found it necessary [sic] to compliment him at the end of the day. His aim seemed to be to please." A week later the teacher reported, "Larry has continued his well-improved behavior in the classroom. His interest in the learning situation remains high, particularly when it is necessary for him to 'listen' (a once very difficult task for him). He has been a pleasing child to teach during these past few days—most cooperative—and seems to be enjoying the approval which he is getting." Three months after medication had begun, at the end of the school year, the school reported, "He had had particularly good behavior concerning [stealing]. . . . He has taken nothing that belonged to the other children. . . . His actions remain calm. . . . He concentrates on his work and no longer distracts other children around him. He is not abnormally quiet however. He seems to maintain a normal amount of energy for a child his age." At home his mother reported that his behavior was substantially improved, his bed-wetting had diminished from once nightly to once or twice a week, and he was somewhat more amenable to discipline. He continued to have negativistic periods and manifested considerable sibling rivalry.

The following fall the mother reported a deterioration in the home situation. Despite her previous reports she related in an excited, exceedingly angry voice, "We are having one wretched year." She bitterly complained that "things hadn't really changed that much. . . . He keeps more to himself than ever before . . . he is not violent but when he is it is like a volcano exploding. . . . He feels unloved, angry at the doctor for giving him medicine . . . blames us, won't do his chores . . . hasn't gotten his allowance for 2 months." His mother's difficulty was not limited to Larry, for one of his older sisters also appeared to be acting up. The mother was incapable of setting limits that were the least bit consistent or sensible and attacked the children unpredictably and irrationally. The problem seemed to be confined to the home, for his new teacher was totally unaware that he ever had had problems.

Simple counseling failed to help the mother. Her angry hypomanic state prevented her from utilizing counseling and her psychological obtuseness prevented her from constructing a rational environment herself. Accordingly it was decided to institute drug treatment for the mother and design an operant program for the child. The mother was placed on phenothiazines—trifluoperazine, 6 mg/day—and for the first time in her adult life became reasonably calm and able to sleep more than 5 hours a night. Her major psychological asset was her intelligence and this enabled her to comply in the construction of a detailed operant program. With the boy's unwilling assistance, eight major household activities were decided upon. These included such tasks as making his bed, cleaning up his room, taking out the garbage, and getting to the church on time. Each of these activities was rewarded with a certain number of "points" per performance per day. These points in turn were convertible for privileges (watching TV each evening, going to the movies, and allowance; a number limit was set to the amount that was redeemable in allowance). The payoff scheme allowed the child to earn a total of 390 points per week. The progression in points earned per week over a 4-week period is indicative of the effectiveness of the scheme: 140; 190; 245; 350. The "point system" allowed the mother to "get off the child's back" and the phenothiazines enabled her to comply with the demands of the system. Under this combined regime the boy's home difficulties diminished to the lowest point they had been at in the previous 5 years.

There is every indication that amphetamine treatment had been able to restore the boy to normal functioning in a tolerable environment (school) but that medication was unable to completely rectify his largely psychogenic difficulties at home. These responded to environmental manipulation which consisted of medication for the mother and the construction of the system of rewards based upon principles of "operant therapy."

Amount of treatment time expended: Initial evaluation, 2 hours; follow-up interviews, 8 hours.

12. Hal

Diagnostic subsyndrome: Mixed neurotic-schizophrenia.

Age at contact: 11 years.

Duration of symptoms: Lifelong.

Duration of follow-up: 2 years.

Etiology: Unknown.

Response to treatment: Moderately good (drug therapy and counseling).

Special features: Initial recognition of the existence of the MBD syndrome but a failure to recognize its role in the generation of "neurotic" problems; time-consuming, seemingly useless, and expensive psychological treatment based on faulty diagnosis. Comparative treatment costs: 2 years in residential day care at $4,000 per year = $8,000; 1½ years of twice-weekly therapy at $30 a session = approximately $4,000; total, approximately $12,000. Cost of second course of therapy (at private rates); less than $200.

The patient, an 11-year-old adopted boy, was referred to a child guidance clinic following 3 years of miscellaneous diagnostic evaluations and treatment programs. At the time of his first contact the parents stated that "it's his behavior and attitude—they have been exactly the same since he was 2½ or 3."

His past history was as follows: he had been adopted at 8 months of age from a foster family who had been caring for him from the time of birth. He was described as a healthy, affectionate baby who ate and slept well and was "very active from the beginning." His developmental history was unremarkable. He crawled at less than 8 months, walked at 11 months, said words at one year and sentences by the age of 2. There were no noticeable coordination difficulties: he was not clumsy and had no trouble learning to fasten buttons or tie shoelaces. Toilet training was "started early" and completed by the age of 2; following training there were no accidents. Temperamentally, both parents felt the boy had always been quite different from his adopted sister. Throughout his life he had been "very active" and easily distracted, had possessed little stick-to-itiveness, and had a marked willingness to give up easily.

From the age of 2 or 3 he couldn't sit still, was restless, was always fidgety and "unable to relax." At about the same time he began "pushing . . . knocking . . . throwing objects." His school adjustment was never easy. In kindergarten his teacher described him as "sassy"—he was unable to conform but would withdraw, get up, and walk around. He refused to do what the other children did and was uncomfortable with implicit comparisons with others. He was definitely noncompetitive. In sports, as in academic activities, he had not participated, feeling he would rather not do than do poorly. His overactivity had diminished by the second grade and he was no longer distinguishable from other children in that respect: his problems had, however, gradually increased in severity. His personal relations had also been distinctly different from those of his sister, also adopted and one year his junior. He was much more strongly attached to his mother than she was and, unlike his sister, he had a transitional object which he had worried into oblivion when he was 10 and it 8. He also manifested separation fears, only gradually tolerating attending nursery school and kindergarten. His parents commented on a large number of behavior problems which had been present from an early age. These included the following: "temper tantrums," marked fearfulness: "as a child he was literally afraid of his shadow—as he has gotten older that has disappeared and now he is afraid of heights, of getting hurt, of insects, of bees;" restlessness and difficulty in falling asleep. The most distressing single group of symptoms consisted of obsessive ones. His parents noticed a concern with orderliness and a tendency to become upset when the pattern of things was changed, which had been present since he was 2½. Since then "nothing ever pleases him . . . from the very beginning his shirt had to be tucked in in a certain way . . . his shoelaces had to be of equal length. . . . If his shirt comes out in a fight he lets himself get beaten up while he attends to tucking it in." He would become upset if he did not have the same lunch every day; not only did the sandwich have to be the same but he would become upset if the bread or brand of potato chips was changed. Hal insisted on wearing the very same clothes every day and his mother complied, washing them every night. When his clothes wore out and had to be *thrown* away or when his mother attempted to substitute another outfit, Hal would throw a prolonged tantrum.

Peer relations had always been less than optimal. Other children made fun of his obsessive habits but did not taunt him since he was quite willing to fight. Both parents were concerned that the boy "might get into trouble" because of his continual ignoring of his parents' requests. Discipline was, and always had been, a problem. The father described himself as "about ready to give up . . . I have tried everything." His mother likewise felt at sixes and sevens and consoled herself by saying "way down deep I feel that Hal knows better." Both parents felt considerable concern about the boy's low self-esteem: "He has a poor opinion of himself—not only can't he accept punishment, he *can't* accept praise from his parents . . . he can't *find any joy.*"

The parents' marriage was a reasonably good one. They had had considerable disagreement over the years about the management of their son. The boy's father felt that the mother had been too encouraging of dependence while the mother stated—not too defensively—that she had always found it necessary to keep a close eye on him, since on those occasions on which she failed to do so the boy had often come close to getting seriously hurt.

Hal's adoptive sister was described as "outgoing . . . has never had any problems adjusting, getting along in school or with other kids . . . she has been a delight."

In the third grade, at age 8, the boy began his model, and at first relatively unsuccessful, career as a psychiatric patient. The sequence was as follows.

1. Examination by a clinical psychologist. The psychologist noted the above-mentioned behavioral difficulties and presented the problem as follows: verbal I.Q. 126, performance I.Q. 132, full-scale I.Q. 132, "very talkative, bright and alert, there appeared to be an almost driven quality about him . . . aggressive to the point where he tried to take over, I had frequently to set very strict confining limits in order to keep him focused on the tasks at hand. I found myself developing a rather negative reaction toward him and note this because this reaction from me is so unusual when seeing a child that I placed some significance in it . . . he was aggressive, anxious and restless. The projective testing reveals more of the same—a highly distractible, disorganized, poorly integrated ego structure in sufficient degree to suggest a possibility of more serious psychopathology. His world is rather disjointed, quite frightening and at times, potentially destructive . . . his responses come in a rush without any deliberation, and are frequently fading and changing, so that there is little stability in his perception of the world around him. One senses an intense struggle in his frantic attempts to identify with an environment which remains essentially alien to him." The psychologist noticed that the Bender-Gestalt was poorly integrated and "suggested gross visual motor impairment." He then went on to comment that "much of Hal's behavior might be well attributable directly to this [neurological involvement] condition" but that neurological treatment would not be useful: "nonetheless this would not change Hal's present personality, which is strikingly suggestive of serious emotional difficulty." He commented further that "the Oedipal scene clearly plays a role in his overall high level of anxiety." The psychologist's cognitive ambivalence was revealed by his request for a "comprehensive neurological examination" and simultaneous recommendation for child psychotherapy.

2. Examination by a neurologist. The neurologist noted that Hal had "rather poor visual and motor coordination" and a suggestion of athetotic posturing of one hand. The neurologist felt that "the behavior problem may be in part produced by the perceptual irregularities and associated difficulties in certain types of thought and these in turn may reduce Hal's ability to cope with the inevitable stresses of growing up." However, he felt that "the major part of the problem is emotional" and was glad the child was to receive psychotherapy.

3. A therapeutic day school and residential treatment center. Here it was observed that "his motor activity can be described as hyperactive but it does not appear to have a driven quality to it. He has much difficulty performing any tasks that are asked of him and he has to have firm limits put upon him so that he can produce. His relationships tend to be generally sado-masochistic and he is primarily concerned about being hurt. He is very fearful that his aggression will get him into trouble and that it will cause him to either hurt others or that his own aggression will even hurt himself. He generally feels that he has to be the one to try and control his own aggression because he cannot rely upon his own parents, especially his mother, to do this for him. However, he finds it difficult to be his own control at this time because he has not been able to master the environment and so he is quite unadult in knowing how to take care of himself. . . . He feels that adults are very helpless, inadequate and unable to control him [an exceedingly accurate perception of the environment]. . . . His hyperactivity seems to be a reflection of his anxiety and his guilt about his lack of impulse control. . . . This appears to be a child who was born with hypersensitivity to smell and taste and from the very beginning began to experience his environment as a very painful place. . . . Although the hyperactivity appears to be mostly related to anxiety at this time, it seems very possible that this is a child who was constitutionally hyperactive." The diagnosis was "Psycho-Neurotic Disorder Anxiety Reaction." Following this evaluation the boy was placed in play therapy, in which he continued for the next 2 years— from 35 to 40 sessions. The goal of the therapy was "allowing the boy to express his aggressiveness and also giving him self-controls. An attempt was made during the year to deal with some of his problems of separation which were quite evident in his behavior at school during the hour. He apparently has to react to his separation problems by becoming aggressive." The parents were also seen by the social worker, who was reported to feel that the parents' "reaction to Hal's behavior had in the past been a great contributor to the pathology that we see in the boy." At the time of discharge his diagnosis was the same and he was referred for private outpatient psychotherapy.

4. *A private psychotherapist.* The boy was seen in weekly play therapy and the parents in weekly meetings. The mother was unable to say whether she felt the boy had progressed but commented that at the end of the year and a half of therapy his school told her that "something must be done." At this juncture she contacted:

5. *A child guidance clinic.* Here the previous history was elicited and the child was interviewed. He was found to be—as previously described—sullen, noncommunicative, and quite anxious. He was placed on *d*-amphetamine, which was gradually increased to 20 mg/day. The parents noticed that there were striking behavioral changes which correlated with sleeplessness. When the dose was decreased the boy's problems reappeared. The parents noted the following changes: a marked decrease in anxiety; far more interest in attending school; willingness to do his school work; a disappearance of behavioral problems in school; increased cooperativeness and easier manageability at home; changed peer relations—"he doesn't have any friends but plays with kids on weekends to a degree." His compulsiveness continued. His medication was then increased to 30 mg/day and his parents were counseled to forcefully insist that he change

his clothes. On this regimen his fussiness—which had persisted from the age of 2–3—began to disappear and in several months it was gone, although his behavioral problems still persisted whenever his medication was stopped. At the time of follow-up his school performance had improved greatly and he was receiving A's in all his subjects.

Amount of treatment time expended: During a 2-year period: Interviews, approximately 6 hours; six telephone calls (approximately 10 minutes each).

References

Agrawal, H. C., Glisson, S. N., and Himwich, W. A. Changes in monoamines of rat brain during postnatal ontogeny. *Biochem. Biophys. Acta,* **130:**511–513, 1966.

Anderson, C. Early brain injury and behavior. *J. Amer. Med. Wom. Ass.,* **11:**113–119, 1956.

Anderson, C., and Plymate, H. B. Management of the brain-damaged adolescent. *Amer. J. Orthopsychiat.,* **32:**492–500, 1960.

Annell, A. L. Lithium in the treatment of children and adolescents. *Acta Psychiat. Scand.,* Suppl., **207:**19–30, 1969.

Aprison, M. H. Neurochemical correlates of behavior. V. Differential effects of drugs on approach and avoidance behavior in rats with related changes in brain serotonin and norepinephrine. *Recent Advan. Biol. Psychiat.,* **8:**87–100, 1965.

Aprison, M. H. Discussion of behavioral changes and 5-hydroxytryptamine turnover in animals. *Advan. Pharmacol.,* Suppl., **6:**261–263, 1968.

Bell, R. Q. A reinterpretation of the direction of effects in studies of socialization. *Psychol. Rev.,* **75:**2:81–95, 1968.

Bell, R. Q., Waldrop, M. F., and Beller, G. M. A rating system for the assessment of hyperactive and withdrawn children in preschool samples. Unpublished manuscript, 1969.

Bender, L. Psychological problems of children with organic brain disease. *Amer. J. Orthopsychiat.,* **19:**404–415, 1949.

Bender, L. Helping reading and general improvement. In Wolff, W., ed., *Contemporary Psychotherapists Examine Themselves.* Springfield, Ill.: Thomas, 1956, p. 271.

Bender, L. A psychiatrist looks at deviancy as a factor in juvenile delinquency. *Federal Probation,* June 1968.

Bennett, E. L., Diamond, M. C., Krech, D., and Rosenzweig, M. R. Chemical and anatomical plasticity of brain. *Science,* **146:**610–619, 1964.

Bergin, A. E. Some implications of psychotherapy research for therapeutic practice. *J. Abnl. Psychol.,* **71:**235–246, 1966.

Bignami, G. Selection for high rates and low rates of avoidance conditioning in the rat. *Anim. Behav.,* **13:**2–3, 1965a.

Bignami, G., Robustelli, F., Janki, I., and Bovet, D. Action de l'amphétamine et de quelques agents psychotropes sur l'acquisition d'un conditionnement de fuite et d'évitement chez des rats, sélectionnés en function du niveau particulierement bas de lears performances. *Psychopharmacologie, C. R. Acad. Sci. Paris t.* **260:**4273–4278, April 12, 1965b.

Blau, A. Mental changes following head trauma in children. *Arch. Neurol. Psychiat.,* **35:**723–769, 1937.

Bleuler, E. (1911) *Dementia Praecox or The Group of Schizophrenias.* New York: International Universities Press, 1950.

Bond, E. D., and Appel, K. E. *The Treatment of Behavior Disorders Following Encephalitis.* New York: Commonwealth Fund, Division of Publications, 1931.

Bond, E. D. Postencephalitic, ordinary and extraordinary children. *J. Pediat.,* **1:**310–314, 1932.

Bond, E. D., and Smith, L. H. Postencephalitic behavior disorders: a ten-year review of the Franklin School. *Amer. J. Psychiat.,* **92:**17–33, 1935.

Bradley, C. The behavior of children receiving benzedrine. *Amer. J. Psychiat.,* **94:**577–585, 1937.

Bradley, C. Benzedrine and dexedrine in the treatment of children's behavior disorders. *Pediatrics,* **5:**24–36, 1950.

Brady, J., and Nauta, W. J. H. Subcortical mechanisms in emotional behavior: affective changes following septal forebrain lesions in the albino rat. *J. Comp. Physiol. Psychol.,* **46:**339–346, 1953.

Broadhurst, P. L., and Bignami, G. Correlative effects of psychogenetic selection: a study of the Roman high and low avoidance strains of rats. *Behav. Res. Ther.,* **2:**273–280, 1965.

Bronfenbrenner, U. Early deprivation in mammals: a cross-species analysis. In Newton, G., and Levine, S., eds., *Early Experience and Behavior: The Psychobiology of Development.* Springfield, Ill.: Thomas, 1968, pp. 627–704.

Broughton, R. J. Sleep disorders: disorders of arousal? *Science,* **159:**1070–1077, 1968.

Burks, H. F. Effects of amphetamine therapy on hyperkinetic children. *Arch. Gen. Psychiat.,* **11:**604–609, 1964.

Capute, A. J., Niedermeyer, E. F. L., and Richardson, F. The electroencephalogram in children with minimal cerebral dysfunction. *Pediatrics,* **41:**1104–1114, 1968.

Chalfant, J. C., and Scheffelin, M. A. *Central Processing Dysfunction in Children.* Washington, D.C.: NINDS Monograph No. 9, 1969. U.S. Government Printing Office.

Chapman, J. The early symptoms of schizophrenia. *Brit. J. Psychiat.,* **112:**225–251, 1966.

Chess, S. Diagnosis and treatment of the hyperactive child. *New York J. Med.,* **60:**2379–2385, 1959.

Clements, S. D., and Peters, J. E. Minimal brain dysfunctions in the school age child. *Arch. Gen. Psychiat.,* **6:**185–197, 1962.

Conners, C. K. The syndrome of minimal brain dysfunction: psychological aspects. *Pediat. Clin. N. Amer.,* **14:**749–766, 1967.

Conners, C. K., Eisenberg, L., and Barcai, A. Effect of dextro-amphetamine on children. *Arch. Gen. Psychiat.,* **17**:478–485, 1967.

Coyle, J. T., and Snyder, S. H. Catecholamine uptake by synaptasomes in homogenates of rat brain: stereospecificity in different areas. *J. Pharmacol. Exp. Ther.,* **170**:221–231, 1969.

Cytryn, L., Gilbert, A., and Eisenberg, L. The effectiveness of tranquilizing drugs plus supportive psychotherapy in treating behavior disorders of children: a double-blind study of 80 outpatients. *Amer. J. Orthopsychiat.,* **30**:113–128, 1960.

Dahlstrom, A., and Fuxe, K. Evidence for the existence of monoamine neurons in the central nervous system. IV. Distribution of monoamine nerve terminal in the central nervous system. *Acta Physiol. Scand.,* Suppl. **64**:247, 37–85, 1965.

Daryn, E. Problem of children with "diffuse brain damage." *Arch. Gen. Psychiat.,* **4**:299–306, 1960.

Davis, G. D. Effects of central excitant and depressant drugs on locomotor activity in the monkey. *Amer. J. Physiol.,* **188**:619–623, 1958.

Doman-Delacato treatment of neurologically handicapped children. Summary statement approved by the Amer. Acad. of Neurol., Pediatrics and others. *Devl. Med. Child Neurol.,* **10**:243–246, 1968.

Drillien, C. M. *The Growth and Development of the Prematurely Born Infant.* London: E. & S. Livingstone, Ltd., 1964.

Dyson, W. Personal communication.

Edelson, R. I., and Sprague, R. L. Conditioning of activity level in a classroom with institutionalized retardates. Unpublished manuscript, 1969.

Eisenberg, L. Dynamic considerations underlying the management of the brain-damaged child. *General Practitioner,* **14**:101–106, 1956.

Eisenberg, L. The management of the hyperkinetic child. *Develop. Med. Child Neurol.,* **5**:593–598, 1966.

Eisenberg, L., Gilbert, A., Cytryn, L., and Molling, P. A. The effectiveness of psychotherapy alone and in conjunction with perphenazine or placebo in the treatment of neurotic and hyperkinetic children. *Amer. J. Psychiat.,* **117**:1088–1093, 1961.

Eisenberg, L., Lachman, R., Molling, P. A., Lockner, A., Mizelle, J. D., and Conners, C. K. A psychopharmacologic experiment in a training school for delinquent boys: methods, problems, findings. *Amer. J. Orthopsychiat.,* **33**:431–447, 1963.

Eisenberg, L., Conners, C. K., and Sharpe, L. A controlled study of the differential application of outpatient psychiatric treatment for children. *Japan J. Child Psychiat.,* **6**(3):125–132, 1965.

Epstein, L. C., Lasagna, L., Conners, C. K., and Rodriguez, A. Correlation of detroamphetamine excretion and drug response in hyperkinetic children. *J. Nerv. Ment. Dis.,* **146**:136–146, 1968.

Eysenck, H. J. *The Dynamics of Anxiety and Hysteria.* New York: Praeger, 1957.

Feinstein, A. R. *Clinical Judgment*. Baltimore: Williams & Wilkins, 1967.

Fish, B. Drug use in psychiatric disorders of children. *Amer. J. Psychiat.*, Feb. Suppl. **124:**31–36, 1968.

Freed, H. *The Chemistry and Therapy of Behavior Disorders in Children*. Springfield, Ill.: Thomas, 1962.

Frisk, M., Wegelius, B., Tenhunen, T., Widholm, O., and Hortling, H. The problem of dyslexia in teenage. *Acta Paediat. Scand.*, **56:**333–343, 1967.

Fuxe, K., and Hanson, L. C. F. Central catecholamine neurons and conditioned avoidance behaviour. *Psychopharmacologia* (Berlin) **11:**439–447, 1967.

Gittelman, M., and Birch, H. G. Childhood schizophrenia. *Arch. Gen. Psychiat.*, **17:**16–25, 1967.

Goldfarb, W. The effect of early institutional care on adolescent personality. *J. Exp. Educ.*, **12:**106–129, 1943.

Goldfarb, W. *Childhood Schizophrenia*. Cambridge: Harvard University Press for Commonwealth Fund, 1961.

Goldfarb, W., and Botstein, A. Physical stigmata in schizophrenic children. Unpublished manuscript.

Goldstein, K. *Aftereffects of Brain Injuries in War*. New York: Grune & Stratton, 1942.

Graham, P., and Rutter, M. The reliability and validity of the psychiatric assessment of the child: II. Interview with the parent. *Brit. J. Psychiat.*, **114:**581–592, 1968.

Greenacre, P. The predisposition to anxiety. *Psychoanalytic Quart.*, **10:**66–94, 1941.

Greenacre, P. The predisposition to anxiety. *Psychoanalytic Quart.*, **10:**610–638, 1941.

Hall, R. V., Lund, D., and Jackson, D. Effects of teacher attention on study behavior. *J. Appl. Behav. Analysis*, **1:**1–12, 1968.

Hallgren, B. Specific dyslexia (congenital word blindness). *Acta Psychiat. Scand.*, Suppl., **65,** 1950.

Hammar, S. L. School underachievement in the adolescent: a review of 73 cases. *Pediatrics*, **40:**373–381, 1967.

Hanson, L. C. F. Biochemical and behavioral effects of tyrosine hydroxylase inhibition. *Psychopharmacologia* (Berlin), **11:**8–17, 1967.

Harlow, H. F. The nature of love. *Amer. Psychol.*, **13:**673–685, 1958.

Hartocollis, P. The syndrome of minimal brain dysfunction in young adult patients. *Bulletin of the Menninger Clinic*, **32, 2:**102–114, 1968.

Harvald, B., and Hauge, M. Hereditary factors elucidated by twin studies. In Neel, J., et al., eds., *Genetics and the Epidemiology of Chronic Diseases*. No. 1163. Washington, D.C.: U.S. Government Printing Office, 1965.

Harvey, J. A. Lesions in the medial forebrain bundle: delayed effects on sensitivity to electric shock. *Science*, **148:**250–252, 1965.

Healy, W., and Bronner, A. F. *New Light on Delinquency and Its Treatment*. New Haven: Yale University Press, 1936.

Heller, A., and Moore, R. Y. Effect of central nervous system lesions on brain monoamines in the rat. *J. Pharmacol. Exp. Ther.*, **150:**1–9, 1965.

Hertzig, M. E., and Birch, H. Neurologic organization in psychiatrically disturbed adolescents. *Arch. Gen. Psychiat.,* **19:**528–537, 1968.

Heston, L. L. Psychiatric disorders in foster home reared offspring of schizophrenic mothers. *Brit. J. Psychiat.,* **112:**819–825, 1966.

Hillarp, N. A., Fuxe, K., and Dahlstrom, A. Demonstration and mapping of central neurons containing dopamine, noradrenaline, and 5-hydroxytryptamine and their reactions to psychopharmaca. *Pharmacol. Rev.,* **18:**727–742, 1966.

Hohman, L. B. Post-encephalitic behavior disorders in children. *Johns Hopkins Hospital Bulletin,* **380:**372–375, 1922.

Hornykiewicz, O. Dopamine (3-hydroxytyramine) and brain function. *Pharmacol. Rev.,* **18:**925–964, 1966.

Huessy, H. R. Study of the prevalence and therapy of the choreatiform syndrome or hyperkinesis in rural Vermont. *Acta Paedopsychiat.,* **34:**130–135, 1967.

Hume, D. *Dialogues Concerning Natural Religion.* In Burtt, E. A., ed., *The English Philosophers from Bacon to Mill.* New York: Random House, 1939.

Hutt, C., Hutt, S. J., and Ounsted, C. A method for the study of children's behavior. *Develop. Med. Child Neurol.,* **5:**233–245, 1963.

Ingram, T. T. S. A characteristic form of overactive behavior in brain-damaged children. *J. Ment. Sci.,* **102:**550–558, 1956.

Iversen, L. L. *The Uptake and Storage of Noradrenaline in Sympathetic Nerves.* London: Cambridge University Press, 1967.

Kahn, E., and Cohen, L. H. Organic drivenness—a brain stem syndrome and an experience—with case reports. *New Eng. J. Med.,* **210:**748–756, 1934.

Kanner, L. *Child Psychiatry.* Springfield, Ill.: Thomas, 1957.

Karczmar, A. G., and Scudder, C. L. Behavioral responses to drugs and brain catecholamine levels in mice of different strains and genera. *Federation Proc.,* **26:**1186–1191, 1967.

Kasanin, J.: Personality changes in children following cerebral trauma. *J. Nerv. Ment. Dis.,* **69:**385, 1929.

Kennard, M. A. Value of equivocal signs in neurologic diagnosis. *Neurology,* **10:**753–764, 1966.

Kety, S. S., Rosenthal, D., Wender, P. H., and Schulsinger, F. The types and prevalence of mental illness in the biological and adoptive families of adopted schizophrenics. In Rosenthal, D., and Kety, S. S., eds., *The Transmission of Schizophrenia.* Oxford: Pergamon Press, 1968, pp. 235–250.

King, F. A. Relationship of the "Septal Syndrome" to genetic differences in emotionality in the rat. *Psychol. Rep.,* **5:**11–17, 1959.

King, F. A., and Meyer, P. M. Effects of amygdaloid lesions upon septal hyperemotionality in the rat. *Science,* **120:**655–666, 1958.

Klaiber, E. L., and Broverman, D. M. The automatization cognitive style, androgens and monoamine oxidase. *Psychopharmacologia* (Berlin), **11:**320–336, 1967.

Klein, D. F., and Davis, J. M. *Diagnosis and Drug Treatment of Psychiatric Disorders.* Baltimore: Williams & Wilkins, 1969.

Knobel, M. Psychopharmacology for the hyperkinetic child. *Arch. Gen. Psychiat.,* **6:**198–202, 1962.

Knobel, M., Wolman, M. B., and Mason, E. Hyperkinesis and organicity in children. *Arch. Gen. Psychiat.,* **1:**310–321, 1958.

Knobloch, H., and Pasamanick, B. Prospective studies on the epidemiology of reproductive causality: methods, findings and some implications. Presented at the Merrill-Palmer Institute Conference on Research and Teaching of Infant Development Feb. 11, 1965 (unpublished).

Koe, B. K., and Weissman, A. The pharmacology of para-chlorophenylanine, a selective depletor of serotonin stores. *Advan. Pharmacol.,* Suppl., **6:**29–47, 1968.

Kosman, M. E., and Unna, K. R. Effects of chronic administration of the amphetamines and other stimulants on behavior. *Clin. Pharmacol. Ther.,* **9:** 240–254, 1968.

Krakowski, A. J. Amitriptyline in treatment of hyperkinetic children: a double blind study. *Psychosomatics,* **6:**355–360, 1965.

Kramer, J. C., Fischman, V. S., and Littlefield, D. C. Amphetamine abuse. *J.A.M.A.* **201:**305–310, 1967.

Krieckhaus, E. E. Decrements in avoidance behavior following mammillothalamic tractotomy in rats and subsequent recovery with *d*-amphetamine. *J. Comp. Physiol. Psychol.,* **60:**31–35, 1965.

Krieg, W. J. S. *Functional Neuroanatomy,* 2nd ed. New York: Blakiston, 1953.

Kulkarni, A. S., and Job, W. M. Facilitation of avoidance learning by *d*-amphetamine. *Life Sci.,* **6:**1579–1587, 1967.

Kulkarni, A. S. Muricidal block produced by 5-hydroxyptryptophan and various drugs. *Life Sci.,* **7:**125–128, 1968.

Kurlander, L. F., and Colodny, D. "Pseudoneurosis" in the neurologically handicapped child. *Amer. J. Orthopsychiat.,* **35:**733–738, 1965.

Laufer, M. W. Cerebral dysfunction and behavior disorders in adolescents. *Amer. J. Orthopsychiat.,* **32:** No. 3, 501–505, 1962.

Laufer, M. W., and Denhoff, E. Hyperkinetic behavior syndrome in children. *J. Pediat.,* **50:**463–473, 1957a.

Laufer, M. W., Denhoff, E., and Solomons, G. Hyperkinetic impulse disorder in children's behavior problems. *Psychosom. Med.,* **19:**38–49, 1957b.

Le Gros Clark, W. S., Beattie, J., Riddoch, G., and Dott, N. M. *The Hypothalamus. Morphological, Functional, Clinical and Surgical Aspects.* London: Oliver & Boyd, 1938.

Levitt, E. E.: Psychotherapy with children: a further evaluation. *Behav. Res. Ther.,* **1:**45–51, 1963.

Levy, D. Primary affect hunger. *Amer. J. Psychiat.,* **94:**643–652, 1937.

Levy, D. *Maternal Overprotection.* New York: Columbia University Press, 1943.

Lurie, L. A., and Levy, S. Behavior disorders—personality changes and behavior disorders of children following pertussis. *J.A.M.A.*, **120B:**890–894, 1942.

Lytton, G. J., and Knobel, M. Diagnosis and treatment of behavior disorders in children. *Dis. Nerv. Syst.*, **20:**314–344, 1958.

McDermott, J. F. A specific placebo effect encountered in the use of dexedrine in a hyperactive child. *Amer. J. Psychiat.*, **121:**923–924, 1965.

McFarlane, J. W., Allen, L., and Honzik, M. P. *A Development Study of the Behavior Problems of Normal Children Between Twenty-One Months and Fourteen Years.* Berkeley: University of California Press, 1954.

Maire, F. W., and Patton, H. D. Neural structures involved in the genesis of "preoptic pulmonary edema," gastric erosions and behavior changes. *Amer. J. Physiol.*, **184:**345–350, 1956.

Mandell, A. J., and Spooner, C. E. Psychochemical research studies in man. *Science,* **162:**1442–1453, 1968.

Margolies, J. A., and Wortis, H. Z. Parents of children with cerebral palsy. *J. Child Psychiat.*, **3:**105–114, 1956.

Mednick, S. A. Schizophrenia: a learned thought disorder. In Nielsen, G., ed., *Clinical Psychology.* Copenhagen: Munksgaard, 1962.

Menkes, M., Rowe, J. S., and Menkes, J. H. A twenty-five-year follow-up study on the hyperkinetic child with minimal brain dysfunction. *Pediatrics,* **39:**393–399, 1967.

Michaels, J. J. *Disorders of Character.* Springfield, Ill.: Thomas, 1955.

Millichap, J. G., and Fowler, G. W. Treatment of "minimal brain dysfunction" syndromes. *Pediat. Clin. N. Amer.*, **14:**767–777, 1967.

Milman, D. Organic behavior disorder. *J. Dis. Children,* **91:**521–528, 1956.

Mizrahi, G. K. Perinatal complications. Unpublished Master's Thesis, University of Copenhagen, 1969.

Montagu, A. *Prenatal Influences.* Springfield, Ill.: Thomas, 1962.

Montgomery County, Md. Board of Education. "Project Focus" report. Unpublished manuscript.

Moore, K. Effects of α-methyltyrosine on brain catecholamines and conditioned behavior in guinea pigs. *Life Sci.*, **5:**55–65, 1966.

Moore, K. E., and Rech, R. H. Antagonism by monoamine oxidase inhibitors of methyltyrosine induced catecholamine depletion and behavioral depression. *J. Pharmacol. Exp. Ther.*, **156:**71–75, 1967.

Moore, K. E. and Rech, R. H.: Behavioral and norepinephrine—depleting effects of disulfiram in reserpine—pretreated rats. *Arch. int. Pharmacodyn.* **180:**413–422, 1969.

Morris, H. H. Jr., Escoll, P. J., and Wexler, R. Aggressive behavior disorders of childhood: a follow-up study. *Amer. J. Psychiat.*, **112:**991–997, 1956.

Mowrer, O. H. Learning theory and the neurotic paradox. *Amer. J. Orthopsychiat.*, **18:**571–610, 1948.

Nauta, W. J. H. Some neural pathways related to the limbic system. In Rainey, E. R., and O'Doherty, D. S., eds., *Electrical Studies on the Unanesthetized Brain.* New York: Hoeber, 1960, p. 1.

Nichamin, S., and Comley, H. M. The hyperkinetic or lethargic child with cerebral dysfunction. *Mich. Med.*, **63:**790–792, 1964.

Olds, J., and Milner, P. Positive reinforcement produced by electrical stimulation of septal area and other regions of rat brain. *J. Comp. Physiol. Psychol.*, **47:**419–427, 1954.

Olds, J. Self-stimulation of the brain. *Science*, **127:**315–324, 1958.

Olds, J. Hypothalamic substrates of reward. *Physiol. Rev.*, **42:**554–604, 1962.

Paine, R. S. Minimal chronic brain syndromes in children. *Develop. Med. Child Neurol.*, **4:**21–27, 1962.

Paine, R. S., Werry, J. S., and Quay, H. C. A study of minimal cerebral dysfunction. *Develop Med. Child Neurol.*, **10:**505–520, 1968.

Palkes, H., Stewart, M., and Kahana, B.: Porteus maze performance of hyperactive boys after training in self-directed verbal commands. *Child Develop.*, **39:**817–826, 1968.

Pats, N. D. *Selected Patient Characteristics and Follow-up Data From the Sheppard and Enoch Pratt Hospital Child Guidance Clinic 1959–1966.* Research Report 3, The Sheppard and Enoch Pratt Hospital, Baltimore (Towson), Md., 1969.

Perez-Reyes, M., Lansing, M., and Lansing, C. The diagnostic evaluation process. *Arch. Gen. Psychiat.*, **16:**609–620, 1967.

Pincus, J. H., and Glaser, G. H. The syndrome of minimal brain damage in childhood. *New Eng. J. Med.*, **275:**27–35, 1966.

Pollack, M., Levenstein, S., and Klein, D. F. A three-year posthospital follow-up of adolescent and adult schizophrenia. *Amer. J. Orthopsychiat.*, **38:**94–109, 1968.

Pollin, W., Stabenau, J. R., Mosher, L., and Tupin, J. Life history differences in identical twins discordant for schizophrenia. *Amer. J. Orthopsychiat.*, **36:**492–509, 1966.

Poppe, K. R. *Conjectures and Refutations: The Growth of Scientific Knowledge.* New York: Basic Books, 1962.

Poschel, B. P. H., and Ninteman, F. W. Hypothalamic self-stimulation: its suppression by blockade of norepinephrine biosynthesis and reinstatement by methamphetamine. *Life Sci.*, **5:**11–16, 1966.

Poschel, B. P. H., and Ninteman, F. W. Excitatory effects of 5-HTP on intracranial self-stimulation following MAO blockade. *Life Sci.*, **7:**317–323, 1968.

Prechtl, H. F. R., and Stemmer, C. J. The choreiform syndrome in children. *Develop. Med. Child Neurol.*, **4:**119–127, 1962.

Pringle, M. L., and Bossio, V. A study of deprived children. *J. Vita. Hum.*, **1:**65–92; 142–170, 1958.

Quitkin, F. and Klein, D. F. Two behavioral syndromes in young adults related to possible minimal brain dysfunction. *J. Psychiat. Res.*, **7:**131–142, 1969.

Rapoport, J. Childhood behavior and learning problems treated with imipramine. *Int. J. Neuropsychiat.*, **1:**635–642, 1965.

Rech, R. H. Amphetamine effects on poor performance of rats in a shuttle-box. *Psychopharmacologia* (Berlin) **9:**110–117, 1966.

Ritvo, E. P., Ornitz, E. M., Gottlieb, F., Poussaint, A. F., Maron, B. J., Ditman, K. S., and Blinn, K. A. Arousal and non-arousal enuretic events. *Amer. J. Psychiat.*, **126:**77–84, 1969.

Robins, L. *Deviant Children Grown Up.* Balitmore: William & Wilkins, 1966.

Rosen, M., Downs, E. F., Napolitani, F. D., and Swartz, D. P. The quality of reproduction in an urban indigent population. I. Birth weight: the differences between mothers of low-weight and of term-size infants. *Obstret. Gynec.,* **31:**276–282, 1968.

Routtenberg, A. The two-arousal hypothesis: reticular formation and limbic system. *Psychol. Rev.,* **75:**51–80, 1968.

Ruch, T. C., and Fulton, J. F., eds., *Medical Physiology and Biophysics.* 18th ed., Philadelphia: Saunders, 1960.

Rutter, M., and Graham, P. The reliability and validity of the psychiatric assessment of the child. I. Interview with the child. *Brit. J. Psychiat.,* **114:** 563–579, 1968.

Safer, D. J. The familial incidence of minimal brain dysfunction. Unpublished manuscript.

Schaefer, E. S., and Bayley, N. Maternal behavior, child behavior and their intercorrelations from infancy through adolescence. Monograph. *Society for Research in Child Development,* **28:**No. 3, 87, 1963.

Schafer, R. *Aspects of Internalization.* New York: International Universities Press, 1968.

Schildkraut, J. J., and Kety, S. S. Pharmacological studies suggest a relationship between brain biogenic amines and affective state. *Science,* **156:**3771, 1967.

Schneider, R. A. and Costiloe, A. P. Effect of centrally active drugs on conditioning in man. *Am. J. Med. Sci.,* **233:**418–423, 1957.

Scott, J. P., and Fuller, J. L. *Genetics and the Social Behavior of the Dog.* Chicago: University of Chicago Press, 1965.

Sheard, M. H., Appel, J. B., and Freedman, D. X. The effect of central nervous system lesions on brain monoamines and behavior. *J. Psychiat. Res.,* **5:** 237–242, 1967.

Shirley, M. A behavior syndrome characterizing prematurely born children. *Child Develop.,* **10:**2, 1939.

Splitter, S. R., and Kaufman, M. A new treatment for under-achieving adolescents: psychotherapy combined with nortriptyline medication. *Psychosomatics,* **1:**171–174, 1966.

Sprague, R. L., Werry, J. S., and Davis, K. V. Psychotropic drug effects on learning and activity level of children. Paper presented at Gatlinburg Conference on Research and Theory in Mental Retardation, March 13, 1969 (unpublished).

Stein, L. Self-stimulation of the brain and the central stimulant action of amphetamine. *Fed. Proc.,* **23:**836–850, 1964.

Stein, L. Facilitation of avoidance behavior by positive brain stimulation. *J. Comp. Physiol. Psychol.,* **60:**9–19, 1965.

Stein, L. Psychopharmacological substrates of mental depression. *Excerpta Medica Int. Cong. Series,* **122:**130–139, 1966.

Stein, L., and Wise, D. Release of norepinephrine from hypothalamus and amygdala by rewarding medial forebrain bundle stimulation and amphetamine. *J. Comp. Physiol. Psychol.*, **67**: No.2, 189–198, 1969.

Stewart, M., Ferris, A., Pitts, N., Jr., and Craig, A. G. The hyperactive child syndrome. *Amer. J. Orthopsychiat.*, **36**:861–867, 1966.

Stott, D. H. *Studies of Troublesome Children.* New York: Tavistock Publications, Humanities Press, 1966.

Strauss, A. A., and Lehtinen, L. E. *Psychopathology and Education of the Brain-Injured Child.* New York: Grune & Stratton, 1947.

Strauss, A. A., and Kephart, N. C. *Psychopathology and Education of the Brain-Injured Child, Vol. II. Progress in Theory and Clinic.* New York: Grune & Stratton, 1955.

Strecker, E. A., and Ebaugh, F. Neuropsychiatric sequaelae of cerebral trauma in children. *Arch. Neurol. Psychiat.*, **12**:443–453, 1924.

Stunkard, A., and Burt, V. Obesity and the body image. II. Age at onset of disturbances in the body image. *Amer. J. Psychiat.*, **123**:1443–1447, 1967.

Sudak, H. S., and Maas, J. W. Behavioral-neurochemical correlation in reactive and nonreactive strains of rats. *Science*, **146**:418–420, 1964a.

Sudak, H. S., and Maas, J. W. Central nervous system serotonin and norepinephrine localization in emotional and non-emotional strains in mice. *Nature*, **203**:1254–1256, 1964b.

Tenen, S. S. The effects of *p*-chlorophenylalanine, a serotonin depletor, on avoidance acquisition, pain sensitivity and related behavior in the rat. *Psychopharmacologia* (Berlin), **10**:204–219, 1967.

Thomas, A., Chess, S., and Birch, H. G. *Temperament and Behavior Disorders in Children.* New York: New York University Press, 1968.

Thurston, D. L., Middelkamp, J. N., and Mason, E. The late effects of lead poisoning. *J. Pediat.*, **42**:120–128, 1955.

Towbrin, A. Cerebral hypoxic damage in fetus and newborn. *Arch. Neurol.*, **20**:35–43, 1969.

Truumaa, A. Some newer practices and trends in child mental health. Unpublished manuscript. Indiana University Medical Center, Indianapolis, Indiana.

Waldrop, M. F., Pedersen, F. A., and Bell, R. Q. Minor physical anomalies and behavior in preschool children. *Child Develop.*, **39**:391–400, 1968.

Wender, P. H. On necessary and sufficient conditions in psychiatric explanation. *Arch. Gen. Psychiat.*, **16**:41–47, 1967.

Wender, P. H., Rosenthal, D., and Kety, S. S. A psychiatric assessment of the adoptive parents of schizophrenics. *J. Psychiat. Res.*, **6** Suppl. 1: 235–250, 1968.

Wender, P. H. Vicious and virtuous circles: the role of deviation amplifying feedback in the origin and perpetuation of behavior. *Psychiatry*, **31**:309–324, 1968.

Wender, P. H. The role of genetics in the etiology of the schizophrenias. *Amer. J. Orthopsychiat.*, **39**:447–458, 1969a.

Wender, P. H. Platelet serotonin level in children with "Minimal Brain Dysfunction." *Lancet, II*: 1012, 1969b.

Wender, P. H., Epstein, R. S., Kopin, I. J., and Gordon, E. K. Urinary monoamine metabolites in children with minimal brain dysfunction. *Amer. J. Psychiat.* In press.

Werner, E., Simanian, K., Bierman, J. M., and French, F. E. Cumulative effect of perinatal complications and deprived environment on physical, intellectual and social development of preschool children. *Pediatrics*, **39**:490–505, 1967.

Werry, J. S., Weiss, G., and Douglas, V. Studies on the hyperactive child. I. Some preliminary findings. *Canad. Psychiat. Ass.*, **9**:120–130, 1964.

Werry, J. S., Weiss, G., Douglas, V., and Martin, J. Studies on the hyperactive child: III. The effect of chlorpromazine upon behavior and learning ability. *J. Amer. Acad. Child Psychiat.*, **5**:292–312, 1966.

Werry, J. S. Developmental hyperactivity. *Pediat. Clin. N. Amer.* **15**:581–598, 1968a.

Werry, J. S. Studies on the hyperactive child: an empirical analysis of the minimal brain dysfunction syndrome. *Arch. Gen. Psychiat.*, **19**:9–16, 1968b.

Whitehead, A. N. *The Concept of Nature.* London: Cambridge University Press, Paperback Reprints, 1964, p. 163.

Williams, R. J. Heredity, human understanding, and civilization. *Amer. Sci.*, **57**:237–243, 1969.

Wise, C. D., and Stein, L. Facilitation of brain self-stimulation by central administration of norepinephrine. *Science*, **35**:299–301, 1969.

Zanchetti, A. Subcortical and cortical mechanisms in arousal and emotional behavior in the neurosciences. In *The Neurosciences*, Quarton, G. C., Melnechuk, T., and Schmitt, F. O., eds., New York: The Rockefeller Press, 1967, pp. 602–614.

Zeilberger, J., Sampen, S. E., and Sloan, H. N. Modification of a child's problem behaviors in the home with the mother as therapist. *J. Appl. Behav. Analysis*, **1**:47–53, 1958.

Zrull, J. P., Westman, J. C., Arthur, B., and Bell, W. A. A comparison of chlordiazepoxide, *d*-amphetamine and placebo in the treatment of the hyperkinetic syndrome in children. *Amer. J. Psychiat.*, **120**:590–591, 1963.

Zrull, J. P., Westman, J. C., Arthur, B., and Rice, D. L. An evaluation of methodology used in the study of psychoactive drugs for children. *J. Amer. Acad. Child Psychiat.*, **5**:284–291, 1966.

Author Index

Subject Index

239